[handwritten note: "...rtha, enjoy these stories. Peter W"]

Peter Winneke is a generosity and life legacy adviser with more than 20 years' experience in strategic, impactful giving – establishing more than 100 philanthropic family foundations in Australia. He assisted many of these families implement a strategic giving program.

As well as being the inaugural CEO of Australia's largest grantmaking family foundation, Peter has served Australia's philanthropic sector with The Myer Foundation, Sidney Myer Fund, The Catherine Freeman Foundation, Philanthropy Australia and the Reichstein Foundation.

Prior to his two decades in the philanthropic sector, Peter had 16 years' experience in the corporate world specialising in insolvency, and mergers and acquisitions. Many years of overseas travel to low-middle income countries during this time developed his passion for philanthropy's ability to address some of the world's inequity and create social change.

Learn more at: peterwinneke.com.au

Praise

"There are those who spend their time surviving -. genuinely wondering how they will have the means to continue living. And there are others who are able to choose what 'luxuries' they will have and how much they can pass on to their children. It is this second group who must read this book... and now. Take your time over a 'luxury decision'... there will always be something else available tomorrow!

But don't delay reading Peter Winneke's marvellous book... every day you put that off is a lost opportunity to explore what might be the most profound and satisfying decision of your life."

Simon McKeon AO, former Australian of the Year

"We need to significantly grow the size of the philanthropic sector in Australia, while also improving the method in which we deploy philanthropic capital. This book will help us get there."

Mark Cubit, donor, co-founder of the Australian International Development Network

"What we need are more innovative approaches to solving the world's toughest social and environmental challenges. Peter's book provides a wealth of inspiring case studies to show us the way."

Paul Ronalds, Founder & CEO, Save the Children Global Ventures

"Pete has been one of Australia's most dynamic philanthropic thought leaders for decades. And not just thought, but action, with years of practical, hands-on experience. A big fan of Chuck Feeney, my dear friend, mentor and worldwide champion of Giving While Living, Pete is a worthy guide on your philanthropic journey."

Dr Dave Kennedy, founder igiveonepercent.org and former Executive Director, The Atlantic Philanthropies Australia

"Our family has been the beneficiary of Peter's deep philanthropic experience as we started our Foundation and learnt how to be good philanthropists. I recommend this book wherever you are at on your philanthropic journey."

Michael Barr, Barr Family Foundation and former Director of Philanthropy Australia

"Strategic giving can have a powerful impact on the community. Peter's passion and experience over many years, captured in this book, will I hope inspire and guide more such giving."

Anna Skarbek, CEO, Climateworks Centre

"My father's generation had a central question. Is there life after death? My dad lived through the depression and fought the Japanese in PNG and knew that this life was fragile and uncertain, so he projected his hope. My baby boomer generation asked, Is there life before death? We were largely secure and prosperous and wanted a good life now.

My kid's generation frames the question as, Is there life tonight? Climate change pessimism, the 24/7news cycles that are unrelenting and depressing, not to mention HECS debts, has narrowed the question to, let's enjoy this moment because who knows? Peter has written an important book which is an invaluable tool for philanthropy. But it also raises the hope question. Giving before I die and doing it well, knowing what is enough for me and my family and what is my purpose resists the deep pessimism and restores hope."

Tim Costello AO, National Living Treasure

GIVE WHILE YOU LIVE

A PRACTICAL GUIDE TO MORE & BETTER GIVING IN AUSTRALIA

PETER WINNEKE

ISBN 978 0 6459442 0 4 (print edition)
ISBN 978 0 6459442 1 1 (digital edition)

www.peterwinneke.com.au
www.givewhileyoulive.com.au

Internal design by Purpose Buzz
Front cover design by Blueboat
Photo by fred kroh fotograf

For

Dad, who taught me to always stand up for what is right, even if it is to your own detriment.

Mum, who is always there for me.

Ange, for your unconditional love.

This book was written on Wurundjeri Woi Wurrung Country, land that was never ceded and a place I am privileged to call my home. I respect and honour the traditional custodians of this land, and Elders past, present, and emerging.

Contents

Preface

Why this book and how to read it

This book seeks to influence more and better giving in Australia. We have created staggering wealth in this country in recent decades and we have a unique opportunity to use part of this capital to tackle significant issues in our community, and beyond our shores.

Prompted by years of backpacking through low-middle income countries whilst working in the corporate world for 16 years, I was searching for more purpose in my life. The result was spending the last 20 years working in the Australian philanthropic sector. Here I met and worked with over 100 high-net-worth families and some very clever community leaders. Whilst there are some terrific stories within our philanthropic sector, the size of the sector is modest, there is little transparency, and many practices have remained unchanged over the last five decades.

I share what I consider to be a pathway to increasing giving levels in Australia and best practice giving. I also provide a critique of the sector and our giving culture. I am passionate about building a stronger country, so I don't do this lightly, and endeavour to do this in a constructive way. Hopefully this will enable us to start a franker conversation on important issues such as how much is enough, how much do the kids need and how we can significantly improve practices within the philanthropic sector. Again, the desired outcome is to achieve more and better giving.

In the absence of many other books being written on the Australian philanthropic sector I have covered topics of interest to high-net-worth families (both new and experienced donors), executives working in the sector, those that are looking to enter the sector and those working within for-purpose entities including fundraisers, who will hopefully gain a useful insight into the opaque world of philanthropy. I have included a list of the most useful books and articles that I have read on the sector over many years.

Given the unusual career path that I have taken – from insolvency services to philanthropy – and my search for purpose in a troubled world, peers thought it might be useful to share some of my personal story. I have endeavoured to keep this brief. This won't be of interest to all readers. If you are just seeking to learn the merits of philanthropy, how a family foundation could be an extraordinary educational tool for your children, best practice philanthropy tips, inspiring case studies from around the world, or tips for foundation CEOs or fundraisers, then just jump straight to those chapters, commencing at chapter 7. I won't mind!

And there is a lot in here! Pick the top five points that are most applicable to your family, given where you are on your philanthropic journey, and work on those. Come back to the book at a later stage and determine other issues to consider.

The book is in five parts:

- Part I: Seeking purpose

- Part II: A better use of wealth

- Part III: Best practice giving

- Part IV: Sector tips

- Part V: Sector reforms required

Given the personal wealth that we have created, we have a unique and exciting opportunity to deploy this capital effectively and create positive change in our community and beyond. We are living our legacy now. With the enormous inter-generational wealth transfer commencing, now is the time for this conversation.

Hopefully this book helps to drive the debate and stimulates more families to think about their use of wealth. If we can show the way via strong leadership, many more will want to get involved and take their families on an exciting journey. Now that sounds like fun!

Peter Winneke

PART I: SEEKING PURPOSE

Chapter 1

Happy man, sad man

"It's a lot more fun to give while you're alive, than to give while you're dead!" – **Chuck Feeney**

Happy man

They say it is dangerous to meet your hero. But there I was on the deck at Kirribilli House with Chuck Feeney walking towards me. It was a warm Sunday in late summer of 2011. Australia's then Prime Minister Julia Gillard AC was putting on a small gathering to recognise the extraordinary work that Chuck and his foundation, The Atlantic Philanthropies, had funded in Australia. At the time, Chuck was the largest giver in Australia ($550 million). And he wasn't even Australian! If I walked down Pitt Street and asked 100 people who Chuck Feeney was, I suspect only one or two would be able to respond correctly.

Chuck was an Irish American who had made a vast fortune from duty free shopping. Chuck's right-hand man in Australia, Dr Dave Kennedy, had been kind enough to include me on the small invite list, given my experience growing giving levels in Australia. Chuck was a little older than I expected. He had a warm smile, but his eyes had a certain intensity that made you concentrate when he spoke to you. Fifteen of the wealthiest Australians were in the room with the Prime Minister, a couple of the PM's advisers, Dave Kennedy and I. Ah, now I know what imposter syndrome feels like!

After an informal group conversation inside we spilled out on to the deck overlooking the glorious harbour. I had a wonderful 15 minute chat with Chuck, one on one. I had prepared a few questions for him in case I was fortunate enough to ask them. I asked him about his greatest learnings in the philanthropic sector, tips for success and how he inspired others to step up and do the same.

Chuck had a vision and mission to share his wealth for the benefit of the community. He was one of the most content people I had ever met. Dave took a photo of Chuck and me, which I have had on my study wall since, which inspires my work every day.

A few years later I was sitting in the dirt on the outskirts of Nampula, Mozambique in the suffocating heat with a young mother with AIDS as she fed her newly infected infant, learning how m2m (Mothers to Mothers) had saved her life and that of her infant. She had been mentored by a local mum who had been through similar issues a few years prior; a 'mentor mother'.

Next stop was a meeting in Berlin with 10 clever strategists and 40 donors, mapping out how to stop/delay the building of 2,000 coal power plants that were in the pipeline around the world over the following decade. If built, they would likely condemn the world to well above a global average temperature rise of 1.5 degrees Celsius.

Soon after Berlin I had the privilege of discussing with Australian First Nations leaders their ambitious and detailed plan to establish a First Nations Voice to Parliament in Australia.

Sad man

Not long after meeting Chuck I sat in the most magnificent study I had ever seen, let alone been in! I was sitting opposite one of Australia's richest men. Perhaps it was considered a library? It was enormous, lined from floor to ceiling with bookshelves. The books all had a similar coloured binding. At one point 'Charles' (let's call him that) was called from the room. I sat there calculating how long it would take me to get from my chair to the far side of the room to check whether the books were real, and then get back to my seat. Too risky, I thought.

'Charles' returned to the large ornate chamber and proceeded to share with me that his kids were fighting over his wealth and were waiting for him to die. I suggested to him that if he moved more of his wealth into his modest family foundation during his lifetime that such a transfer could not be disputed upon his passing. As I walked out of his grand home, I reflected that 'Charles' seemed to have little purpose in his life, was drifting in his final years and was probably the saddest man I had ever met.

Just imagine

But on this particular day, as I stood in the late afternoon sun looking over Sydney Harbour, I could see how satisfied Chuck was. I could see his extraordinary humility. He wouldn't rest as there was always more to do, but wow, there was a content man. As I wandered out the Kirribilli gates heading towards the airport, I reflected on a unique day.

Imagine the positive impact in Australia if we could create 100 Chuck Feeney's here! Imagine the impact on our medical facilities, the environment, our education system, our mental health system and our First Nations people. Imagine the positive impact we could make on our Pacific neighbours, and further abroad. Just imagine …

Chapter 2

We have the wealth and intelligence to solve every issue

"It is what difference we have made in the lives of others that will determine the significance of the life we lead." – **Nelson Mandela**

A true test of a civil society

Many years ago I read Jeffrey Sachs', *The End of Poverty,* a *New York Times* bestseller. Sachs is a world-renowned economics professor. He cut his teeth advising Latin American countries in the 1980s on how to end hyperinflation and reduce external debts. Since the 1990s he has worked with many African countries as they attempted to 'escape from poverty'.[1]

The End of Poverty provided a vision of the steps to transform impoverished countries to prosperous ones. Sachs' book had a profound impact on me. My conclusion from reading his book: we have the wealth and intelligence to solve every issue on the planet, if we could be inspired to do so. I felt as if my eyes had been opened.

A true test of a civil society is how we treat those less fortunate and our for-purpose organisations. (I don't use the term 'not-for-profit'. When discussing our most important entities, why do we define them for what they are not? The team members of these entities are driven by purpose. So I, and many others, refer to them as for-purpose entities.) Do we assist

---

1. https://www.jeffsachs.org

building up their organisational capacity so they can thrive and achieve their mission of assisting those less fortunate and without a voice? Such support cannot be left to government alone due to a range of factors including: budgetary constraints, funding risk with taxpayers' money and not having the necessary skills.

"If you're not pissed off at the world …"

Many years ago Kasey Chambers, Australian country and western singer wrote a song called, *Ignorance*. It has a line in it that reached out and slapped me on the face: "If you're not pissed off at the world, then you're just not paying attention." Yes, there it is right there for me. Why do so many of us not pay attention, or if we do, we look the other way? Is it all too hard? Do we not know where to start? Is it because our friends are doing little? How could we address this? How could we inspire people to do more?

It's a beautiful, thoughtful song, but not one to listen to after a bad day at the office!

Peter Singer AC, world-renowned philosopher from the University of Melbourne and Princeton University, provides a fascinating illustration on this issue. The pond illustration. On your way to work you pass a young child drowning in a shallow pond. Despite wearing your new expensive shoes and suit, and knowing that your heroics will make you late for work, of course you wade in and save her. Who would not? We all agree that we would. However, Singer goes on to argue that 5.4 million children under 5 died in 2017 from preventable or treatable causes. This includes measles, malaria and diarrhea, conditions that either don't exist in the western world, or if they do, they are rarely fatal. Singer argues these children are vulnerable to these diseases as they don't have safe drinking water or no sanitation, and when they fall ill their parents can't afford any medical treatment.

Singer suggests people consider their own situation. We could donate a relatively small amount of money, considerably less than the expensive shoes or other items that we don't really need such as nights out, new clothing, new cars and home renovations. He asks if it is possible that by choosing to spend money on such things, rather than contributing to an effective charity, we are leaving a child to die, a child that we could have saved?[2]

Indeed, Singer challenges us to more deeply consider our obligations to those living in extreme poverty and suggests that "… it may not be possible to consider ourselves to be living a morally good life unless we give a great deal more than most of us would think is realistic to expect human beings to give."[3]

I agree with much of what Singer says. However, I take a pragmatic approach to giving. Most in the western world won't give up their lifestyle, so I wouldn't suggest that they do. But for many families with surplus wealth I feel we can take them on a journey and inspire them to share more.

A better use of wealth

The Sustainable Development Goals (SDGs) were adopted by the United Nations in 2015 as a world-wide call to action "… to end poverty, protect the planet, and ensure that by 2030 all people enjoy peace and prosperity". There are 17 integrated SDGs.[4] As I write, these targets will not be achieved, particularly post Covid-19, but we have the ability to get there in the years post 2030, if we are committed to doing so. The SDG Goals Report 2022 suggests we have considerable work to do.[5]

Singer suggests that from his research, a major objection to people doing more is a lot of money has been given to help poor people in low-income countries yet "… there are still many millions living in extreme poverty, so isn't it all just a hopeless, insoluble problem?"[6] Singer points to the work done by the late Hans Rosling (with his son and daughter-in-law), showing that in many areas, the world is in a much better state than we think, with the status on extreme poverty, girls

2. https://www.thelifeyoucansave.org.au

3. Peter Singer, *The Life You Can Save*, The Life You Can Save, 2019, p. xxiii

4. https://sdgs.un.org/goals

5. https://unstats.un.org/sdgs/report/2022/

6. Peter Singer, op. cit., p. 45

finishing primary school, average life expectancy, levels of vaccinations of one year olds, all in much better shape, and improving, than we think.[7]

So Singer argues that it is a myth that we are not making progress on many issues around poverty.[8]

From my observations some people will never care. They are simply caught up in their own world and somewhat self-absorbed. However, I think there are many others who are concerned about these issues, they do want to take action, but don't know what to do or how to get started. Hopefully the sharing of my experiences in this book might get more people started on an exciting journey with their family, using some of their wealth to create positive change in the world.

7. Hans Rosling, *Factfulness*, Sceptre, 2018

8. Peter Singer, op. cit., p. 46

Chapter 3

Early days

"The measure of who we are is what we do with what we have."
– Vince Lombardi

Growing up

Born in Melbourne in 1965 I had a very comfortable upbringing. We were not a wealthy family (by western world standards), but Mum (Heather Paton) and Dad (Michael Winneke) worked hard to put their three children through private schools.

I was the second child, after my sister Caroline. Younger brother Richard followed me five years later. I don't think there was much cash left over after school fees. Dad was an old fashioned lawyer, more interested in solving his clients' problems than making money from them. There were no fancy cars or fancy holidays. Dad got sick in his early 50s so Mum stepped up and worked in several retail jobs to help pay the bills.

However, we lived in a nice house in Barkers Road, Kew, in Melbourne's inner eastern suburbs and from conversations around the kitchen table I knew we were better off than most in the world. I had a good education at Scotch College, and we learnt from the strong values of our parents and grandparents.

Of course, when I think of the early days, Mum is the first thought that comes to mind. Mum was the constant. Mum was always there. She had met Dad whilst he was studying law at the University of Melbourne. Mum and Dad courted when Mum commenced her Bachelor of Arts at the University. They became engaged in 1961.

It wasn't long before Caroline and I arrived. In the mid-1960s many mothers did not join the workforce, and Mum was no exception. Mum and Dad took the view that Dad would be the breadwinner and Mum would run the household.

We rarely dined at a restaurant or got takeaway food. Such activities were seen as expensive and unhealthy. Dad also liked his 'meat and three veg'. Fish and chips or takeaway Chinese food might happen four or five times a year. This was a real luxury and a delight for the kids!

I did the local paper round for a few months. I would wake at 5am and in the dark ride my bike up to the local newsagency. I would collect my papers and deliver them to my given route around the local streets. My first job didn't last long as the pay was terrible!

Dad's parents, Henry and Nancy Winneke, lived behind us, and Dad's younger brother, John, lived behind them with his first wife, Kaye, and their three kids, Andrew, Chris and Anna. Dad and John had grown up in our house. In the early 1960s Henry and Nancy built a smaller home in the back garden for themselves. Mum and Dad bought the old family home from Henry and Nancy in the mid-1960s. We shared a driveway. The three adjacent homes were linked by gates and there was a family dinner on many Sundays. I'm not sure how the in-laws felt about this, but the young cousins loved it! There was plenty of running between houses and kicking the footy in the court alongside Uncle John's house.

Rich and I played plenty of cricket in our front driveway. With a gravel driveway there was plenty of sideways ball movement. Given I was 5 years older, Rich got fit chasing the ball!

Dad

Dad was a lawyer, ran his own firm and practiced most forms of law ("better to be an all-rounder in life son"). However, he specialised in sport law and defamation. He had some interesting clients that included: Australian Olympic Committee, Moonee Valley Racing Club, North Melbourne Football Club, the Australian Golf Union and Channel 9 Melbourne. He was a gregarious cigar-smoking, whisky-drinking storyteller, sometimes fiery character who seemed to know everyone in

Melbourne in the 1970s/80s/90s.

Dad achieved an amazing amount. Probably in a moment of apprehension, I once asked him whether he had been ambitious. He said not particularly, but simply people had kept asking him to join various boards and committees. He had been a Melbourne City Councillor at the age of 34, a Melbourne & Metropolitan Board of Works Commissioner, a member of the Victorian Arts Centre Building Committee (with Ken Myer AC and Sir Ian Potter – whose families I would later connect with in the philanthropic sector), and a Trustee of the 'Ash Wednesday' 1983 Bushfire Public Appeal, amongst other notable tasks.

I learnt a lot from Dad. The key learnings were:

- humility: we are all equal. We all have different skills, from different backgrounds, but everyone is a human being, and should be treated with dignity

- material possessions: are superfluous and not a measure of a man's character

- life is about people: everybody has a story – if you ask and listen, you will probably learn something interesting

- work ethic: most achievements in life are through hard work, not talent

- detail: read it and understand it, as it is critical, and this will give you an advantage as many will be too lazy to do so

- people: many are over-rated, particularly those coming with big reputations.

Anglesea, Flinders & the Howqua

Each January we would spend a wonderful two weeks at the shared holiday house of Mum's family at Anglesea. If I wasn't surfing at the beach with Caroline, I would be playing cricket with Rich in the open garage under the house. Easters were spent in a very old, rented house at Flinders. This usually involved a lot of kicking the footy, and golf at the Flinders Golf Club.

Perhaps the best thing Dad did for us as children was our camping trips to the Howqua in the stunning Victorian high country. From the age of 8 until about 15, every January Dad and half a dozen other fathers and their children headed to the Howqua region for 10 days.

These trips were run by The Lovick family, tough mountain cattlemen who had run livestock on the high plains for many years. Old Jack was the patriarch. He was a tough old bugger and was seen still riding a horse at the age of 80 with 2 plastic hips! John and Charlie were his wonderful sons.

We would ride horses for several days on mountain trails and then the remaining week was on the back of 4-wheel drive vehicles. These vehicles had a tray back. Bags would be thrown in and a tarp thrown over the top, secured by rope. Most of the dads sat inside the vehicles. However, the kids would jump on the back. Our job was to hold on to rope so we wouldn't fall off the back! This was great fun, particularly as we drove across beautiful mountain passes.

Places visited usually included: King Billy, Wonnangatta, Bogong High Plains and Dargo. The scenery was simply stunning. Being January, it was usually very hot. We would 'skinny dip' in the rivers and go spotlighting for rabbits at night. A real highlight was racing the horses across beautiful places such as the Bogong High plains. We would absolutely 'fly' as we galloped across the plains – incredibly exciting and exhilarating! Not a helmet to be seen.

We would sit around the campfire each night, cooking marshmallows on sticks. If the weather was clear, we would sleep in our sleeping bags under the stars. If it was overcast, we would move under large tarps. If you needed a 'bog' you would have to grab a spade and toilet paper, walk into the forest, dig a hole and squat. It was great for young kids to be away from the 'luxuries of life', such as flushing toilets and running hot water, for a couple of weeks.

Our Howqua trips were some of my favourite memories of my early years.

Sport

Sport was always in our lives. Dad had been a great athlete: he represented Victoria in amateur Australian Rules Football, opened the bowling for Richmond (District Cricket, the forerunner to Premier Cricket) and played pennant golf for The Metropolitan Golf Club off a handicap of 2.

I loved team sports, but also played golf and tennis. Footy and cricket got most of my attention. The learnings from team sport are enormous: learning from a young age to work as a team; realising that everyone has different strengths and weaknesses; building a work ethic; leadership; dealing with failure individually and as a collective; learning to play in the right spirit; and being humble in victory.

It all builds resilience. I think the number one trait that we should try to instil in our children is resilience. Team sport greatly assists with this and many of these learnings can be applied to the workplace.

I had dreams of playing for the Hawthorn Football Club and was asked to train with their junior squad. (I think mainly as my uncle John had played in their inaugural premiership team in 1961.) However, I was clearly not tough enough or fast enough, and was shown the way to the gate very quickly!

Government house

My grandfather, Sir Henry Winneke AC was appointed Victoria's Governor in 1974. Papa was the first Australian born Victorian Governor. He was appointed for a five-year term, which was then extended for a further three years. This was right through my secondary school years. In those days of a smaller Melbourne the Governor was more widely known. My school nickname quickly became 'Henry'. This didn't worry me, but initially as a shy kid I probably would have preferred to have come from a lower profile family.

Henry was widely known as one of Victoria's most popular Governors as he was a real people person. During his period as Chief Justice of Victoria he and his mate, Sir Henry Bolte, the then Victorian Premier, would regularly sit through the night sharing stories and bottles of scotch. They would then be up at the crack of dawn, Henry B to run the State and Henry W to run the Courts!

Upon Papa's appointment, he and Nana moved into Government House. I have very fond memories of our visits to Government House. These visits were quite frequent during the summer months, where we would wander through the massive gardens, climb the tower to look at the stunning views over the Botanic Gardens, the Yarra River and the city, swim in the pool and play on the grass tennis courts. We would love these visits and they are fabulous memories.

School

I enjoyed school but was quite shy until about 4th form (now called year 10.) In the final years of school I was given several leadership positions which forced me out of my shyness. I was young for my year and in 1982 started my HSC year (now VCE) 16 years of age. Becoming a school Prefect, House Captain, one of the senior cadet leaders and captain of the 2nd XI cricket team put me right out of my comfort zone and helped slowly develop my leadership skills. School assemblies were held most days in the large Memorial Hall. It held around 1,000 students. The first time I addressed the school assembly at the end of year 11 I was to read the daily notices. I walked up to the stage and nearly froze as I looked at the sea of faces staring at me. I mumbled my lines incoherently and left the stage as quickly as I could.

It was at school that I met life-long friends Graeme Hamilton and Andrew Stern. We all went on to Monash University together. There were lots of fun times with Hammo over many years growing up. My favourite memories with Sterny were when he and I led an under 19 Old Scotch Football Club team to a premiership.

Whilst I didn't know what I wanted to do after school I knew that a degree was important to keep my options open. I can remember thinking at the time that this was serious stuff and as I wasn't a brilliant academic (I certainly didn't have maternal grandfather Sir George Paton's Rhodes Scholar genes!) I realised that I had to work harder than the next guy. This was something that I learnt from Dad and have basically applied throughout my life. In the final term I thought I needed to apply myself even further. As a result, I went to the library every lunchtime to study. I had worked out that there were many extra 'study hours' I could gain in this way. And besides, I had plenty of time in the future to play footy and cricket!

Upon reflection, and with the benefit of experience, I probably could have planned my study technique a little better and used my time more wisely. However, it was all worth it and I am proud of my discipline and how I applied myself. Prior to the final exams we had to lodge our university preferences. Whilst I still had very little understanding of what I wanted to do after school I included law and commerce at the top of my preferences. Previous academic results had indicated that I would probably not obtain the straight As to gain entry to law school. I was not concerned with this as law looked very dry to me.

This was an interesting point as I hailed from two generations of judges (soon to be three.) Henry Christian Winneke (County Court Judge), Henry Arthur Winneke (Supreme Court Judge and later Chief Justice) and later (uncle) John Spence Winneke AC (the first President of the Court of Appeal). Almost without fail, every week of my life as far back as I can remember people asked me, "Are you going into the law?" (Later, the question became, "Are you in the law?") I never felt any pressure on this issue. Mum and Dad certainly helped with this as none was applied from them. Dad actually said to me several times, "Don't go into the law." I never asked him whether he meant this, or it was his way of relieving any perceived pressure on me. I do know that he had become very cynical with the legal profession with its focus on specialisation and making money.

In the weeks leading up to the exams I would set the alarm for 5am and get up and do two hours of study before breakfast. I had realised that my brain was very clear in the morning and with no noise or distractions I could achieve a lot at that hour. This is a pattern I then continued throughout my life. I love reading biographies – a great way to learn about history and high achievers, and I can't recall a high achiever that didn't get out of bed early.

Anyway, the hard work paid off as I got into Economics at Monash University – by one mark!

I had certainly won the 'parent lottery'. I have always been aware of this, and for years have said that I am, 'the luckiest guy alive'. What should I do with this luck?

Chapter 4

University life and career formation

"Everyone is dealt a group of cards at birth. With them come possibilities and responsibilities. What one does with them is up to each one of us; and the sum of those choices, constitute our lives." – **Nicolas Berggruen**

Monash University

In March 1983 I commenced a degree in Economics (Accounting Major) at Monash University, when 'there was only one Monash' i.e. there was only one campus, which was the Clayton campus. Since that time the University has expanded at a rapid rate. Uni was a magical time of my life. Little responsibility and so much fun and freedom. I obtained my driver's licence and an old yellow Galant to get around in. Uni was also a great place to meet many new friends, from many walks of life. The long-lasting benefit of Uni was not some amazing educational legacy; it was the life-long close friends that I made such as Paul O'Bryan and Anthony Garnham. There were many others I met that I still see decades later.

I found the standard of lecturers to be ordinary and the course content incredibly theoretical. But the pace at Uni was leisurely; we had about 12 to 14 hours of lectures and tutorials each week. If you organised your weekly schedule cleverly at the commencement of each year you could get at least two days off.

There always seemed to be something to celebrate: getting

assignments done, passing exams, watching the Hunters & Collectors play at the Union building, regular 21st birthdays, winning the America's Cup and regular Hawthorn premierships!

To buy all those celebratory beers at Uni required money, notwithstanding that a pot of beer at the nearby Notting Hill Hotel was only 90 cents in the mid-1980s! I held a number of part-time jobs over my time at Uni. These included:

- waiter at Leonda function centre on the Yarra in Hawthorn

- legal clerk at Dad's office in Melbourne

- summer internship at Rundles, the accounting firm of Dad's mate and amateur football legend, Noel Rundle

- summer internship at accounting firm, Arthur Andersen (AA).

In year 10 we had started to have more choice over our subjects. At about this time I started to make a stream of important life decisions not based on what I wanted to do, but on what I did *not* want to do! I chose to do humanities-based subjects as I didn't enjoy the sciences. I chose to study economics/accounting at Monash as I wasn't interested in the other courses on offer. After Uni I accepted a job at AA as, ironically now, it had a great reputation and I didn't like the other options for me. I fell into the audit division as tax looked really dull.

I was thankful to AA Manager (future Partner) Simon Jones for taking a punt on me. AA generally hired those with straight distinctions. With the many distractions at Uni, I wasn't achieving those! When I thanked Simon years later, he said he could see that I had personality and leadership potential. Subsequent to the summer vacation work with AA in 1985/86, AA asked me to commence with them full time in 1987. For some time, Tony Jones (an old Uni mate) and I had discussed a 6-month world tour at the completion of Uni. I can recall meeting with the Recruitment Manager at AA in early 1986, Keith Ryall, to discuss my full time start date in 1987. I had rehearsed a corny story about my desire to have six months leave without pay in my first year with AA, to travel, and about the 'real life' experience that I would gain and how this would make me a more 'rounded' person.

I guess there was an element of truth in this. However, I simply wanted to see the world, and Jonesey and I had heard that graduates at the 'Big 8' accounting firms as they were known then (AA, Price Waterhouse, Coopers & Lybrand, Peat Marwick, Arthur Young, Ernst & Whinney, Deloitte, Haskins & Sells and Touche Ross) spent half their working day photocopying documents. Now that didn't sound like fun, nor much of a learning curve. Far better to be exploring the delights of Europe!

This amuses me as I reflect on it years later, now paperless. AA talked about going 'paperless' in the late 1980s. I see so many are still to get there nearly four decades later!

USA & Europe

Over many years I had saved $15,000. So, Jonesy and I were set. The 'around-the-world' plane ticket was acquired for $1,500. This enabled us innumerable stop-offs, as long as we kept heading east. The first leg was booked, and Jonesy and I jetted out in mid-February 1987, very excited about the adventure ahead, with backpacks secure in the hold. I arrived home about six months later, and wow, there were some amazing experiences in between, which included the exhilarating, fun, scary and romantic. A great adventure for two sheltered 22-year-old lads from the eastern suburbs of Melbourne!

We had three wonderful weeks cruising around the west coast of the USA in a Chevrolet. We flew to London and joined a two-week Contiki tour through the major tourist destinations in Europe. There was a party every night, so I challenged myself to not fall asleep whilst on the bus each day as we motored to our next destination. Through great discipline, mission accomplished! The tour ended in London, where we bought an old Mercedes-Benz diesel van (which we named 'Flash', as it looked far from it!) for £1,500 from a guy at Waterloo Station. Before we handed over the cash, we asked to see the engine. I'm not sure what we were looking for, but it seemed an appropriate question given the transaction. As we strode confidently to the front of the vehicle, the owner said, "Ah guys, the engine is at the back."

Over the next 4 months we drove over 20,000 kms through Europe. After crossing the English Channel in a ferry (no Chunnel back then) via Belgium and driving into Paris, we travelled down the west coast of France, into Spain, Portugal, Switzerland, Austria, Liechtenstein, Yugoslavia (behind the 'iron curtain'), Greece and the Greek Islands, Hungary, Czechoslovakia, East and West Germany, The Netherlands, Denmark, Sweden, Norway and then Scotland, Wales and back to London.

Jonesy was a great travelling companion and encouraged me to open my mind up to different cultures. I can recall him early in the trip in Paris, not understanding something on the restaurant menu, and ordering it anyway as he was keen to sample French cuisine!

Of course there were no mobile phones in the 1980s, so communication was difficult. Our parents had no idea where we were at any time! Imagine that today? Once a month I wrote a long letter to Mum and Dad, which had the dual role of informing them what we were up to and also becoming my trip journal.

As a young guy, I wasn't seeking to change the world. I was simply seeking adventure. However, I do recall reflecting at the time that the overt display of wealth in Monaco seemed extravagant given some of the poor towns we drove through. Perhaps some seeds were being sown?

The trip was a formative experience for me. Travelling for 6 months on the other side of the world, with almost no contact with family and friends at home, is a powerful way to build self-belief. So many stories! But that's a very different book for another day …

Arthur Andersen – audit

Prior to my overseas travel I had commenced full time with AA in the Audit Division in December 1986, on a graduate salary of $21,000 p.a. Clients included Plumrose Australia, Clemenger Advertising and Repco. One day I drove to Albury to conduct a stock-take of Plumrose's Yoplait yoghurt division. I can recall walking into the giant cold rooms comprising a vast quantity of huge vats of yoghurt. I was supposed to inspect all of them. It was freezing in there. A quick peek into a couple of them was enough for me and I was out of there. There appeared to be a lot of yoghurt – I thought the work-in-progress in the balance sheet seemed ok! On the guilty long drive home down the Hume Highway, I realised that the audit 'care factor' was not high. This was one of the first indicators to me that perhaps auditing was not the answer for me.

Upon my return from my 6-month world tour I returned to AA's audit division. As the weeks went by, I quickly developed a distaste for auditing. The role of the auditor is to basically 'verify' other peoples' work. Whilst the role was important, why would one wish to do that?

However, I had a dilemma. Whilst I still had no idea what I wanted to do career-wise, I had decided that in the long term it would be good for my resume if I completed my Professional Year (PY) with the Institute of Chartered Accountants, to become a chartered accountant. To undertake PY you had to be working with a chartered accounting firm. Prior to commencing you had to have worked for 12 months with such a firm. PY comprised four subjects completed over 12 months. This meant I would need to be at AA for at least two years. Was it possible to tolerate auditing for two years? I thought not. If I don't have my heart in something, I'm not very good at it. I thought this would not augur well for my career. Action was needed; but what?

Arthur Andersen - insolvency

I literally bumped into the solution. Mark Mentha was a Senior Manager in AA's Insolvency Division (later renamed Corporate Recovery). He later founded KordaMentha with Mark Korda. Mentha was a bit of a 'lad' and I had got on well with him when we had initially met. I had been learning AA's auditing process and he was teaching The Insolvency Training School to young insolvency graduates.

I was having another ordinary day in the Audit Division at AA's office at Collins Place when I turned a corner in the corridor and literally bumped into Mark. He asked, "How are you?" I said, "Not very well," in a typically frank response. When he asked why, I told him I wasn't enjoying the audit experience. He suggested I consider transferring to the Insolvency Division. He briefly explained the nature of the work: receiverships, liquidations and special investigations of companies in financial difficulty. He then organised for me to meet with John Spark the next day, at the time the sole insolvency partner in the Melbourne Office. There was a strong rumour that John carried a shotgun in the boot of his car. Well, the nature of the role is that you deal with some upset directors and creditors whose lives have been tipped upside down. My 20 minutes with John went well and I was offered a position in the Division effective immediately. With limited knowledge of the Division and the nature of the work, I accepted. It sounded interesting, and surely it couldn't be as boring as auditing?

That fortuitous meeting with Mark led to seven enjoyable years in the Corporate Recovery (Insolvency) Division. Led by John and Mark, and later Mark Korda, Mike Humphris, John Georgakis, Laurie Fitzgerald, David Winterbottom and Ross Cooke, there was a real sense of camaraderie in the Division. It was primarily male staff, with plenty of testosterone. However, there was a terrific sense of teamwork. We worked hard and played hard. It was a strong team, with some real characters including: Paul Ward, Janet Toy, Dave Ward-Ambler, Tim Le Cornu, Hugh Piper, Anne McNabb, Peter Derbyshire, Roger Grant, Graeme Hazeldine, Wendy Fowler, Mike Symons and Hamish Tadgell. I hired Hamish over two jugs of beer at the now extinct Phoenix Hotel in Flinders Street. The 1980s were a different time!

When I joined the division there were eight staff and it didn't rate highly in the marketplace. When I left seven years later there were about 100 staff and we were the preferred insolvency practitioner in Melbourne. It was very satisfying to be part of this team, and eventually to be a team leader in such a strong environment.

Jobs I worked on included Budget Rent a Car, Brashs, Otto Wurth smallgoods and Cherry Lane Fashion Group. One receivership that I worked on was a small electronics manufacturer based in Geelong. With the partner and manager of the job in Melbourne negotiating the terms of the sale of business, at the age of 22 I had to terminate the services of the 30 staff. This was the first time that I had to terminate staff myself, a very nerve-wracking experience and I was shaking as I addressed the group. As I locked up the warehouse hours later in the dark, I wondered whether anyone was waiting for me in the isolated car park. It was a brisk walk to the car. Unfortunately, I subsequently had to terminate staff on many occasions (at AA and later at Southern Cross Broadcasting), but you never forget your first time.

I did my Professional Year in 1988. This was a tough year. I was working hard establishing my career at AA, whilst studying part-time for my PY. Serious discipline was required for a socially minded 23 year old. However, it was a terrific learning to see how much one could achieve each week.

Secondment to London

In mid 1990 I commenced a 12-month secondment to AA's London Office. I arrived in London after two months spent exploring the west coast of Canada: British Columbia and Alberta. As Australian insolvency law was based on the insolvency law in the UK the transition wasn't difficult. However, everything was on a far larger scale. The London office had a terrific team with a bunch of gregarious characters, and of course London was a great base to further explore the UK and Europe with London-based Aussie mates Anthony Garnham and Brett Corfield.

On the way home a year later I met Jonesy in Nairobi, and we spent an extraordinary two months exploring Kenya, Tanzania, Zimbabwe, Namibia and South Africa. Africa is an assault on your senses. The sights, the sounds, the smells. Everything was way beyond anything that I had experienced before. Other than the amazing scenery, the animals and friendly people, the issue that stood out for me was the poverty at every turn. Everyone was scrapping for a living, hustling, trying to earn a dollar. I was starting to see how inequitable the world was. It was another clear reminder of how fortunate I was to be born in Melbourne. This luck didn't sit well with me. It seemed very unfair that I could wave my Australian passport, jump on a plane and return to my easy lifestyle at home.

Seven years of insolvency work was enough for me. I didn't want to be a career insolvency person, I didn't want to be a partner at AA and I wanted to move away from professional services. However, I was walking away with great memories, lots of learnings and some life-long friends.

I was very grateful for the opportunities that Mark Korda and Mark Mentha had provided me. I didn't realise how much I had learnt until I left AA. How to write a letter, how to write a client report, how to run a meeting, how to negotiate, how to cope when you were out of your depth, how to think on your feet, how to deal with difficult people, how to diffuse a heated meeting, how to act professionally at all times and the meaning of fantastic service.

Years later (shortly after 2000), I found it extraordinary when AA imploded. Due to reputational issues based around just a few of the thousands of world-wide partners, the firm ceased to exist. It was an amazing reminder that reputation is really all that matters to many organisations (and individuals for that matter), particularly those in professional services. You can spend years building a reputation, and it can be lost in a matter of moments.

During my insolvency days I had developed a healthy scepticism. Just because someone says something doesn't mean it is true. Look behind the words. Be curious. Ask questions. Delve a little further. Little did I realise at the time that this would be ideal training for the philanthropic sector! But my journey would not take me there immediately.

Media

The next stop was the media sector. This wasn't a burning desire. As part of my drifting nature at the time, I just happened to see an advertisement in the Australian Financial Review for an interesting role with a company that had growth opportunities, and recruiter Peter Tanner AM did the rest.

In mid 1995 I commenced as Corporate Analyst at Southern Cross Broadcasting (Australia) Limited (SCB). I primarily worked with Tony Bell (CEO) and Eddie Chia (Financial Controller and Company Secretary). The market capitalisation of SCB at the time was $65 million. When I left 8 years later it was over $500 million. By 2002 our television and radio outlets reached 94% of Australia's population and net profit had increased from $4 million to $35 million. It was an exciting ride!

The mantra was growth, and we were constantly on the lookout for media companies to gobble up. Acquisitions included:

- Radio 2UE (Sydney) and 4BC (Brisbane), which completed our national talk network given existing ownership of 3AW (Melbourne) and 6PR (Perth)

- Radio 6MMM (Perth)

- NWS9 (Channel 9) Adelaide

- Telecasters Australia Ltd (Ten Network regional affiliate in northern NSW and rural Queensland).

At one point we even considered acquiring the Ten Network, a much larger listed media entity that provided the bulk of our television programming.

My responsibilities included due diligence on acquisitions, restructuring acquired businesses, improving margins on existing businesses and negotiating Certified Agreements with trade unions.

After several years I sought to inject more purpose into my role. In the late 1990s I had been reading what Dame Anita Roddick was doing at The Body Shop–beauty products retailer–and her view that business could be a force for good. I found this fascinating and inspiring. I unsuccessfully tried to convince the CEO that SCB should establish a foundation and contribute 0.5% of net profit each year to the foundation, and establish a corporate community program that would have included a workplace giving program and a workplace volunteering program. I was convinced that any decent size businesses would all have such programs in years to come and that SCB should be a market leader.

There were some terrific general managers on the SCB team, including Mark Colson, Graham Mott, David Bacon and Denis English. A fun aspect of working at SCB at the time was that Corporate Head Office was based in the 3AW studio in Bank Street, South Melbourne. This brought me into regular contact with the 'radio personalities' of the day including Neil Mitchell AO, Dean Banks, John Burns, Ross Stevenson, Ernie Sigley, Shane Healy and David Hookes – former Test cricketer and terrific guy who tragically died so young. Some serious egos there!

Whilst it was a challenging position, fun, and with a good learning curve on how to run a publicly listed company, it dawned on me that a key part of my role was determining how many people we could sack without impacting the ratings. Not so inspiring. Also, when I seriously analysed my position, my role was to essentially create wealth for the 4,000 SCB shareholders. I knew many of the names on the share register, and they were already wealthy. Not so meaningful. I was on the wrong pathway.

I'm fortunate that I have never found it difficult to form relationships with people. I think curiosity helps. Everyone has a story and I love teasing it out. As I have wandered through life, I have collected people along the way who I thought had strong values and cared about the world. As I reflect on my time in the Australian media industry, it is interesting that I keep in touch with very few colleagues from that sector.

Chapter 5

My search for purpose

"The tragedy of life does not lie in not reaching your goal. It lies in having no goal to reach. It is not a calamity to die with dreams unfilled, but it is a calamity not to dream." – **Benjamin Mays**

A hollow feeling inside

I had enjoyed the corporate world for 16 years; eight years with Andersen and eight with Southern Cross Broadcasting. Aged 36, I had been reasonably well remunerated and had learnt a lot about the commercial world. Life was great: a good job, reasonably well paid and I owned my own little house.

Every winter I would leave the cold Melbourne air and spend three to four weeks backpacking in low-middle income countries. I wasn't looking to 'save the world'; I was simply seeking adventure off the well-worn tourist trail. Destinations included Africa, the Himalayas, western Asia, southeast Asia, the Middle East, Central America, South America, the Caribbean, and the Pacific Islands. There was something exhilarating about boots and backpack on, fending for yourself in an isolated part of the globe. I felt alive!

I was very privileged. In one bored, self-indulgent moment in my mid 30s I calculated that I had visited 52 countries. I lived a glamorous, extravagant life. However, I had a hollow feeling inside. My life really consisted of Aussie rules football, cricket, beach, travel, beer and girls. And not necessarily in that order. I drank too much back then. As I later reflected upon it, it was because I was a little bored.

When I looked in the mirror I thought 'I don't have enough purpose in my life'. I was searching for more meaning. To psychologists, purpose is an intention to achieve goals that are personally meaningful and make a positive impact on the world.[1] As I was in my mid 30s, I guessed that I had about 30 years of working life to go. Would I pass the 'rocking chair test'? I wanted to be able to sit in my rocking chair at 80 and reflect on my working life as having made some meaningful contribution to the world. We are all custodians of our world, and we all need to ensure that we leave it in better shape than when we entered it. Surely, I could make a positive impact on the world in some small way.

We seemed to be living in the era of self-gratification. There is nothing wrong with growing the personal balance sheet, but should this be our major focus? The 1990s saw the rise of the adulation of 'celebrity' assisted by new technology. A further pointer towards the focus on self.

I was surrounded by white-collar professionals. I wondered why more weren't doing some form of community work. In the 1990s, the topics at the dinner parties that I was attending primarily circled around the rapidly rising Melbourne property market, home renovations, European sports cars, luxury overseas holidays and private schools. That's fine, but I didn't find it very stimulating.

Years of travelling in low-middle income countries had changed my perspective on life. I had grown up in a sheltered world and travelling had broadened my horizons. I had seen the real world, and how most lived. It was not pretty. The world was not in good shape: poverty, hunger, conflict, climate change and eroding democracy.

Learning from those who have gone before

From my mid 20s I had taken the view that some part of my life should always be dedicated to the community. I can't quite recall where this came from – I think it just evolved. Deep in my subconscious were the learnings from watching the actions of my grandparents and parents.

I have never had a strong faith in my life. My parents sent me to a Presbyterian school and I attended Sunday School as a child, at the

---

1. https://greatergood.berkeley.edu/topic/purpose/definition

Frank Paton Memorial Church in Deepdene, named after my maternal great-grandfather, Rev. Frank Paton. My great-great-grandfather was John G. Paton, legendary Scottish Presbyterian minister who in the mid 19th century was trying to convert cannibals in the New Hebrides (now Vanuatu). It was odd to read John G. Paton's autobiography, *Missionary to the New Hebrides.* He should have been killed (and eaten) on numerous occasions by the locals. I should never have been born!

I had watched as my grandmother, Alice Paton, sat in her study for hours at a time and read aloud into a microphone the driest of voluminous legal textbooks, which was taped in order that vision-impaired students could study law. I can still hear her strong voice booming through her home. Extraordinary diligence. She was involved with many other community initiatives. Alice had been a polio sufferer, wearing a brace on her leg since early childhood. I never heard a complaint from her. She always focussed on those worse off than her.

Such action leaves an impression on young minds.

Alice's husband, Sir George Paton, had been the Vice-Chancellor of the University of Melbourne from 1951 to 1968. Being in that position, when there was only one university in Victoria, resulted in him being involved with many community initiatives. These included: being Australian delegate at the League of Nations Assembly in Geneva in 1938, arguing for more scholarships for Asian students (in order to foster relationships, not increase Uni income!), sitting on the board of the Melbourne Theatre Company and being the Australian Secretary of the Rhodes Trust (he was a former Rhodes Scholar), amongst other positions.[2]

Dad's father, Sir Henry Winneke, with his wife Nancy, had served the Victorian community for many years as Governor of the State.[3]

I recall not telling anyone at school or Uni that both my grandfathers had a knighthood for community service, for fear of sounding like a tosser! As I matured, I was very proud of the family histories.

Mum had been heavily involved with many community groups,

---

2. J. R. Poynter, *Australian Dictionary of Biography*, Volume 18, Melbourne University Press, 2012

3. Robert Coleman, *Above Renown: The Biography of Sir Henry Winneke*, MacMillan Australia, 1988

including the Royal Women's Hospital board and the Lady Mayoress' Committee. Dad had also felt a sense of civic duty. He regularly did pro bono legal work for many organisations.

Dad always stood up for what is right, even if it was to his own detriment. I have such admiration for this quality. It takes courage and seems to be rare. I have reflected on this many times over the years.

There was a far greater sense of civic duty in Mum and Dad's era – not so long ago. Our grandparents had lived through wars and depressions. It was automatic that you helped others. I'm not sure this trait is as prevalent today. Our generation has become the 'me' generation. We have everything. And if we don't, we just go down to the shop and buy it, on credit. It is very much focussed on satisfaction of self. This rarely provides inner satisfaction.

I think there are opportunities to turn this around, which we shall explore soon.

Volunteering

In 1995 when Peter Tanner had recruited me for the position at Southern Cross Broadcasting, he had sat on the board of The Reach Foundation (now known as Reach). Reach was a community organisation assisting youth at risk, encouraging them to ignore peer pressure and develop their own identities. It had been established by Brownlow Medallist Jim Stynes OAM, and Paul Currie. Reach was seeking to establish an inaugural Ball which was to be a key annual fundraiser. Peter asked me to Chair the inaugural committee with Jim's assistant, Amanda Freeman. I got my old mate Andy Stern involved, we put a committee together and held Reach's first Ball at the Melbourne Tennis Centre in 1996.

I ran this Annual Ball Committee for five years, with Amanda & Sterny, bringing in new committee members each year to bring fresh ideas and a broader audience. I then decided it was time to assist another community group. Soon after I bumped into old Uni colleague, Sonia Kent. Sonia had been asked by socialite Lillian Frank to head up a 'new generation' fundraising committee for The Royal Children's Hospital Melbourne. Sonia was looking for assistance. I joined the committee and in the next four years we held a variety of functions including race days, balls, cocktail parties and dinners at exclusive restaurants.

Bill Perkins, energy trader and author, suggests the aim in life should not be to maximise wealth, but to maximise your life experiences.[4] Many people around me seemed to be focussing primarily on wealth creation – whether this was a conscious decision or whether they were subconsciously copying those around them – they didn't seem content. What did I really want in life? What life experiences were I seeking?

Over these fundraising years I not only assisted with the raising of a few hundred thousand dollars, I always managed to have a lot of fun! I noticed how raising money for others gave me such an inner sense of satisfaction. Something was shifting inside me.

I will now discuss Jordan Kassalow's fascinating book, *Dare to Matter,* co-authored with Jennifer Krause[5]. Back in the late 1990s Kassalow's book had not been published, but it would have helped me think through meaning and purpose in my life, as my search for purpose was intensifying.

---

4. Bill Perkins, *Die With Zero*, First Mariner Books, 2021, p. 171

5. Jordan Kassalow & Jennifer Krause, *Dare to Matter*, Citadel Press Books, 2019

Chapter 6

Dare to matter

"If you are neutral in situations of injustice, you have chosen the side of the oppressor." – **Desmond Tutu**

Skoll World Forum

Several years ago I went with a client to the Skoll World Forum. Established by the Skoll Foundation (Jeff Skoll, eBay founder) and held in Oxford in April each year, Skoll is an annual gathering of one thousand donors and social entrepreneurs seeking to "… accelerate innovative solutions to the world's most pressing problems."[1] The Skoll secret sauce is to find smart social entrepreneurs, back them and then help scale up their work via the strong Skoll network.

You need to have your self-esteem in place when you first wander into Skoll. At the first morning tea I turned to the guy on my right and asked what he did. He said he was developing a social enterprise to sell, 'Avon lady' style, subsidised medical goods to mums in sub-Saharan Africa providing jobs to locals at the same time (Living Goods).[2] OK. I turned to the woman on my left and asked what she was doing. She said she was developing a social enterprise in Mali, Senegal and Tanzania that focussed on moving smallholder farms out of poverty by providing mobile layaway opportunities, allowing farmers to purchase seeds and

---

1. https://skoll.org/skoll-world-forum/

2. https://livinggoods.org

fertilizer in small increments (myAgro).[3]

Ah right, well I might just wander off to the loo and reflect on why my life ambition is so low!

Skoll is a different world. It is a forum of big vision, big ideas and big ambition, all seeking to solve problems across entire communities by changing the system. Sure, there is some ego there, but it is exhilarating. The buzz in the room and at all the little cafes and pubs in the Oxford village where meetings were taking place at all hours was amazing.

Jordan Kassalow

Skoll is where I met Jordan Kassalow. As I soon discovered, most people attend Skoll not for the plenaries or the breakout groups, but because a lot of social entrepreneurs and large donors from around the world have all landed in Oxford at the same time. Some don't even buy a ticket – they just organise meetings in the township.

The client I was with was funding a dozen social entrepreneurs working on major social issues, primarily in Africa. We had determined that it would be inefficient to employ two team members to wander around Africa searching for people to support as others were already doing that. We developed a 'follow strategy'. We knew Sam Morgan and Nina Gene at the New Zealand foundation, Jasmine Social Investments (JSI), we trusted them and liked the way they did their due diligence. JSI travelled to Africa every year to meet with partners on the ground, prepared due diligence and updated reports, shared it with us and the client generally matched the funding that JSI were providing. Efficient and effective.[4]

To share intelligence, JSI collaborated with Big Bang Philanthropy, a world-wide group of like-minded donors working on some of the world's most pressing issues.[5]

Kassalow founded Vision Spring, which is "creating access to

---

3. https://www.myagro.org

4. https://www.jasmine.org.nz

5. https://www.bigbangphilanthropy.org

affordable eyewear so that people living on less than $4 per day can see well to do well".[6] The day that I met him he was exhausted. He had flown in from the USA and headed to ten half-hour briefings with donors. We were meeting number 10! He was still impressive as he laid out his vision for the organisation, how they were tracking, and the challenges and needs for the forthcoming three years.

A few years later Kassalow co-authored the book, *Dare to Matter*,[7] a book that I wish he had written 25 years earlier. It is one of the better books that I have read on seeking purpose in life. He states that you don't need to be a billionaire, give up your day job or wait for retirement to make a difference in the world. Kassalow tells his story of, against his better thoughts, following his father's profession and becoming a successful New York optometrist. However, on a hiking trip when he was young, he thought he must be alive for some reason and he swore that, "I will matter".

He poses the thoughtful statement, "Just imagine a world where everyone dared to matter." He goes on: "Imagine a world where all people acted as if the world's present and future lay in their hands, hinged on their choices, turned on the axis of their dedication and the courage to be as exquisitely consequential as they have been created to be". And then he wonders: "Imagine how we might feel about ourselves to wake up each morning knowing that today is a day when the world can be different because we are in it."[8]

Dare to Matter follows Kassalow's journey as he struggles with lack of purpose whilst simultaneously developing a successful optometrist business. He reflects on how he wasn't asking himself the right questions at a young age, which would have led him more rapidly to the life that was right for him. He would have focussed earlier on what his friend describes as putting "… who we are at the forefront of what we do, not in the background." Kassalow: "If you dare to matter you will find fulfilment

---

6. https://visionspring.org

7. Jordan Kassalow & Jennifer Krause, op. cit.

8. Ibid., p. 18

and … your feet will not fail you."[9]

Kassalow realises that he can use his optometry skills to assist others in the world (via Vision Spring), whilst still maintaining a decent income to support his family.

He argues that each of us can't win a Nobel Prize, but we can all matter if we seek to. Through the book Kassalow provides a practical way for the reader to take thoughts—on seeking purpose and mattering—from thought to action. He does this by exploring important questions about the reader, their strengths, resources, beliefs and values. This should provide the reader the motivation to create change in the lives of others, fuelling life-purpose but also enabling the reader to have a decent quality of life.

Actor Jim Carrey says: "The effect you have on others is the most valuable currency there is."[10]

Given the pressing issues that the world faces, and the lack of strong political leadership, it's easy to give up, but Kassalow argues that if each of us *dare to matter* we can lead a more fulfilling life and create positive change. The reader's task is to determine the issue that you are best positioned to assist with. And this can be done by still having a reasonable income. If we can see the potential in ourselves, and become less focussed on self, we can see the world's potential.

Another useful book, *Career to Calling* is more a 'how-to guide' than memoir.[11] It's a very practical guide to moving from a career to your 'calling' and bringing more purpose to your life.

You are living your legacy now

During one of the many lockdowns in Melbourne during the Covid-19 pandemic I went for a walk with a former client. Roger was in his mid-60s. We walked the beautiful streets of Hawthorn, near where he lived. He and his wife had built a successful business and seemed to be in the

---

9. Jordan Kassalow & Jennifer Krause, op. cit., p. 27

10. Jim Carrey, The Meaning: https://www.youtube.com/watch?v=Z0ZrkBCnfxw

11. Annie Stewart, *Career to Calling*, Impact Press, 2019

midst of a successful transition of leadership to the next generation. He was spending a large percentage of his week on his family foundation, working with subject-matter experts on major issues in the world, such as the World Mosquito Program.

Roger had a huge amount of purpose in his life. As I drove home I reflected that he was one of the more content people that I knew. He was 'mattering' on a daily basis.

Kassalow quotes Mark Twain: "The two most important days in your life are the day you are born and the day you find out why."

My friend Jack Vincent, American author, has a great saying: "You are living your legacy now". We make conscious choices about the type of legacy we wish to leave. As we lie on our deathbed, will we be content with our choices? I suspect Roger will be. How was my legacy looking? It was never too late to start.

PART II: A BETTER USE OF WEALTH

Chapter 7

Why philanthropy?

"We make a living by what we get, but we make a life by what we give." –
Winston Churchill

I researched numerous 'for-purpose' entities in Australia. I was seeking an organisation with a mission that I was interested in and a culture that would suit me. It made sense to use the commercial skills that I had developed in my career. It would have been dopey for me to paint fences as I wasn't skilled at such work, would probably do a shoddy job, which would then have to be rectified by professionals within a short amount of time. I wanted to maximise my impact.

Over many years of overseas travel I had seen first-hand the world's inequity. This had been hammered home to me on many of my travels through low-middle income countries such as Nepal, Peru, Bolivia, Cuba, Guatemala, Vietnam, Kenya and Tanzania. Poverty and lack of opportunity. I would do some exploring, have some fun and then return to my western lifestyle. On every trip I became more aware of the unfairness that the locals could not jump on my plane.

I had also seen and read of many instances where generosity had had a positive impact on communities. I had witnessed examples where, at the request of the locals, travellers had assisted to expand a school, build a library or donate books. I was developing an interest in, and growing passion for, philanthropy's ability to address some of this inequity that I was seeing.

While significant wealth had been created in Australia in recent decades, for many reasons we had not developed a strong culture of giving.

Philanthropy defined

Philanthropy has transformed our nation and built many of the institutions that we take for granted today. In my home city of Melbourne alone, if I take a morning walk through the Botanic Gardens, need a procedure at the Epworth Hospital, take my elderly mum to The Florey Institute of Neuroscience to discuss Alzheimer's disease, drop my son at the University of Melbourne, take my aunty to get her new Cochlear hearing implant fitted, get a friend an appointment at Headspace, meet with my new immigrant mentee, buy the new novel from a Stella Prize winner, visit the New Masters' exhibition from Europe at the National Gallery of Victoria and catch a show at the Melbourne Theatre Company, all of these activities can occur due to the generosity of others. Yet usually we do not know the significant impact that philanthropy has had over decades at each of these institutions. Its influence is often unrecognised.

The Macquarie Dictionary defines *philanthropy* as the "love of mankind, esp. as manifested in deeds of practical beneficence". Philanthropy means people assisting fellow mankind and the community with their time, talent and/or treasure. Volunteering Australia tells us that we are quite good at volunteering. As of April 2022, despite complications due to Covid-19, 56.7% of Australians had undertaken some form of volunteering in the previous 12 months.[1] We volunteers are the backbone of many vital community groups around the country.

The focus of this book is the giving of 'treasure' – financial giving – and when I refer to philanthropy or giving, I am primarily referring to financial giving by high-net-worth families. This has been my focus for many years as this is where there is enormous scope to do much more and much better. Of course, you don't need to be a high-net-worth family

---

1. Volunteering Australia, *Submission to the Productivity Commission Review of Philanthropy*, May 2023, p. 5

to be generous, and the same principles raised in this book apply at any scale, whether you are a high-net-worth family or simply wish to share a percentage of your income.

The true test of a civil society is how we treat those less fortunate than ourselves. From my travels I wasn't convinced we were doing a good job. Philanthropy plays a critical, undersold role in any society. Major issues in the community cannot be solved by governments alone. Philanthropy Australia, the sector peak body, summarises philanthropy's role:

> *Philanthropy is uniquely placed to address these challenges by providing critical support to leaders, individuals, organisations and communities who are working so hard to make this world a better place. While philanthropy constitutes a relatively small proportion of the overall funds needed to address these challenges, it often provides the critical support that makes a real difference – kick-starting new ways of addressing disadvantage, taking risks where governments don't, providing immediate and responsive support in times of great need, and lifting up diverse voices to shape policy development.*[2]

Philanthropy's uniqueness

Philanthropy provides funding that impacts millions of people's lives each year. Many of our most iconic for-purpose entities would not survive in the same shape without philanthropic funding. Of course the philanthropic sector brings much more than cash when it seeks to address issues in the community. It can also bring skills, networks and passion to the table. On some occasions these latter resources are equally as, or more important in getting the job done.

---

2. Philanthropy Australia, *A Blueprint to Grow Structured Giving*, April 2021

Philanthropy has a unique place in our community. It:

- brings independence to the debate

- has an asset base that allows it to take a long term view

- can be a powerful change agent

- can take risks that others can't e.g. governments with taxpayer revenue

- can disseminate knowledge to others in the field

- is not answerable to voters at election time

- can bring critical non-cash resources to the table e.g. leverage, skills and networks.

Generally I believe families should act where they have passion. If the arts are your passion, well that's where you should focus. Personally I would be spending more time on what I consider the big issues within our community that need addressing: climate change, First Nations Australians, our fraying democracy and assisting our neighbours in the Pacific region.

I do think we need to reflect on Peter Singer's thought that, given a world of pressing humanitarian needs, some giving is morally dubious.

Interestingly, an old colleague, David Allen and I often pondered over the water cooler that if we could 'fix' parenting (i.e. improve parenting 10-fold so that many more kids would have a healthy and safe upbringing), then this would address many issues in our community.

As governments around Australia face increased budgetary pressures, philanthropy's role will grow. Of course it is important that philanthropy not replace the work of government, but it can meet unmet need. If a service is clearly a government responsibility, then it should remain so. As philanthropy marches in the front door, government shouldn't be wandering out the back door.

Philanthropic partnerships with government can be critical for the largest social issues. Success can often depend on working with or around government. Larger funders will need to take advice on how best to work with government to maximise impact. And government needs to get better at engaging with the philanthropic sector to maximise outcomes. There is often a role for philanthropy to take risks that perhaps governments can't, to test ideas, and if the pilot works then to pass over to governments so the program can be scaled up.

In a post Covid-19 world localised giving has become more of a priority. Philanthropy can empower communities to shape their own future through local intermediaries such as community foundations.

Philanthropy can also provide an independent voice to a debate crowded with vested interests. A great example of this independence in action is the positive impact that the ClimateWorks Centre, seed funded by The Myer Foundation (TMF) and in partnership with Monash University, has had on climate change policy in Australia.[3]

Paul Ylvisaker was a long-time dean of American philanthropy. He said, "Philanthropy is society's passing gear."[4] Philanthropy is a vehicle to try and make change occur.

As we will discuss throughout the book, philanthropy can provide great joy and satisfaction to families as they work together on a common goal. Many of the families that I have worked with were surprised with the level of joy their foundation had brought to their family, and expressed regret that they didn't commence their giving journey earlier.

My research

I did significant research on the philanthropic sector in Australia, as well as on the sector in the USA, Canada, United Kingdom and Europe. I could see that the sector in 2002 in Australia was small, was really a 'cottage industry' and needed to grow. There were few families engaged in the sector in a large, strategic way. I could also see that there were very few professionals in the sector in Australia attempting to drive the growth of the sector.

---

3. https://www.climateworkscentre.org

4. Rockefeller Philanthropy Advisors and the Stanford Social Innovation Review, *Powerful and Innovative Ideas for Grantmakers, Investors, and Nonprofits*, 2006

A 'light bulb' went off in my head. I believed that there was an opportunity for me to grow the philanthropic sector in Australia and to encourage high-net-worth families to get involved via establishing a family foundation. Looking back now, I'm not sure how I thought I would do that!

I made numerous 'cold calls' to CEOs and directors of large foundations seeking opportunities. These included Dorothy Scott AM (Ian Potter Foundation), Michael Liffman AM (ex TMF), Sandy Clark AO (TMF, Sidney Myer Fund and William Buckland Foundation) and the late Darvell Hutchinson AM (Helen McPherson Smith Trust). Dorothy suggested I call Mary Wooldridge, at the time the CEO of the Foundation for Young Australians, and later to become a Victorian Member of Parliament. Mary was very helpful and provided many suggestions, as well as insights into the sector.

I initially thought the right pathway for me might be community foundations. They had grown significantly in the USA during the 1980s and 1990s. The position of General Manager of The Lord Mayor's Charitable Trust, now known as the Lord Mayor's Charitable Foundation (LMCF), was advertised. Despite having no experience in the sector, I was short-listed for an interview. At the time in 2002, LMCF had a very low profile.

There I was, sitting in the boardroom in the Melbourne Town Hall opposite five 75-year-old white male trustees (including Darvell). I mounted my case for why I should be chosen. Twenty-five years earlier LMCF had been a household name in Melbourne. Now it had been forgotten. I argued that the Trust needed a 'shake-up' to again become a household name to encourage families to give. I knew at the time that I was taking an assertive stance. I meant what I said. However, I also thought that to be the successful candidate (and knowing I would likely be competing with individuals with significant sector experience) that I might need to take a stance on a couple of issues. Perhaps the trustees agreed that I was a touch challenging; I got a polite "thanks, but no thanks" letter from them!

I then started discussions with the other community foundation in Melbourne – the Melbourne Community Foundation, now known as the Australian Communities Foundation (ACF). I met the Chair, Hayden

Raysmith AM, director Marion Webster AM and then, over a meeting and a lunch, met the majority of the board. I thought I was in with a reasonable chance to take up the position of General Manager with ACF. Seeking growth, for the first time in their history, they were considering appointing a leader with a commercial background, as opposed to someone from the community sector.

As I was going through this process Mary Wooldridge rang and asked whether I had heard that a newly created position as Finance and Administration Manager at The Myer Foundation had become available? I had not. A window was opening …

Chapter 8

The first step into the sector

"Never lose your sense of outrage … There has to be in all of us a moral thermostat that flips when we are confronted by suffering, injustice, inequity, or callous behaviour." – **Paul Ylvisaker**

Sleepless nights

I was interviewed by a recruitment agent, and by Charles Lane, then CEO of The Myer Foundation (TMF) and Sidney Myer Fund (SMF). The interview with Charles went well. A second interview was organised with Charles, Andy Myer AM (TMF Director) and Janine Ferguson, Chief Financial Officer with The Myer Family Company (MFCo). I mentioned in the interview my family's link with the Myer family, recalling stories that Mum had told me years earlier about Sidney Myer's (the penniless immigrant who had founded the Myer Emporium) wife Merlyn regularly discreetly popping cheques into grandfather, George Paton's pocket when he was Vice-Chancellor at the University of Melbourne. Sidney and Merlyn Myer had been major supporters of the University.

The interviews must have gone well as I got the job. I halved my pay and in January 2003 commenced with TMF. I remember getting the first (significantly reduced) pay cheque thinking, "I'm pretty sure I know what I'm doing!" Charles was looking for someone with a finance background to get TMF's financial affairs in order, as well as improve its systems and processes.

Prior to taking the role at TMF I had had two sleepless nights. I thought I was being seriously considered for the role at the Australian

Communities Foundation. My ambition was to grow the Australian philanthropic sector. That was a major part of their mission. Of course, the finance role at TMF had no such mission. We make many decisions each week, but few have a significant impact on your life.

Despite my ambitions on sector growth, I concluded that whilst I had read extensively about philanthropy, I had little practical experience, and I would be best served by spending two years learning the ropes with the Myer family, meeting the key players in the sector and then move to a body charged with growing the sector. Given the senior position of the Myers in the philanthropic sector and the small size of the sector at the time, I met most of the key players within eight weeks!

In addition, a key factor in my thinking was that I had noticed a new form of family foundation, Prescribed Private Funds (now Private Ancillary Funds) had been introduced in Australia in 2001. I could see that their potential to create impact via high-net-worth families was likely to be larger than community foundation sub funds, as the latter generally have a significantly smaller average corpus.

Entering a new world

When I joined TMF it was as if I had entered another world. I remember thinking, "These people in the philanthropic sector actually care about the world and want to leave it a better place than how they found it." I had not encountered that in my 16 years in the corporate sector. It was fascinating.

In early 2004 I was appointed Company Secretary of TMF and in early 2006 I was appointed secretary of SMF.

TMF resided on the 45th floor of 55 Collins Street at Collins Place. It was on the corner of the floor, with the rest of the floor taken up by The Myer Family Office (MFO). MFO had been established in 1986 to provide a range of investment and financial services to Baillieu Myer AC (Bails), son of Sidney Myer. Within a short period of time many other Myer family members were being served by MFO. In 1999 the range of services was opened up to non-Myer family members. By the time of my arrival at MFO in 2003 it had about 35 staff: accountants, tax advisers, investment advisers and in-house lawyers.

A bright idea

Sitting at my desk in my first year at TMF with my 'selfish hat' on I thought, "I must be in one of the best places in Australia to do what I want to do – to grow the philanthropic sector." If we could package up all the skills on the floor – accounting, tax, wealth management, legal, the Myer family's wealth of philanthropic experience gleaned over decades – TMF's grant making skills and connections with the community, then we had a powerful combination to grow the philanthropic sector in Australia.

The 'Myer' name was one of the most trusted in the philanthropic sector in Australia. So I set out to replicate Rockefeller Philanthropy Advisors in the USA, a reputable philanthropy consulting house, which had spun out of The Rockefeller Foundation in 2002 and was sharing the Rockefellers' philanthropic experience with other families.

I first had a conversation with Graham Reeve, Managing Director of MFO, about establishing a philanthropic services division within MFO. Coincidently I knew Graham as he was a former Andersen tax partner. It seemed to be logical to me as, by definition of being a MFO client, all MFO clients had the capacity to get involved with philanthropy if they chose to. However, if the MD didn't want such a team, it was unlikely to go further. Graham agreed that the idea made sense and said that a philanthropic team had previously crossed his mind. Well, I was keen to implement it.

I then discussed the issue with senior Myer family members including Baillieu Myer (Mr Myer to me!), Rupert Myer AO, Andy Myer and Martyn Myer AO, and also with Graeme Sinclair AM, long-standing CEO of MFCo. MFCo was the wealth management vehicle for the Myer family (and at the time owned 100% of MFO). All indicated an eagerness for the issue to be pursued.

A tense Myer family meeting

The next step was a Myer family meeting to discuss the issue. The meeting was held in the MFCo boardroom, with senior Myer family members in attendance. Graham Reeve and I laid out our strategic plan for the implementation of MF Philanthropic Services (MFPS), that I had developed. I had heard that there was reticence by some family members for MFPS to go ahead. However, no-one had expressed that to me.

The matriarch of the family was Lady Southey AC, the youngest of Sidney Myer's four children. When her first husband had passed away (the winemaker Ross Shelmerdine) she had married Liberal Party power broker, Sir Robert Southey AO. Lady Southey, as I had been instructed to call her until she requested otherwise, was a very strong-willed woman. Her service to the community was extraordinary, over many years across many sectors, and she drove a Red Cross ambulance until late in life.

At the conclusion of our presentation, Lady Southey stated that there were plenty of other players in Melbourne who could grow the philanthropic sector and that she did not want to see the Myer family being seen to make money from philanthropy.

I respectfully pointed out to Lady Southey that these 'other players' were not doing a strong job growing the sector, which was stagnant. This was awkward as some of these were her friends and colleagues, including the industry peak body, Philanthropy Australia, of which she was the President at the time. I also advised that MFO would most likely not benefit financially from MFPS for some years. I suggested that when MFPS did make a surplus, I would be happy for the MFO board to direct it to appropriate for-purpose entities.

This confusion and uncertainty were similar to that met by the Rockefeller family in the early 2000s in the USA when they established Rockefeller Philanthropy Advisors.[1]

It was a tense but respectful debate between Lady Southey and me. No decision was made at the meeting.

---

1. Emma Beeston & Beth Breeze, *Advising Philanthropists*, Directory of Social Change, 2023, p. ix

The birth of MF Philanthropic Services

Thankfully the MFO board shortly after agreed that the establishment of MFPS made strategic sense and it was confirmed – MFPS would be created!

In July 2004 I remained in the same office, but my employment transferred from TMF to MFO. I thought of the old saying, "Careful what you pray for, as you just might get it!" What had I done? I had been so focussed on establishing MFPS that I had had little time for thought. I had left the 'comfortable' environment of TMF after only 18 months and created an enormous amount of work for myself, as well as the risk that the creation of MFPS may not work! Where would that leave me? And now I had a pregnant wife.

Upon reflection, it was interesting that the 38-year-old guy who had dated some amazing women, but had never looked like getting married, finds his purpose in life and there suddenly standing in front of him is Ange. Ange is intelligent, down-to-earth, gorgeous, warm, caring, rational with a sense of humour. Perhaps the timing of our connection was coincidental? I'm not sure it was. We clicked over a six-hour dinner at a pub in Port Melbourne. It was apparent immediately that we held similar strong values and interest in the community sector. We were engaged within a year of meeting and then married at sunset at Uluru, the heart of Australia, in mid 2004. In the following three years two gorgeous (well, most of the time) young boys arrived: Mike and Ed. I am very fortunate to have Ange by my side as we wander through life.

I needed to march on. I could feel it was 'my calling'. This was how I could 'matter'. I was already getting bored at TMF, as the challenges weren't great enough. I wanted to use my commercial skills to build a business in something that I thought particularly meaningful: growing the philanthropic sector in Australia. There was a unique opportunity to significantly grow the sector and make positive change in our community. And I thought MFO was the place to do it. It was a little daunting, but exciting. Best get some clients, I thought!

I had studied the work of several philanthropic advisers in USA. These included: Tracy Gary (brought out to Australia by Jill Reichstein OAM and the Reichstein Foundation), The Philanthropic Initiative and Rockefeller Philanthropy Advisors. I had also read the Stanford Social Innovation Review, Harvard Business Review and many books on philanthropy. The resources that I believe are the most useful are listed in the appendices to this book.

MFPS offered a range of services to clients:

- developing the family philanthropic vision

- engaging the next generation

- establishing the appropriate philanthropic entity

- grant research

- monitoring and evaluation of grant recipients

- secretariat, accounting and administration.

I am deeply grateful for Rupert Myer walking around to my office stating that his family foundation would like to become a client of MFPS. We had our first client. We were up and away!

In all meetings representing MFPS, I had Lady Southey on my shoulder i.e. an imaginary miniature version of her, watching and listening to how I conducted myself. I was very aware that as I grew the philanthropic sector, I was representing the Myer name, and I thought if she was 'always with me', then I would act in an appropriate way that she and the Myer family would be comfortable with.

Chapter 9

Australia's giving culture

"Money is like manure: it's only good if it is spread around."
– **J. Paul Getty**

We have staggering wealth

Staggering wealth has been created by Australians in recent decades. Wealth creation has gone to new levels. The *AFR Rich List 2023* indicates that the top 200 wealthiest families in Australia have aggregate wealth of $563 billion, with 141 billionaires. To make the list in 2023 you needed wealth of $690 million. The aggregate wealth of the list is up from $180 billion only 10 years ago, according to the *AFR's Rich List 2013*, when there were 36 billionaires. To make the list in that year you needed $235m. We have 58,000 Australians with wealth above $10 million.[1]

We are yet to build a culture of giving

Given that the bulk of Australia's wealth has only been created in the last 3-4 decades, it is not surprising that we are yet to build a culture of giving. The Myer family is into its 5th generation of wealth. I am sure there are other families in Australia that have had significant wealth for five generations, but I have been asking people for many years, and no-one has provided me with another name.

---

1. Credit Suisse, *Global Wealth Databook*, 2022, p. 130

The evidence suggests that the giving levels of high-net-worth individuals (HNWIs)[2] in Australia remains low:

- total structured giving (using a vehicle designed to enable giving) in 2020 was only $2.5b[3]

- 46.4% of the 14,816 taxpayers earning over $1 million p.a. did *not* claim a tax deduction for a gift to charity i.e. it seems likely they didn't make one[4]

- despite the *Rich List* suggesting there are 141 billionaires in the country (which suggests to me that there would probably be 175+), you can still count on one hand the number of foundations in Australia with a corpus of over $1 billion

- within the AFR's 2023, *Philanthropy 50* list of the country's 50 highest givers, 38% of those listed had passed away. And if you gave away $5 million you would still make the list

- nearly all the individuals mentioned on both the *Rich List* and *Philanthropy 50* are giving small %s of their net wealth. Many listed in the top 50 of the *Rich List* are not mentioned in the *Philanthropy 50*

- in 2022 donations from the top 50 philanthropic foundations, trusts and estates ($942 million) on the *Philanthropy 50* list represented just 0.25% of total wealth for the top 50 ($376 billion)[5]

---

2. HNWIs: net wealth >$10m

3. Philanthropy Australia, *A Blueprint to Grow Structured Giving*, April 2021

4. McGregor-Lowndes, Balczun & Williamson, *An Examination of Tax-Deductible Donations Made by Australian Taxpayers in 2019-20*, QUT, September 2022, p. 99

5. P. Flatau, L. Lester, J. T. Brown, M. Kyron, Z. Callis, and K. Muir, *High Net Wealth Giving in Australia: A Review of the Evidence*, Centre for Social Impact, August 2022, p. 14

- only three of those on both the 2022 *Philanthropy 50* list and the *Rich List* donated more than 0.75% of their wealth last year[6]

- over twenty years after the establishment of Private Ancillary Funds (PAFs), we still only have 2,060 PAFs,[7] despite Credit Suisse advising that around 58,000 Australians have wealth of >$10m[8]

- many public ancillary fund sub funds have a minimum sub fund size of only around $10,000-$20,000 (some start as low as $2,000), yet we still only have around 2,000 sub funds in Australia[9].

There are some historical reasons that Australia's giving culture lags behind the USA:

- "It (USA) operates in an environment which is resistant to the idea that the state has a prominent role to play in the provision of welfare and higher education services, cultural facilities and community assets"[10]

- "US philanthropy is not just an option which wealth provides but is a defining characteristic of the elite"[11]

- traditionally Australian income taxes were higher than in the USA, and we have had a stronger welfare safety net, so we have relied on governments to address a community issue for us

---

6. Ibid., p. 14

7. Philanthropy Australia, *Insights from Australian Philanthropy's Response to the Covid-19 Crisis*, 27/2/23, p. 15

8. Credit Suisse, *Global Wealth Databook*, 2022, p. 130

9. Philanthropy Australia, *A Blueprint to Grow Structured Giving,* April 2021, p. 8

10. Theresa Lloyd, *Why Rich People Give*, Summary, 2004, p. 8

11. Ibid., p. 8

- the USA is an older country with a significantly higher population than Australia. The Americans have had generations of wealth, whereas the bulk of the wealth in Australia has only been created in recent decades

- some American states have inheritance taxes, which encourages some to give whilst they are alive. There are no inheritance taxes in Australia

- Americans have been much better than Australians at marketing philanthropy products like donor-advised funds, which have grown enormously in the USA. Public ancillary fund sub funds have been poorly marketed in Australia

- generally, Americans are more comfortable talking about success, including financial success, which includes discussing their gift giving. This is common in the USA. In Australia we have few role models that are happy to discuss their giving, and we still seem to be struggling with the 'tall poppy' syndrome, where we seem to like to criticise successful people ('cut down the tall poppy').

In the last 20 years, the Australian Government has implemented many tax initiatives and structures to incentivise increased giving levels in this country, including the introduction of PAFs in 2001.

It is interesting to note that across all Australian individual taxpayers, on average we only donate 0.4% of our assessable income. And 71% of us do not claim a deduction for a gift to a charity. Most of us could triple our donation level to 1.2% and see no noticeable change to our lifestyle.[12]

Daniel Petre AO has funded numerous reports on Australia's giving culture in the last two decades. They all highlight our lack of generosity. The most recent was in 2022 with the Centre for Social Impact's comprehensive, *High Net Wealth Giving in Australia*. It concluded that, "... Australia's giving record remains relatively low compared with other wealthy countries. Donations by Australians are estimated to make up

---

12. McGregor-Lowndes, Balczun & Williamson, op. cit., p. 99

0.81% of Gross Domestic Product compared to the United Kingdom (0.96%), Canada (1%), New Zealand (1.84%) and the United States (2.1%)."[13]

We need to change the culture

The reasons for low levels of giving by HNWIs in Australia are primarily cultural:

- most of the wealth in Australia has been created in recent decades and we are yet to develop a culture of giving

- Philanthropy Australia, the peak body, was only established in 1977 (initially called the Australian Association of Philanthropy) and it wasn't until 1988 that The Myer Foundation, Ian Potter Foundation and other foundations provided funding to build the peak body secretariat

- we rarely openly talk about our giving

- the 'tall poppy' syndrome still exists in Australia, and we don't celebrate individual success as naturally as some other countries

- we are still learning to celebrate giving. *Australia's Top 50 Philanthropic Gifts*, cataloguing some of the best and most innovative gifts in our history, is a rare example of doing just that.[14] Philanthropy Australia's, *Australian Philanthropy Awards* have only been running since 2016

- many of our philanthropic role models have long passed away e.g. Sidney Myer, Sir Ian Potter, Sir Vincent Fairfax

- we have few living, public exemplar philanthropic role models for others to aspire to

---

13. P. Flatau, L. Lester, J. T. Brown, M. Kyron, Z. Callis, and K. Muir, op. cit., p. 13

14. The Myer Family Company, *Australia's Top 50 Philanthropic Gifts*, 2013

- there is very minimal peer pressure on HNWIs in Australia to give away material sums of money. Whilst the USA has a different history and culture to Australia, generally in the USA if you are financially successful, it is almost a given that you share it, and in fact you may be deemed a social pariah if you do not. There is peer pressure to act

- upon the passing of a 'successful' businessperson in Australia, there is discussion about their achievements in business, but there is little discussion about their contribution to the community through giving, or lack of, as there was in the USA when Apple founder, Steve Jobs, passed away.

When businessman and renowned philanthropist, Sidney Myer passed away in 1934 it is said that 100,000 people lined the streets of the Box Hill cemetery where he was to be buried.[15] This was approximately 10% of Melbourne's population at the time! For which businessperson in Australia would that occur today?

So, we are starting from a fairly low base. I think once we educate families on efficient structured giving, the satisfaction of working with their family on common goals, the impact that they can have in their chosen areas and the joy of giving, we can start a revolution of increased giving.

---

15. Michael Liffman, *A Tradition of Giving*, Melbourne University Press, 2004

Chapter 10

Chuck Feeney

"Chuck has set an example … he is my hero and Bill Gates' hero. He should be everybody's hero." – **Warren Buffett**

My inspiration

We met Chuck Feeney in chapter one. Chuck has been my inspiration for many years. Chuck was an Irish American businessman and philanthropist. He was a co-founder of Duty Free Shoppers Group. Driven by a belief that the best use of wealth is to help people, Feeney founded The Atlantic Philanthropies (AP) in 1982. Initially his giving was anonymous. Over the years he was persuaded that if he went public then it would influence others to do more. Chuck said he didn't want to "blow his horn" but that, "… eventually we became synonymous with anonymous".[1]

By the time AP ceased operation in 2020, the foundation had made grants of more than USD8 billion.

Feeney summarised his mission in a few sentences. "I see little reason to delay giving when so much good can be achieved through supporting worthwhile causes. Besides, it's a lot more fun to give while you live than give while you're dead!"[2]

---

1. Conor O'Clery, *The Billionaire Who Wasn't*, PublicAffairs, 2013, p.309

2. https://www.forbes.com/sites/stevenbertoni/2020/09/15/exclusive-the-billionaire-who-wanted-to-die-brokeis-now-officially-broke/?sh=6bd2cb813a2a

For years I have asked people, "Who is Australia's greatest philanthropist? Someone who has gifted $550m to the country." (Only recently overtaken by an Australian.) Very few guessed Chuck Feeney!

A leader amongst leaders

Feeney is known as the 'spiritual leader' of the overseas Giving Pledge. Chuck didn't want toys. He had a distaste for ostentation and was well known for his frugality and humility. He didn't own houses, he travelled in 'coach class' and wore simple clothes.

Bill Gates – Microsoft and Gates Foundation cofounder – said of Chuck:

> "Chuck created a path for other philanthropists to follow. I remember meeting him before starting the Giving Pledge. He told me we should encourage people not to give just 50%, but as much as possible during their lifetime. No one is a better example of that than Chuck. Many people talk to me about how he inspired them. It is truly amazing."[3]

American John Arnold, Founder of Arnold Ventures said:

> "Chuck pioneered the model where giving finishes late in life, rather than starting. He was able to be more aggressive, he was able to take bigger risks and just get more enjoyment from his giving. There's great power in giving while living. The longer the distance between the person who funded the philanthropy and the work, the greater the risk of it becoming bureaucratic and institutional – that's the death knell for philanthropy."[4]

---

3. https://www.forbes.com/sites/stevenbertoni/2020/09/15/exclusive-the-billionaire-who-wanted-to-die-brokeis-now-officially-broke/?sh=6bd2cb813a2a

4. Ibid.

Chuck took the learnings from his business career and applied them to his giving. "… dynamism, vigilance, and the informed risk-taking investment inherent in entrepreneurial work – together with making good relationships and personal engagement a priority. In business, as in philanthropy, he had always sought an independent, strategic edge where potential was often greatest."[5] Chuck didn't operate from the 'ivory tower'. He liked to make site visits to 'kick the tyres'. "Spending is not a big problem, but spending it meaningfully is", Chuck reflected.[6]

Big bets

AP liked to make big bets, particularly focussed on health and medical research, higher education, human rights and reconciliation, children and ageing. Some of Atlantic's many wins include:

- promoted reconciliation and peace in Northern Ireland and South Africa

- strengthened major health care facilities in Vietnam

- strengthened biomedical research facilities in Australia

- transformed university infrastructure in Northern Ireland and the Republic of Ireland.

For big ideas Chuck sought five layers of leverage. AP's financial commitment was often subject to significant funding from:

- the intended recipient

- local large donors

- the State Government

5. Conor O'Clery, op. cit., p. 348

6. Ibid., p. 392

- the Federal Government.

Of course with Chuck's 'giving while living' philosophy, AP was a limited life foundation, not a perpetual foundation. Limited life foundations are still very rare in Australia.

You can learn more about Chuck and AP from the foundation's website, which has, in detail, documented its journey and learnings, including very useful papers on their 'Top 10 Lessons', 'Advocacy for Impact', 'Operating for Limited Life', 'Strategic Litigation' and 'Government Partnerships & Engagement'.[7]

Former AP CEO, Chris Oechsli said, "Chuck's gift to philanthropy is his challenge to high-net-worth individuals to apply both their wealth and their considerable personal skills to making a difference in people's lives now, in the donor's lifetime."[8]

Chuck thought deeply about the little money he required to live and how his kids should forge their own paths. Despite his achievements around the world and in Australia, Chuck is still not well known here. If we can encourage a few 'Australian Chucks', to 'give while you live', they could be great role models here and introduce many more Australian families to the joy and satisfaction of giving.

---

7. https://www.atlanticphilanthropies.org

8. Conor O'Clery, op. cit., p. 393

Chapter 11

How much is enough?

"If your identity is tied to what you own, it's hard to give it away."
– **Rosemary Santos**

Never enough

In my experience families create wealth, buy assets such as a nice car (or two), a nicer home, a holiday house and build an investment portfolio. Then they seek to create more wealth to do a large renovation to create an even better home and then buy a holiday house in a better street. And then a boat would be nice … There never seems to be enough. Wealth creation becomes a never ending cycle.

When John D. Rockefeller was asked how much was enough, he answered, "Just a little bit more."[1]

Wealth creation is the result of many factors. Yes, hard work and intelligence are key factors. But Warren Buffett thought there are other factors too. "My wealth has come from a combination of living in America, lucky genes and compound interest." [2]

In addition Buffett said:

> *"My luck was accentuated by my living in a market system that sometimes produces distorted results, though overall*

---

1. John C. Bogle, *Enough*, John Wiley & Sons, 2009, p. 238

2. https://givingpledge.org/pledger?pledgerId=177

it serves our country well … I've worked in an economy that rewards someone who saves the lives of others on a battlefield with a medal, rewards a great teacher with thank-you notes from parents, but rewards those who can detect the mispricing of securities with sums reaching into the billions. In short, fate's distribution of long straws is wildly capricious."

Three ways to use your wealth

Fundamentally there are only three ways to use your wealth:

1. *Spend it all*
High-net-worth families usually have a level of wealth that is too high to spend in their lifetime.

2. *Give it to your kids or family*
Providing significant assets and income streams to children in Australia is very common. However, it can be fraught with danger, even if managed very carefully.

3. *Give it away*
The final option is to work with your family, with assistance from relevant experts, and have the privilege and satisfaction of tackling major issues in our community. As Chuck Feeney says when explaining his 'giving while living' philosophy, "I see little reason to delay giving when so much good can be achieved through supporting worthwhile causes today."[3]

Industrialist, and once the richest man in the world, Andrew Carnegie took the view that people should administer their wealth on behalf of the community. In 1889 he wrote:

---

3. https://www.atlanticphilanthropies.org/videos/chuck-feeney-giving-while-living

"... this then is held to be the duty of the man of wealth: To consider all surplus revenues which come to him simply as trust funds, which he is called upon to administer ... in the manner which, in his judgment, is best calculated to produce the most beneficial results for the community."[4]

Carnegie then went further: "The man who dies thus rich dies disgraced."[5]

We know Gina Rinehart AO has too much to spend in her lifetime and given the litigating with her children, it is unlikely that they will receive a material amount of her wealth. So it is likely that she will be giving it away, either during her lifetime or upon death! Hopefully this is done strategically and directed to issues of high importance to the nation and the world. Just imagine the fun and satisfaction she could be having doing this whilst she is alive.

At a party given by a billionaire on Shelter Island, Kurt Vonnegut informs his pal, Joseph Heller, that their host, a hedge fund manager, had made more money in a single day than Heller had earned from his wildly popular novel *Catch-22* over its whole history. Heller responds, "Yes, but I have something he will never have ... enough."[6]

So how much is enough?

Many people are aware that they have more than they need. They are aware that the assets that they have accumulated and/or inherited are significantly more than they will ever spend, or wish to share with their family. However, we often don't do the detailed work to determine what our 'surplus' is. For some there are also emotional reasons for not wishing to 'let go' of wealth. For others there is a fear that wealth could be lost if financial markets turn downwards. And so we sit on our wealth

---

4. Andrew Carnegie, *The Gospel of Wealth*, 1889, p. 12

5. Ibid., p. 15

6. John C. Bogle, op. cit., p. 1

and keep accumulating.

The calculation of the surplus can help with the 'letting go'. There are simple steps to assist with determining the surplus:

1.Calculate your financial needs

Determine, via spreadsheet, your financial needs during the estimated remainder of your life. Consider issues such as:

- your lifestyle

- the family's education needs

- holidays

- ageing parents

- your own aged care needs

- medical emergency buffer

- family emergency buffer

- how much to leave the kids (see next chapter)

- other

- a contingency amount.

2. Calculate your surplus

Once you have considered your net wealth and financial needs, and made assumptions about future annual income and capital growth from your portfolio, you will be able to determine your surplus.

3. Determine the use of your 'surplus'

Discuss with your family, and relevant experts, how you can maximise the use of your surplus to create constructive change in the community in an area(s) that your family is passionate about.

When families do this calculation, they are usually surprised at how high the 'surplus' is. And so the process of 'letting go' of wealth becomes easier.

I had a client who did exactly this calculation a number of years ago. A liquidity event was approaching, so mum and dad sat down and with an Excel spreadsheet determined, in detail, their financial needs. This included a very modest bequest for their children. They were surprised by the size of the surplus and when the cash landed in their bank account a few months later they immediately transferred the 'surplus' into their family foundation.

Claude Rosenberg, founder of RCM Capital Management, has been through the same process:

> *"I listed our income and the value of our assets, estimated the total investment returns … compared the results to a specific budget that included our needs, some luxuries, a reserve for our children's futures, and enough to cover our philanthropic outlays. The conclusions were startling. It was as if I had literally found money. To my surprise, I discovered that we had dramatically understated our potential. We could afford to give, or spend, much more. Since we were basically happy with our standard of living, and since our income and our asset ownership left a sizable cushion for us, we concluded that we could have been sharing more of what we had. A lot more! So we weren't as generous as we had imagined."*[7]

The view of Rakesh Khurana, Harvard Business School Professor, was, "I will create value for society, rather than extract it."[8]

---

7. Claude Rosenberg Jr, *Wealthy and Wise*, Little Brown & Co, 1994, p. 4

8. John C. Bogle, op. cit., p. 123

Warren Buffett had an interesting take on his wealth:

> *"The reaction of my family and me to our extraordinary good fortune is not guilt, but rather gratitude. Were we to use more than 1% of my claim checks on ourselves, neither our happiness nor our well-being would be enhanced. In contrast, that remaining 99% can have a huge effect on the health and welfare of others. That reality sets an obvious course for me and my family: keep all we can conceivably need and distribute the rest to society, for its needs."*[9]

In 2006 Buffett announced that the bulk of his fortune would be gifted to the Bill and Melinda Gates Foundation.

'How much is enough?' can be asked by those with different levels of wealth at different points in our life. Even those with lesser means can choose not to spend more than they need and give away the excess.

John Bogle, founder of investment company, The Vanguard Group, reflected:

> *"But I know that each one of us can profit by some moments of quiet introspection about whether our lives are driven far too much by the accumulation of things, and not nearly enough by the exercise of bold commitment to our family, to our work, to a worthy cause, to our society, and to our world."*[10]

Do children want mum and dad to work harder, or spend more time with them? Most kids would want to spend more time with their parents. Bill Perkins, energy trader and author, argues that at some point you are depleting your kids' 'inheritance' (i.e. their experience memories) because you are spending less time with them creating wonderful

9. https://givingpledge.org/pledger?pledgerId=177

10. John C. Bogle, op. cit. p. 192

experiences.[11]

Interestingly, Perkins also believes that you can't be generous when you are dead, even if you make gifts via your Will. You no longer need the money, and the transfer of assets is legally enforced, "… so how can that be generous?"[12]

Does money make you happy?

Certainly creating initial wealth provides comforts and makes life a little easier. It allows you to buy healthy food, put a nice roof over your head in a nice suburb, you can buy a car that doesn't break down, you can go to nice restaurants, buy a nicer drop of wine and take exotic holidays. Most of us would get excited by these ideas.

However, John Bogle argues money can provide a level of happiness, but as we get used to our higher level of material wealth, it turns out to be a transitory sort of happiness.[13] We can buy items which give us a short boost in happiness, but then we drop back to the prior level as the new possessions don't add to the feeling of living a meaningful life.

Ryan and Deci argue that it's not money that determines our happiness but the presence of a combination of three attributes:

1. autonomy—the extent to which we have the ability to control our own lives

2. maintaining connectiveness with other human beings, in the form of love of our families, our pleasure in friends and colleagues, and an openness with those we meet in all walks of life

---

11. Bill Perkins, op. cit., p. 95

12. Ibid., p. 97

13. John C. Bogle, op. cit., p. 230

3. exercising competence, using our talents, inspiring and striving to learn.[14]

Giving to an area that you are passionate about ('autonomy') provides a great way to bring more purpose to your life by working with your family and for-purpose partners ('connectiveness') and using your skills for good ('competence') in an outward-focussed way.

> *"We experienced directly what the studies on happiness show—that once the basics are covered there is no correlation between how much money one has and how happy one is—but there is a high correlation between having meaningful work and meaningful relationships to one's health and happiness."* – Ray and Barbara Dalio[15]

We could transform the world, and our families, if more of us thought about how much is enough and then used the surplus constructively in the community.

---

14. Richard Ryan & Edward Deci, *American Psychologist*, January 2000

15. https://givingpledge.org/pledger?pledgerId=185

Chapter 12

How much to leave the kids?

"Leave enough for your kids to do anything in life, but not enough to do nothing." – **Warren Buffett**

Families in countries with long-established wealth, such as the USA, have grappled with the issue of children and inheritance for a long period of time. Given the bulk of Australia's wealth creation has occurred in recent decades, this is a relatively new issue for most high-net-worth (HNW) families here, and in my experience is not given enough thought.

This issue of inheritance has always fascinated me. It is a very personal issue, which evokes very different views from people. However, I find it unusual that one would leave significant income streams to their children. In such cases the children then 'don't need to get out of bed in the morning'.

Carnegie, Gates and Buffett

One of America's richest men in 1889, Andrew Carnegie, wrote in *The Gospel of Wealth*, "I would as soon leave my son a curse as the almighty dollar." Carnegie further claimed that poverty, not wealth, was the "only school capable of producing the supremely great, the genius", and that inherited wealth robbed the inheritors of their self-respect and blocked the fittest from advancing. Carnegie's view was that no society could reach its highest potential if it gave the rich an advantage over the poor in attaining positions of leadership and responsibility.[1]

Bill and Melinda Gates and Warren Buffett, amongst many others, plan to leave their children very small portions of their estates. If money is supposed to provide a security blanket for children, perhaps one should ask, "How little is too little?" as opposed to, "How much is too much?"

I have seen some families take the view that the security blanket can be the provision of a small to modest sized house. And nothing more. This aligns with Buffett's excellent quote, "Leave enough for your kids to do anything in life, but not enough to do nothing."

Self-esteem

We get our self-esteem from our achievements in life, not our inheritance. Leaving a child a small to modest sized house would ensure they could enter the property market as an owner and not pay rent or pay off a mortgage. A roof over the head provides some security. This would assist the next generation to follow their passion and take up the career of their choice, regardless of the pay. This is an enormous head start in life, which allows one to follow one's dreams. But by leaving no income stream this means that one needs to get out of bed each day to work to put food on the table, build skills and a life, and be a role model for the next generation. This would also hopefully ensure they got the best out of their talents.

I believe it is prudent to provide this gift to children when they most need it, early in their careers when they are yet to build an asset base. This will have the most impact. And of course, advise them that no further inheritance is forthcoming, so they get on with their life, and are not waiting for you to die.

It is easy to mount the case that to be given a small to modest sized house is too much as most of us learnt to save and pay off the mortgage. But for HNW families I think it is about right. You may wish to set aside an extra sum for the grandchildren's education and medical emergencies.

---

1. David Nasaw, *Andrew Carnegie*, Penguin Books, 2006, p. 349

"Part of the reason for believing that my wealth should be given back to society and not, in any substantial percentage, be passed on to my children, is that I don't think it would be good for them. They really need to get out and work and contribute to society. I think that's an important element of a fulfilling life." – Bill Gates

Trustafarians

From my experience these families are rare, with most HNW families leaving the majority of their wealth to the children, to continue the family dynasty and so the kids can have all that they need. This can be a dangerous proposition.

I have seen many, what a friend of mine calls, 'trustafarians', those that don't really work, but sit on family office investment committees, watching money being managed by professionals. Whilst I have seen families successfully manage large bequests to their children, I have seen a greater number of families manage this process poorly, leaving kids' lives adversely impacted. This can occur for a range of reasons: their initiative has been stunted, it has built a sense of entitlement, they don't know their place in life, lack of dreams, and lack of trust in others. This can result in low self-esteem.

One client I worked with grew up with very little. He built a very successful business and amassed significant wealth. I established a foundation for him into which he gifted a small sum. He had several children. One day I was gently exploring with him the notion of what one should leave their kids. He explained that he and his wife had endured many hardships early in their life, and they didn't want their kids to endure the same hardships. I chatted with him in some detail about the difficulties he had faced, and how it built his work ethic, resilience and self-esteem, which made him the individual that he was. I then asked him why he wouldn't want his kids to have these same experiences, to build their character. He didn't have an answer.

> *"Wealth is created. If that wealth is all passed on to another generation, its benefits often are greatly underutilized, as those who inherit the wealth view their mission as one of maintaining it. The better path is one that allows wealth to be activated as a force to make the world a better place through endless avenues."* – Dan and Jennifer Gilbert[2]

I have spoken on this delicate issue publicly on many occasions. It certainly gets some people fired up. In one article I discussed the dangers of leaving kids significant income streams. One client spoke to me irately and asked whether I was accusing he and his wife of being poor parents, and whether I was the 'inheritance Nazi'? An emotional issue indeed!

Learn to work

James E. Hughes, Jr. is an American adviser who has worked with HNW families around the world for decades and published many books on families and wealth. He has a strong view on 'work', which he shares in a conversation with Charles Collier, former senior philanthropic adviser at Harvard University.

Collier:

> *"Why does the third or fourth generation tend to dissipate the family financial wealth?"*

Hughes:

> *"Basically, they do not learn to work. Work in its deepest dimension equates to a calling. Discovering your calling is*

---

2. https://givingpledge.org/pledger?pledgerId=201

the most important task an individual can undertake ...".[3]

Giving versus inheriting

As usual Warren Buffett took a different approach to most. He told his kids they would inherit very little, but he made substantial gifts to each of his kids' family foundations.

American businessman, Michael Bloomberg said:

> *"... and if you want to do something for your children and show how much you love them, the single best thing by far is to support organizations that will create a better world for them and their children. Long term, they will benefit more from your philanthropy than from your will. I believe the philanthropic contributions I'm now making are as much gifts to my children as they are to the recipient organizations."* [4]

Billionaire businessman, Manoj Bhargava said:

> *"My choice was to ruin my son's life by giving him money or giving 90+% to charity. Not much of a choice. Service to others seems the only intelligent choice for the use of wealth. The other choices especially personal consumption seem either useless or harmful."*[5]

We could transform the size of the philanthropic sector in Australia overnight if families gave more consideration to the critical issue of

---

3. Charles W. Collier, *Wealth in Families*, Harvard University, 2003, p. 43

4. https://givingpledge.org/pledger?pledgerId=172

5. https://givingpledge.org/pledger?pledgerId=167

inheritance. We need to show families how thoughtfully their wealth can be used for the benefit of the community. A good start is by getting the kids engaged in the community when they are young.

Chapter 13

Engaging the next gen in the community

"For of those to whom much is given, much is required."
– John F. Kennedy

As parents, Ange and I believed it was important to instil an ethos of caring and giving within our children. A strong community supports each other, particularly the most vulnerable. An individual without empathy is usually an individual without a soul.

Sharing

When our boys were about five years of age, they started receiving pocket money. This is a great opportunity for kids to learn about financial responsibility. They received $3 per week. They were given a 'Moonjar' moneybox which had three named coin slots:[1]

1. save

2. spend

3. share.

The boys had to put the coins in a slot, with a minimum of $1 going

---

1. https://moonjar.com/index.php/products/classic-moonjar-moneybox/

into the 'save' and 'share' slots each. This sparked a conversation on day 1, with one of the boys asking, "Dad, why do I have to share my money? It's mine!" With the 'spend' money the kids could spend as they chose, so there were some learnings about the value of money. A couple of times a year we would pull out the 'share' money and the kids had to make decisions on for-purpose entities to gift the money to.

(There was an awkward moment one year when there were some coins missing from one of the 'share' boxes. It's fair to say that Dad was unimpressed. There was a 'teachable moment' right there!)

Once or twice a year we would have family volunteering days. A number of these were managed by Kids in Philanthropy (KiP)[2] . KiP creates volunteering programs for school aged children to assist with the needs of disadvantaged young people. It provides a safe environment for kids to take their first volunteering steps.

Ange and I sat down to dinner with the boys most nights of the week. At least twice a week cricket and footy talk was banned and we would have a conversation on a topical issue in the community; these can start at a young age. Sometimes we used cards with topic prompts purchased from The School of Life,[3] or we would just make them up e.g. 'Do you think the world is fair?' 'Should capital punishment be reintroduced?' 'If you could have dinner with any four people in the world, living or dead, who would it be and why?', and 'What traits do you not want to inherit from your parents?' (I thought, "Mum's insane positivity" was a bit harsh!).

We sponsored two students at the School of St Jude in Tanzania[4] . These boys were a similar age to our boys. Letter-swapping provided opportunities for our kids to learn about education in that country, as well as some of the other challenges faced by the citizens of Tanzania.

I'm aware of families who use Kiva to teach their kids how some people struggle financially.[5] Kiva enables crowdfunding loans to expand

---

2. https://kip.org.au

3. https://www.theschooloflife.com

4. https://www.schoolofstjude.org/our-school/

5. https://www.kiva.org

financial access to help underserved communities thrive. The parents, with their kids, go online and discuss the small loans that they would like to make.

Trips to low-middle income countries can be powerful for children. You don't need to say much. Kids are like sponges, and they see the differences in living conditions and lifestyles. Seeing inequality at a young age can build an appreciation of different cultures, and gratitude.

As the kids got older Ange and I would leave newspaper articles on world issues on the kitchen table for our kids to read over breakfast. Sometimes these were simply on how hard the Australian cricket captain had to work on his rehabilitation after his back injury.

Rites of passage

When our boys each turned 15, I took both of them (separately) on Arne Rubinstein's, The Rites of Passage Institute (RoP), 'The Making of Men' camp.[6]

I had met Arne many years before when he approached me to see whether any of our Myer Family Office clients would fund his work seeking to support boys and girls successfully make a safe, healthy transition into adulthood. As a General Practitioner he could see the myriad of issues that teenagers were facing. He had seen that many Indigenous communities around the world had some form of rite of passage from (in the case of boys) boy to man. He could see western communities tended not to have such practices and how this impeded the growth of boys to men. He set out to build one.

RoP runs a number of programs. Arne and his team have trained some incredible facilitators, who are skilled in providing a safe environment for sharing stories between fathers and sons. I had heard good things about The Making of Men camp helping transition teenage boys from boy behaviour into respectful, considerate and confident young men. So I signed up with my eldest son.

RoP has the most beautiful property in the hinterland near Mullumbimby, 20 kilometres from Byron Bay. The first action upon

6. https://ritesofpassageinstitute.org/making-of-men/

arrival is to hand in your mobile phone. Most of the 20 dads agreed that that was a good start, although I could see a couple hesitating! Over the next four days there is an informal, but scripted, process of storytelling and sharing of information between the dads and the boys. Some of these conversations were incredibly deep and emotional, as dads shared some of their life challenges, and at other times you were rolling around in laughter at a silly experience a dad had shared! Many of these conversations were under the stars around the campfire at night. There were also a bunch of fun activities.

The aim of the camp is not to repair any damage between a father and son. Rather, it is a terrific way to build an avenue for better conversations between fathers and sons. There are also programs for mother and sons, and daughters.

There is more, but I can't reveal too many details, to ensure that all have a similar experience. On both of the camps that I attended, the dads were joking about who was getting the most benefit – the fathers or the sons! It was a unique experience on both occasions that I attended, and both boys and I benefited greatly from the experience.

One of the RoP camp instructors has developed an App, iyarn.[7] It is a useful tool to check-in with kids on how they are feeling on the major issues in their life e.g. family, friends, school, work. You both provide a number out of ten for your agreed categories, at agreed intervals, which then acts as a conversation starter. I have found that boys (and men too) are more likely to provide an honest response via a number than words.

Teachable moments

We were always looking for 'teachable moments' with our boys. It is not their fault that they live in a privileged part of the world, but I think it is important that they learn that they are fortunate and that hardship in life is all relative.

Several times I have recommended principal/author, John Marsden's, *The Art of Growing Up* to families who were new parents. There are lots of learnings and case studies on how to raise resilient children.

---

7. https://iyarn.com/iyarn-for-you/

A philanthropic family foundation provides extraordinary learning opportunities for children. To maximise the learning opportunity they should be given a voice to share their views. If this is not done in an authentic way, they will quickly drift away.

One client I worked with didn't establish his foundation until he retired. He had quietly accumulated a decent level of wealth over many decades and decided that nearly all of it would be gifted into the family foundation. He then brought his middle-aged son, who had little corporate experience, on as a foundation director. The ageing father knew that this would be a wonderful experience for his son and that given his interest in community, the son would be an engaged Chair. The father, independent directors and I supported and educated the son to be the Chair, so the succession worked well when sadly the father died. The son now spends a large percentage of his time running the foundation and due to his passion for the role, does a great job.

There is significant evidence to show that those that learn to give when they are young, tend to give more throughout their life.[8] And they will operate differently to previous generations. Dr Geetha Murali, Room to Read CEO, sees that "… younger generations … are developing a strong sense of social consciousness early and are looking to engage with causes earlier in their lives, leading to larger gifts during wealth transfers and longer giving trajectories that are more focussed on specific missions."[9]

Kids won't always engage with a family foundation, or similar activities. Against my advice one client forced their teenage child to participate with the family foundation. Of course, he then totally disengaged for some years. Provide them the opportunities and they will engage in their own way, at their own pace, in their own time.

---

8. https://www.socialventures.com.au/sva-quarterly/insights-to-grow-philanthropic-giving-for-not-for-profits/

9. Andrew Milner, *Views from the receiving end*, Alliance Magazine, March 2023, p. 62

Chapter 14

Educational tool for the next gen

*"Success means using your knowledge and experience to satisfy yourself.
Significance means using your knowledge and experience to change the
lives of others."* – **Bob Buford**

Choking on my beer

One Thursday evening in Sydney I spoke at a wealth management event
about the extraordinary educational tool that a family foundation can
be for the next generation. At the end of the session I took my first sip
of beer when a middle-aged man approached me, and said, "I'm sorry, I
can't stay for drinks, here is my card, please call me on Monday as I would
like you to set up a $x million (insert very large number) foundation
for our family." I looked down at his card and said (in a voice hoping
it sounded like I had these conversations every day), "Ah certainly Bob
(name changed). Have a nice weekend and I will call you on Monday."
And then Bob scurried off to his next event.

Bob and his wife (I'll call her Betty) had had a liquidity event and
were planning to establish a foundation and manage it themselves. From
my talk Bob twigged to the extraordinary educational tool that a family
foundation could be for his children. Over the next few years Bob and
Betty became my 'poster people' for best practice in this area.

A family foundation is a microcosm of a business. On this occasion it
is in the business of creating positive change within the community. This
provides many 'teachable moments' for children.

Responsibility of wealth, governance

Bob and Betty discussed the responsibility of wealth with their children and advised them that the family was establishing a family foundation. Here was an opportunity to instil an ethos of giving and caring within future generations, develop collaborative and leadership qualities and build a deepened connection with each other and the outside world. We have surplus to our needs; let's share it. When I suggested that we run a half day philanthropic vision workshop with the entire family, Bob and Betty could see the opportunity to unify the family in a common goal, and to test and express values.

Bob and Betty could see the governance learnings for the kids via the foundation. It was the kids' first exposure to the family wealth. The children over 18 years of age joined Bob and Betty on the board, and those younger attended as meeting observers. There would be quarterly board meetings, a board charter was developed with the kids, board papers were provided, minutes were taken and there were accountabilities. It was a little awkward when one of the kids had not actioned an item between the first and second board meeting. There was some eye-rolling from the diligent siblings. A lesson had been learnt.

Investment strategy

Whilst Bob and Betty had the experience to quickly develop an investment strategy themselves for the foundation, again they saw an opportunity for the kids to learn financial literacy. Tenders were called from several wealth managers to develop an investment strategy and manage the foundation's investments. This process took months, prior to a manager being selected, but the vast amount the children learnt about investing was clear.

This process occurred just prior to the 'global financial crisis' (GFC) in 2007/08. Given the over-heated markets at the time, Bob and Betty were astute enough not to fully invest, but given they were investing for the long term they didn't want to hold 100% cash. Ten percent of the corpus was invested into local and overseas equities, with the balance remaining in cash. The initial GFC market correction occurred around 4 months later. At the foundation board meeting a month later the family was told that the equities investments had dropped in value by around 15%. The youngest child (mid-teens) looked astounded that this could occur, and asked, "Where has the money gone?"

There was another learning right there!

A few years later Bob was keen for the foundation to make a modest investment in a pub which was a social enterprise with a large percentage of profits to be given to for-purpose entities. I had run a few pubs in my insolvency days, so knew how fickle consumers can be with their drinking habits and I understood the dangers of a cash business. I reviewed the business plan and advised Bob not to invest the intended modest sum. Bob was aware that it was a high risk investment, but he was keen for his kids to watch a social entrepreneur in action. Unfortunately the business collapsed 2 years later but again there were many learnings for the kids.

I'm sure Bob followed that social entrepreneur, as some years later he went on to have great success with another social enterprise, which has enabled it to provide significant funding to for-purpose entities overseas.

Creating change, measuring impact

The major business of a family foundation is to create positive change in the community via its investing and grantmaking activities. To create such change is a huge challenge and results in significant learnings for the kids. In addition, it is important to measure the impact of funding partners and evaluate the foundation's performance. All nature of businesses need to focus on this, in some shape or form, so this is useful in many careers.

Bob and Betty also quickly realised that taking the kids on site visits (in Australia and overseas), well away from their leafy suburb, to 'learn on the ground', provided significant learnings on seeing tangible progress and the challenges faced by their funding partners.

The family glue

Of course if we move away from these tangible arguments about the educational tool a foundation can be, simply put, a family foundation provides the next generation engagement with the community and an understanding and appreciation of the needs of those who are perhaps less fortunate.

Bob and Betty mentioned numerous times to me over the years how much joy the family received from being united in a common goal (the foundation's vision) and the great debates that regularly occurred amongst family members. In addition they talked about how the family foundation was an important vehicle to enhance the family's culture.

I saw this at the second board meeting. Bob was a strong character and had a view on most issues. A terrific debate arose on an issue between two of the kids. As the debate developed, I noticed Bob put his pen down, push his chair back and watch and listen, with a smile on his face. It was working … [1]

The Myer family, now into its 5th generation since a young Sidney Myer landed in Australia in 1899, says philanthropy is the "glue that sticks the family together".

---

1. A 30-minute training course years earlier at Arthur Andersen had taught me to sit in a meeting where you could see all attendees. (Well, it was an American firm!)

Chapter 15

Philanthropic vision

"The only thing necessary for the triumph of evil is for good men to do nothing." – **Edmund Burke**

A successful entity needs a strong vision, a tight measurable strategic plan and a strong team with a deep commitment to success. A family foundation is no different.

Our role at The Myer Family Office was not to tell families what to do; it was to guide them. Larry Kramer, President of The William and Flora Hewlett Foundation in the USA, gave the opening keynote address at the 2018 Philanthropy Australia conference in Melbourne. In his opening remarks he stated that he assumed there was a wide variety of focus areas within the room of 600 attendees. However, he stated that if you weren't working on climate change and the fraying democracy levels around the world, then you were kidding yourself, as everything is impacted by these two issues.

Effective altruism

Effective Altruism (EA) has been defined a number of ways, but put simply it is about doing good better. The goal is to remove personal preferences and use evidence to determine how to maximise the outcomes from your giving.[1]

---

1. https://www.effectivealtruism.org

It was inspired by the work of Australian philosopher, Peter Singer, that led to the formation of *Giving What We Can.*[2] This was one of the first organisations focussed on EA.

A simple example of EA is Singer's 2013 TED Talk where he compares two solutions for blindness. The first one is training a guide dog, and the second is funding charities that can cure one person in a low-middle income country of trachoma for between $25-$50. "It costs about $40,000 to train a guide dog and the recipient so the guide dog can be an effective help to a blind person … or you could cure between 400 and 2,000 people of blindness. I think it's clear what's the better thing to do."[3] I agree in principle and wish more would adhere to it by focussing on the world's most pressing needs.

Simon Lewis, one of the co-founders of the Australian International Development Network, shares his view:

> *"As a largely migrant country, as a very wealthy country, as a country on the doorstep of the world's largest developing economies, and as a country similarly exposed to the regional and global threats of our time, now is the time for Australian philanthropy to lead a new wave of private capital investment into solutions for our region, and beyond."*[4]

It is estimated that only around 12% of Australian giving currently goes offshore.[5]

Now I thought this made a lot of sense. And after reflection agreed with Larry Kramer's keynote speaker comments. But if I thumped the table and told families this is what they should be doing, then they would walk out the door. We need to be pragmatic. We shouldn't lose sight of the critical importance of community, and people should get engaged with

2. https://www.givingwhatwecan.org/about-us

3. https://www.thelifeyoucansave.org.au/blog/is-there-such-a-thing-as-bad-charity/

4. Conversation with author, 6 April 2023, https://aidnetwork.org.au

5. ACNC, JBWere Philanthropic Services: https://www.youtube.com/watch?v=p9QgDEaIYxA

issues that they are passionate about.

In my view my role as a philanthropic adviser was to encourage families to do more and better giving. If that meant they commenced by giving to donkeys, well that's okay. With apologies to Rupert's donkeys, I thought I could eventually guide them to issues that had more significance within their community and to the world. "You can't get people to improve their swing if they don't take up golf in the first place!"[6]

Philanthropic vision workshops

Based upon best practice offshore, I developed a philanthropic vision workshop for our clients. Each workshop was tailored to a family's needs.

The aim of each philanthropic vision workshop was to bring the family together, provide everyone with a voice, develop the family's philanthropic vision and strategic giving program. This would assist with maximising the outcomes from the foundation.

We provided some 'homework' to all family members to complete a few weeks prior to the session. This included several questions around their individual values, the family values, experiences that have deeply impacted them, what excites them about the world, what angers them or upsets them, their existing giving activities (including volunteering), what they would change in the world with a 'magic wand', and their aspirations for the foundation. We would also seek their views on where the foundation should focus, including target groups and geography (e.g. primary school students in regional areas).

We then brought the family together for a half day workshop to develop the family's vision and strategy. This would include group discussions on:

- principles of good governance

- focus areas that the foundation would target

---

6. Emma Beeston & Beth Breeze, op. cit., p. 192

- types of philanthropic strategies

- programmatic tactics

- grantmaking fundamentals

- common problems and pitfalls

- strategies for success.

We would discuss best practice philanthropy and issues such as considering whether the foundation would be perpetual or have a limited life. Consideration of this issue was important to discuss early in the foundation's journey as it impacts strategy.

The provision of a voice to all family members must be authentic. A family member once suggested to me that the workshop was really, "… just going through the motions as dad would never give up control anyway!"

Where there had been significant family giving prior to the establishment of a more structured approach to giving, we would prepare a pie graph summarising the family giving to date into focus areas. This usually provided some surprises where the bulk of the funds had been distributed. A family that had thought it was primarily assisting kids in disadvantaged communities, could suddenly see that in the previous five years 40% of funding had gone to the arts, unrelated to children.

I ran many of these sessions over the years. Sometimes the kids were in their 40s. Other times they were in their early teens, which in my view was the perfect time to hold such conversations, when their brains were in their formative years. The youngest family participant to have attended such a workshop was eight. I had suggested to dad that that was probably too young, but he had insisted she was mature for her age, which turned out to be correct. When I asked her in the family's workshop what in the world made her sad she said, "When people eat little piggies." Big brother found this most amusing, but stifled his laughter after a quick glare from mum.

The dad rang me the next morning, a little emotional and very thankful. He said that it was the best family conversation they had ever had, and that it long continued, in the car on the way home and over the family dinner that night.

In the days following the workshop we would document the philanthropic vision, the major focus areas and the giving strategy.

On one set of preparatory papers, a son advised that one of the most difficult moments of his life was his fear prior to telling his dad that he was gay. That was an insight into how much we were being included within family conversations.

These workshops were a highlight of the work that we were doing. It was always a privilege to be invited into intimate family conversations. They were always great conversations. They were fun too!

This work engaged all family members, provided them a voice, developed a family vision and provided a plan for the work of the family foundation to commence. Families were starting to see that philanthropy would not only transform the lives of others, but could strengthen family relationships.

Chapter 16

The power imbalance and humility

"It's amazing what you can accomplish if you don't care who gets the credit." – **Harry Truman**

There is a, not often discussed, power imbalance in the philanthropic sector; one party has a pot of cash, and the other party seeks access to it in order to achieve its mission.

At a breakout session at a Philanthropy Australia conference a number of years ago, the keynote speaker of the conference, Larry Kramer, President of the Hewlett Foundation stated that the 'power imbalance' in the philanthropic sector was a myth and didn't exist. There were awkward glances around the room. The convenor of the session, Kristy Muir, then CEO of the Centre for Social Impact, pulled him up at the end of the session and strongly disagreed, suggesting that his position of privilege possibly resulted in him not seeing the imbalance. This drew hearty applause from the room.

In order to have a trusting relationship with its funding partners, foundations must tread very carefully with this imbalance. The most effective way to deal with this is to bring humility to the relationship. A foundation can only achieve its goals if it has talented partners working on the ground. In practice, plaudits are often given to the donor. It is towards the partners (grant recipients) where the plaudits should go. True partnership requires humility.

Doug Balfour in *Doing Good Great* talked about changing the focus of accolades *from* being given when the gift is made, *to* when the issue is solved.[1]

When you are a grantmaker you receive a lot of plaudits. The oldest philanthropy joke is, "When you join the philanthropic sector, you have told your last bad joke!" You get plaudits for providing time for grantseekers, for turning up and for listening and for paying a grant. One client I worked with was an extraordinarily humble couple from whom I learnt a lot. This couple would always flip this on its head. They would say, "Please don't thank us. It is your team doing the work on the ground every day. For that we are very grateful, and we would like to thank you for your time today and your constant efforts."

Provide the accolades to your partners, not to yourself. This is not only appropriate but will also assist build their supporter base. I learnt early on that if a partner is achieving goals, it has a bigger impact if you share this with your relevant network rather than talking about yourself.

Large foundations need to be very mindful of not being arrogant. I have seen, and heard of, countless occasions over the years where large foundations are failing in this regard. We need to ensure that all foundations and their staff:

- are respectful on all occasions

- have clear guidelines on how they operate and their focus areas

- respond and make decisions in a timely manner

- listen: they are not the experts—their partners are. Don't tell their partners how to run their team, spend their money or achieve their goals.

I have heard many stories of grant seekers spending considerable time having discussions with foundation staff and then completing detailed grant applications to be told months later that it was 'off strategy'. I have heard of many occasions where foundations have not returned phone calls or not done so in a timely manner. There is a large foundation

1. Doug Balfour, *Doing Good Great*, Geneva Global, 2015, p. 67

in Australia that regularly takes 9+ months to make a decision on discussions with partners. On most occasions this time span is totally inappropriate.

I have a painful recollection of an occasion when our team took what we thought was a good idea to a board. The idea was rejected quite quickly. Our team had become so focussed on the idea that we sought more detail from the potential partner and reworked the paper for the board's next meeting, who rejected it a second time. In hindsight I should have met with the Chair after the first meeting and discussed the likelihood of the board's approval of the idea. The result was wasting considerable time for the grant applicant over a six-month period.

Tom Keenan, in his thesis on charity/funder relationships, argues that the, "… fractured nature of the charity/funder relationship results in a combined output significantly below its potential."[2]

It is important that foundations show leadership here. Don't let partners thank you; you should be thanking them as they are in the trenches on a daily basis using their expertise, trying to create positive change in our community. Donors achieve very little without their partners, and so that is where the accolades should be directed.

---

2. Thomas W Keenan, *Charity and Funder Relationships: Unlocking the Potential*, 2021, p. 222

Chapter 17

Is philanthropy harmful to society?

"Greatness, it turns out, is largely a matter of conscious choice, and discipline." – **Jim Collins**

The debate around philanthropy

Before we delve into a conversation around best practice philanthropy and powerful case studies, we need to explore another little-discussed issue: whether philanthropy can be harmful to society.

Some argue philanthropy is harmful to society. They believe it is simply providing high-net-worth individuals (HNWI) public influence, sometimes with the goal of changing public policy, whilst receiving a tax break resulting in a loss to Treasury. They further argue that philanthropy cements HNWIs' place in society and is unaccountable. Some assert that a much better approach would be to increase taxes for HNWIs, with elected governments to determine the distributions to ensure they are directed to the greatest need in the community.

Melissa Berman, CEO, Rockefeller Philanthropy Advisors sums this up well: "... The system of capitalism and the power imbalance that underlies much philanthropy are under question, and thus the legitimacy of philanthropy is in doubt."[1]

Oliver Wendell Holmes, the American jurist, once said, "I don't mind

---

1. Emma Beeston & Beth Breeze, op. cit., p. x

paying taxes; they buy me civilisation." Of course, philanthropy can only be morally justified if it uses its subsidy from the public purse (i.e. tax concessions) to buy civilisation to a degree not less than that which can be bought by the State.[2]

Three recent books question the value of philanthropy to society. To build knowledge and self-awareness, I recommend every donor and philanthropic practitioner read, as a minimum, the three books discussed below and consider the authors' arguments.

Just Giving: Why Philanthropy is Failing Democracy and How it Can Do Better, Rob Reich

Reich mounts the case that whilst we laud wealthy donors, philanthropy may not provide the benefits we think it does and it may in fact be undermining democratic values. It does this as it is the wealthy in our society wielding and maintaining power via their giving, and using private assets for public influence, with tax breaks attached.

However, Reich does concede that philanthropy, "… under certain circumstances and structured by certain policies … has an important, first-best role to play." In addition he argues that foundations could survive scrutiny, "… provided they operate in a particular role, namely as 'discovery' mechanisms for innovation in social policy that the state and market are unlikely to undertake."

Winners Take All, Anand Giridharadas

Giridharadas argues that members of the global elite use their wealth and influence to preserve systems that concentrate wealth at the top at the expense of societal progress. He mounts the case that societies' biggest problems should be solved by public institutions and elected officials. From my experience the benefits of philanthropy done well outweigh the downside, but Giridharadas makes you reflect on your giving strategy and what you are trying to achieve.

---

2. Professor Dorothy Scott, *Visionary Philanthropy: Looking Back to See Ahead*, Philanthropy Australia Conference, 10 October 2005

Dark Money, Jane Mayer

Reading *Dark Money* revealed the contentious side of philanthropy, whereby significant sums with little transparency were spent over many years by the Koch brothers, and other billionaires in the USA, to secretly fund right wing think tanks, academic institutions and media groups in order to pursue government influence.

Philanthropy has a strong role to play

I don't agree with all that these three authors argue, but it does give us much to reflect on. We must be aware of the possible shortcomings of philanthropy in order that our actions are for the community benefit, and not other spurious reasons, whether intended or otherwise. Significantly increased transparency in the Australian philanthropic sector will assist.

We must be very careful to not downplay the role community organisations play in not only delivering change but as the source of ideas behind the change. We must be careful that we don't take the patronising view that wealth and philanthropy know best. Warren Buffett's son, Peter, in 2013 wrote a piece in *The New York Times* where he noted philanthropy had become *the* vehicle to level the playing field but the main effect of this was "conscience laundering" to "… enable the rich to sleep better at night". He suggests that the answer lies in listening to those that have ideas and the ability to create change and then providing the risk capital for those ideas.[3]

How do we deal with the massive foundations such as the Bill and Melinda Gates Foundation? Given their enormous size they have out-sized influence within their focus areas, and for most of their history their board has consisted of just Bill, Melinda, Bill's dad and their mate Warren. (The board has since grown significantly in size with a number of independent director appointments.) The foundation has had some wonderful successes, but its funding of poorly performing schools in the USA was controversial with very mixed success. And its leaders

---

3. https://www.nytimes.com/2013/07/27/opinion/the-charitable-industrial-complex.html

can't be unelected. Chapter 22 (Case Studies) includes MacKenzie Scott's contrasting approach of 'yielding' control.

The Australian philanthropic sector currently has many weaknesses. That does not mean that we should shut the sector down. The sector has an extraordinary opportunity to create positive change in our community and further abroad. Let's focus on addressing the weaknesses so that the sector can thrive, and capital can be effectively deployed in a transparent way for the benefit of the community. There is no reason that we cannot do this. Surely this should be our aim.

Chapter 18

The Myer Family Office: growing the sector

"The immense capacity of imaginative individuals to impact the world is both boundless and mysterious." – **Peter Karoff**

Selling philanthropy

Our mission for the Philanthropic Services team at The Myer Family Office (MFO) was to grow the philanthropic sector, deploy capital wisely and provide great service. It was certainly a point of difference in the high-net-worth individual (HNWI) services market. Many provided estate planning, wealth management and tax and accounting services, but very few provided philanthropic services in 2004. This resulted in it being a 'door-opener'. Families that ordinarily MFO couldn't get to see were curious about these philanthropic services.

Earlier I discussed the extraordinary educational tool that a family foundation can be for the next generation. I quickly determined that this was the best selling point for philanthropy. HNWIs were often keen to learn more about this, how our team could implement this and how their family would benefit.

A key to the early success of MF Philanthropic Services (MFPS) was my ability to do the subtle sell of philanthropy and respectfully use the Myer family's trusted name with its seven decades of giving experience. Of course, my passion to diligently pursue leads was useful. If I saw that a family had had a liquidity event, I would find some way to be connected with them and seek a discussion on philanthropy. Another method was to sidle up to a target at a large meeting or conference and get a cup of tea at the same time they did. I would pretend I didn't know them and start small talk before introducing myself and launching slowly into a broader discussion.

I found that when you are very passionate about what you are selling, you quickly become quite good at it. It was fun too! I now had real purpose in my life.

Target: $1 billion

I think my drive to succeed was partly driven by my usual fear of failure and wondering what I would do if MFPS did not succeed! A return to the commercial world, and its (often) lack of purpose did not appeal. However, the real drive was led by my desire to grow Australia's tiny philanthropic sector and my vision of establishing 200 foundations, with an average corpus of $5 million. This would provide an aggregate corpus of $1 billion. A yield of 5% would spin off an additional $50 million p.a. to distribute to community groups, and hopefully much higher if clients were happy to also distribute capital.

My timing was good, as the boom of the 1990s/2000s was continuing. Extraordinary wealth in Australia had been created over the previous 30 years. It was an exciting time and we established nearly 50 family foundations in the first five years, with an aggregate corpus of nearly $150m. In addition to Victoria, we picked up clients in New South Wales, South Australia and Western Australia. On each occasion I got very excited when a new client confirmed the 'go ahead' to establish a new foundation. It was the start of a new journey for the family.

I always had a large pipeline of potential clients. However, patience was needed. Often it took over 3 years from an initial conversation to foundation establishment.

Gifts to a family foundation are generally tax deductible (depending on the structure.) In a meeting with a husband and wife considering establishing a family foundation, I could see they were excited to establish a foundation. However, one of them was clearly hesitant. I asked her what was on her mind. She asked if funds placed into the foundation could ever be 'retrieved' by the family? I advised that as it was a Private Ancillary Fund ('PAF'), with gifts to the Fund being tax deductible, that the funds could not be returned to the family.

It was exciting to know that with the establishment of each new foundation more funds were locked away for community benefit, forever.

Building the team

During the first year of MFPS establishment I employed former media colleague Lynne Simnett (always upbeat) to provide administration support. Then in mid 2007 I employed Jodie Belyea (a community warrior) part-time to provide grant research services to our clients.

The business continued to expand and in March 2009 I put on Tamara Logan (ex The Myer Foundation grant researcher) to job share with Jodie. Soon after I employed Lauren Casey as Assistant Client Adviser, effectively a chief operating officer, to manage all the client accounting and administration issues, as well as assist with marketing.

As we won more business Louise Kuramoto joined the team, ex World Vision and a bundle of energy (later CEO, The Jack Brockhoff Foundation). Further strong growth enabled me to employ a senior research manager, Stacey Thomas, ex Telstra Foundation (later Philanthropy Australia board member and CEO, The Wyatt Trust). When Stacey moved to Adelaide, I replaced her with Amanda Miller OAM, ex lawyer and Australians Investing in Women Manager (later Philanthropy Australia Chair) and Lou Doyle, ex Social Ventures Australia and Effective Philanthropy (later CEO, Besen Foundation.) The administration team was always strong and included at various times Harriet Dwyer (later Director, Impact and Innovation, Hireup), Nancy Ranner (nee Piche and later Grants Coordinator, National Foundation for Medical Research and Innovation), Thomas Lopez (later Relationship Manager, Australian Communities Foundation), Michelle Dempster and Lisa Jacobs, all great operators with a strong understanding of great service.

You are only as strong as the team, and one of my proudest achievements has been to recruit outstanding individuals. I always looked for individuals with strong values, curiosity, a strong work ethic, and who were team players and had a passion to create positive change in the community.

To watch so many of them move on to senior positions in the philanthropic and for-purpose sectors has been a personal highlight for me.

It was hard work but exhilarating to help families start their philanthropic journey. We worked with some amazing families and had the privilege of being invited into their homes and offices, to be included in very personal conversations.

Connecting money to ideas

I really saw my role as a connector. A connector of money to good ideas. I had the privilege of knowing many families who were happy to share some of their wealth and attempt to tackle some of the ills in society. I had also developed many connections with outstanding for-purpose CEOs, who had plans in place to tackle some of these issues. The trick was to connect the money with the right ideas i.e. like-minded individuals. I always had a strong team to do the due diligence, to ensure a strong measurable plan was in place, so we could take the ideas to mission-aligned clients.

It was an honour to spend time with individuals like Bails Myer. I found it incredible that Bails was a son of Sidney Myer, the founder of the Myer Emporium. His dad had passed away so many years earlier, in 1934! One day I was sitting with Bails in his study at Cranlana, the old Myer family home, discussing his private foundation. We were overlooking the beautiful garden. It dawned on me what special moments these were. I learnt much from him. This included:

- when discussing a possible $0.1 million grant, he asked a for-purpose CEO what he would do with $10 million. The CEO did not have a coherent response. Bails was testing the CEO's vision

- when Bails received a grant application from a large entity assisting homeless people, he was given the option of funding a rehabilitation program or a building refurbishment. He chose the latter as he knew few other donors would

- in a meeting, if a technical term was used that he didn't understand he would say with a twinkle in his eye, "Now I understand what that means, but you may need to explain it to Peter here …"

Bails loved Chuck Feeney's 'give while you live' approach. Bails was also conscious that philanthropy is not just about money, but it is also about bringing to the table other critical resources such as expertise and networks. He once said to me (not in an arrogant way but more to reinforce the point), that he had an infinite amount of money, but a finite amount of time.

Doing enough?

Once, on a site visit, I wandered through the extensive slums of Mukuru, just outside Nairobi, Kenya. Everything seemed broken. The tin shanties lining the streets looked like they would blow over with the next gust of wind, roads had severe potholes, electrical wires were hanging loose, rubbish was everywhere, and sewerage in the street left a rotten stench. By now I had two young teenage boys who were receiving an excellent education in Melbourne. As I laughed with the gorgeous young smiling faces walking beside me, I could not help but reflect on the far greater opportunities in life that my boys would receive, compared to the youngsters beside me. It was hard not to be overpowered by the injustice in the world. Surely as a race we could do better?

The MFPS team established over 100 family foundations and worked with some amazing families, a small number of whom had gifted a material percentage of their wealth into their foundation. However, this was rare, and the majority of families gifted a small percentage of the family wealth in the foundation. My view at the time was that this was okay. That it was a stepping stone in the right direction; we have established a family foundation and capital has been put into it.

One example was in the early days of MFPS. A family whose wealth was approximately $100m (with plenty of liquidity) had agreed that we establish a PAF for them. The founders then told me they would gift $2m to the foundation. I was surprised that the gift would only be 2% of the family wealth. However, I was convinced that once we had brought mum and dad and the kids together, run a philanthropic vision workshop with the family, documented their vision and giving strategy, and introduced the family to impressive mission-aligned entities, that the family would be inspired to take further action and build the corpus of their foundation.

But this did not occur. Whilst the foundation strategy was being successfully implemented by our team in its early years (so we thought), and we had connected the family to some terrific partners who were having some successes, no further funding was gifted to the foundation. This was a common story.

I was confused:

- had we not inspired these families to do more?

- had we not introduced the families to the right for-purpose entities?

- were we failing as a team?

- were we failing as a nation?

- why do we not share more of our wealth?

- were most families only going to commit 1%-2% of the family wealth to the community? Was this a reasonable commitment, given it was more than most?

- had I become too biased in my thinking?

- was I missing something?

With my experiences from my extensive travel to low-middle income countries, I could see that we lived in a world of pressing environmental and humanitarian needs. I considered that if I created wealth of $100 million (excluding our home), then our family could live on no more than

$20 million, and so donate $80 million to for-purpose entities and/or our family foundation. Was my thinking a bit wacky and utopian?

I had one client who was worth around $300 million. When we established his foundation, he gifted $1.5 million to it. Fours later he had doubled his wealth to over $600 million. He maintained just $1.5 million in his foundation. On one occasion I had spent months trying to meet with him to discuss his foundation's strategy. I eventually received a message from him via a third party that he, "wasn't feeling philanthropic at the moment". Had I failed here? Or do some people naturally not share? If not, why not? How could we shift this?

Getting grumpy

It wasn't for me to judge what one did with their $20 million, $50 million or $250+ million, but after over a decade running the MFPS team, working alongside amazing for-purpose teams and seeing what they could achieve in the community with additional capital (they were all under-capitalised), I began to wonder if I was becoming a little judgemental about the size of wealth that families seemed to think they needed to live on. Perhaps it was time for me to move on.

The MFPS team established over 100 foundations in the 11.5 years that I ran it. Many people said that was an amazing outcome. I didn't see it that way. With the wealth in Australia, with my connections, with the Myer family's connections and with the connections of most of our clients, I felt we should have established closer to 500 foundations during that period.

I asked families to consider discussing the success of their foundation, including the engagement of the kids, with their relevant friends in order to encourage other families to establish a foundation. Due to the lack of a strong giving culture in Australia, and the lack of role models, clients were usually very reluctant to do this, for fear of being seen to 'preach' to their friends.

All I was suggesting was that if your family was having such a unique time collectively working together to attempt to address issues in the community, wouldn't your friends want to know about that, and consider having similarly thoughtful family conversations and getting the same levels of satisfaction?

I was surprised that the MFPS team did not receive more internal support at MFO, particularly given we were The *Myer* Family Office, and considering the rich history of giving by several Myer family members. Philanthropy/community did not appear to be a high priority for a number of my MFO senior executive colleagues.

More broadly, in my view MFO was a lost opportunity. MFO had been best placed to be the multi-family office in Australia that not only grew family wealth, but also assisted families develop their estate and succession planning with a focus on instilling strong values in the next generation, including via a better use of wealth with more of a focus on community. MFO's focus was primarily on building financial capital, with little focus on building a family's human and social capital. This was unusual, as in my experience parents are more worried about their children becoming productive adults, as opposed to growing the family wealth.

The outcome could have been a better adjusted next generation and better outcomes for the broader community, as opposed to simply building a family dynasty primarily focussed on wealth preservation plus growth. The potential to shape families was enormous. The majority of the executive team (other than Graham Reeve and a couple of others) had a different focus, which I found was a missed opportunity.

A few years later MFO merged with another entity and the MFO name and opportunity seemed lost.

After much thought I resigned. I was tired and I was grumpy with the modest size of many of the foundations that we had established. I was grumpy with the slow growth of the philanthropic sector more broadly in Australia. It was time for new leadership and fresh ideas.

I was incredibly grateful to the Myer family for providing me with the opportunity to pursue my dream – to grow the philanthropic sector in the country. Graham Reeve provided me a lot of autonomy to get on with the job.

The next opportunity

The 2015/16 summer was approaching so Ange and I took the boys on a memorable road trip to Mt Kosciuszko, Parliament House and the inspiring National Portrait Gallery in Canberra, the Bradman Museum in Bowral and the beautiful southern beaches of NSW.

After a wonderful break over summer, I was totally re-energised. I commenced working with one (anonymous) family. This was a family who had similar values to me and similar views on wealth and giving. They had worked out 'how much is enough?' They considered that leaving significant wealth to the next generation would likely be detrimental, so their significant 'surplus' was gifted to their foundation. They also had a Chuck Feeney-type approach: give while you live. They were keen to make a significant immediate impact on their focus areas. It was a limited life foundation, with the plan to close the doors within 20 years.

It was certainly a little unusual going from a high-profile role in the Australian philanthropic sector, championing those who spoke publicly about their giving in order to inspire others, to then working with an anonymous family. I thought it might be a nice change to be able to focus on one family and just a few focus areas. Of course I really valued the family's approach to wealth and could see the impact that the foundation could have given the sizeable balance sheet. The family was passionate about impact, and this was where their focus was. It was a unique opportunity.

I also thought at some stage I might be able to convince the family to tell their story, to inspire others. They are yet to do that publicly, but they have been happy to talk 'within the tent' and speak with appropriate families and small groups that they might be able to influence, about their giving philosophy and strategy.

Whilst working with this family we narrowed the focus areas, developed the strategy in each area, built the team to implement the strategy and then with an investment mindset, practised what I would consider to be best practice philanthropy. Of course we did not get everything right; no-one does. However, it was a very thoughtful way to consider how to create impact. During this time I hired some unique individuals who are all making significant contributions to the community. These included Sam Rogers, Keryn Slade, Steph Kenealy, Stefan Stoev, Chris Sadler, Seri Renkin OAM, Adrian Appo OAM, Nick Taylor, Aidan Rowley, David Baulis, Carly Quonoey and Susan Overall. We worked hard, but we also had a lot of laughs!

Many lessons from working with this unique family over a number of years are sprinkled throughout this book.

PART III: BEST PRACTICE GIVING

Chapter 19

Best practice giving—the basics

"I wish more people of means were not satisfied with just doing good in the world". – **Doug Balfour**

I have worked in the philanthropic sector for 20 years with over 100 families, some of whom have decades of philanthropic experience. Others were new to the sector but with smart philosophies. I have seen many successes and failures over the years (mine included). In this section of the book I summarise what I believe to be best practice giving.

Principles

- rule #1: do no harm. Be aware that giving can cause harm if done in an ill-informed manner. Seek advice from experts

- you are the custodians of capital to be used for charitable purposes. You have a duty to seek to maximise impact

- humility: you are unlikely to be the expert on the issue, so seek out those who are. Showing humility will build trust, so that an open and honest relationship can be established. Your partners (grantees) don't thank you for your time, you thank them

- seek the views of those with lived experience, where applicable, and preferably provide them with decision-making ability

- focus: pick one or two focus areas only (preferably one), build expertise over time, and make fewer but larger grants. Don't 'spray and pray'

- let the market know where and how you operate, so the relevant good ideas can find you

- know yourself: if you have a large corpus then focus on big bets. Like venture capital, if 1 in 10 bets comes off, then you will have great success

- if you have a more modest balance sheet, develop a focussed small grants program

- continuous improvement is vital—constantly self-evaluate and be open to mid-course corrections if required

- don't re-invent the wheel: search for those who are already working on similar issues and learn from them. Don't restrict your search to Australia

- be curious. Ask questions. Talk less. Listen and reflect. I gather Buddha said, "If your mouth is open, you are not learning"

- embrace risk. Be bold; philanthropy has the ability to take risks. If you are not making mistakes, you aren't taking enough risks

- exit strategy: if you seek to exit from a partner, do so via an appropriate staged exit plan. This is never without notice

- don't look for quick fixes. Take a strategic view and be patient

- discipline is the key – stay focussed.

Use the right tools

- foundations have a bunch of tools in their toolkit. Don't just think of a grant. Consider the power of blended capital – use the right tool for the job, whether it be a grant, debt, equity or a combination:

  - if you can only move forward with a grant, then that is fine. But if your partner (grantee) simply has a short-medium term cashflow issue, then debt could be used. When the debt is repaid the funds can be recycled for use with another partner

  - if you are trying to encourage more of an investment mindset with a partner on a venture, an equity instrument could be appropriate

- use leverage e.g. convene meetings of like-minded donors and subject matter experts, in order to share and learn from each other, make introductions to your partners through your networks, offer matched funding to grow partners' donor bases and speak at conferences to amplify the issue

- with one client we used a stack of tools, primarily advocacy, within the theory of change to seek the goal of reducing carbon emissions. The client funded partners to:

  - encourage politicians and corporates to change by showing voter/consumer support for change

  - show governments that change is possible, detailing the changes required

  - be proactive with the media to share these strategies (e.g. 'stranded asset' became a common term in the financial press—this was not by accident!)

  - litigate to challenge existing and new fossil fuel infrastructure

- shift finance: educating investors about the financial risks of climate change in order to shift capital flows

- impact invest to stimulate clean technology investments

- collaborate with others. Put the ego aside. Too many in the philanthropic sector want to lead. If someone else has a great plan, back it. This will enable you to operate beyond your budget, share ideas and systemically target issues in the community

- collaboration includes letting go of power and transferring cash to pooled funds where subject matter experts make the decisions. It's also a great way to learn from experts and discover new partners. This approach will maximise outcomes compared to foundations operating in a fragmented manner. Pooled funds are far more common in Europe and the USA

- where possible, assist for-purpose entities achieve sustainability, and move away from dependence

- seek to provide long term unrestricted funding, as opposed to project funding. This will enable your partners to get on with their mission with some budget certainty and spend less time fundraising. The pandemic increased the level of unrestricted funding given the urgent needs of for-purpose entities. We need to ensure such funding continues. Many foundations have a long list of 'funding exclusions' on their website (e.g. capital expenditure, travel, wages, overheads). This amuses me. I don't know how they determine such items! Surely it is up to their partners, the experts, to determine how and where funds are spent

- ensure partners have the ability to set goals, track milestones and measure impact. If they can't, help them get there.

Impact investments

- use the entire balance sheet to achieve your mission: ensure the investment strategy of the foundation is aligned with the foundation's mission. If a foundation is distributing 5% of its corpus each year, why would you only use 5% of your net assets to target the mission, when you could use up to 100%? Get the balance sheet working too. I still regularly see cases where this doesn't occur

- impact investments have the intention of generating measurable social and environmental outcomes, alongside a financial return. To solve all issues in our community we will need significant sums of patient capital (i.e. no expectation of a quick return). There will be opportunities for most foundations to seek impact investments to further the mission of the foundation. Impact investing can catalyse impact by triggering additional flows of capital from other investors

- philanthropy can play a key role by assisting entities to become 'investment ready', supporting proof of concept, taking a first loss position within an investment and attracting other investors. Impact investing can also change the mindset of for-purpose entities, getting them to think through taking additional risks as they invest in innovation and growth, driven by an increase in availability of capital

- impacting investing is not the focus of this book. However, the philanthropic sector should be leading the discussion on impact investing and showing the way. Bodies such as Impact Investing Australia, amongst others, have significant resources to explore.[1]

---

1. https://impactinvestingaustralia.com

Staff

- when hiring, seek:

  - people with strong values, with a passion to change the world

  - those from outside the sector who bring an investment mindset

  - people who are smarter than you

  - strategic thinkers (test via case studies)

  - those that are curious

- seek lived experience within the team. For one client I appointed a First Nations man to lead the First Nations team and a Paralympian to lead the disability team. (I loved Nick's humility. He would say to me, "Yes Pete, I have lived experience. But I have the lived experience of one man.") Such appointments are common sense, but I don't see many First Nations' Australians or those with a disability in the philanthropic sector in Australia

- I usually employed results-driven 'generalists' with the above attributes. Particular expertise can be hired in. Employing specialists can result in a fixed way of thinking and hinder strategy agility

- encourage a culture of sharing of failures, for others to learn from, and lessons learnt should be a 'what' hunt, not a 'witch' hunt[2]. For one client I introduced a 'Failure Report', whereby the team was encouraged to share failures via a quarterly report, to be discussed with the team and shared with the board to try and ensure we were learning from our failures

---

2. Doug Balfour, op. cit., p. 85

- ensure teams don't operate in silos. Build relevant practical meetings into the calendar so that cross-collaboration can occur, and learnings are shared

- develop an appropriate learning program for each team member. Where are they heading? What skills do they need to get there? What are the appropriate education programs that they should be undertaking to assist your foundation achieve its mission? This behaviour occurs at successful corporates, and should also occur within the philanthropic sector

- seek practical learning opportunities for the team. Early in my journey Rupert Myer could see that I would benefit from a trip to north-east Arnhem Land where I would see, first hand, the entrepreneurial Indigenous activities that were occurring on the ground. So he paid for my trip, which resulted in me learning a lot

- get staff into the office to learn, share and build a strong culture.

Life of foundations

It is important to consider the lifespan of a foundation at inception, as it impacts strategy. Nearly all family foundations that I have worked with in Australia have been established in perpetuity i.e. their life will continue indefinitely.

There are natural arguments for perpetuity: if the capital is wisely invested it may grow to support the community over a long period of time, the family legacy lives on, future generations can be engaged in the family foundation, income can be used in the future to tackle problems that we are not aware of today, and the total gifts made by a foundation over time can far exceed the foundation's initial funding.

In my early days in the philanthropic sector I was a 'perpetuity man'. If the funds were wisely invested they could benefit the community for generations to come. With experience, I have changed my view. I think the case for a limited life foundation, where the foundation has a finite life, is overwhelmingly strong:

- a dollar spent today will go further than a dollar spent tomorrow

- distributing large sums quickly to a small number of areas is likely to have a bigger impact than distributing funds in smaller sums across a wide variety of areas over a long period of time

- why tie up significant capital and drip feed funding to major issues that we could address today?

- the wealth creators tend to be more passionate about the community than future generations, so use that passion to tackle the mission today

- I have seen examples where future generations felt a family foundation was an obligation that they didn't want in their lives

- let future generations create wealth to solve future problems, some of which we are not aware of today.

I do find it odd when I see foundations focussed on time critical issues such as climate change, where the issue needs to be addressed today, but such foundations only distribute their income to the issue. If the foundation achieves a yield of 5%, it is using 5% of its assets to tackle the issue, with the remaining 95% not being utilised. (Granted that part of the balance sheet might also be tackling the issue via impact investing.)

At every philanthropic vision workshop that I ran I would ask families to consider the lifespan of the foundation. It was always amusing to watch the facial expressions: "Peter, you have just established our family foundation, and now at our first meeting you are asking us to consider an end date?"

As already discussed, I have seen on many occasions the benefits of the wealth creator unified with the second and third generation as they worked on a common goal. However, the fourth generation rarely knows the wealth creator, and in my experience the family passion can wane over time. There is a danger with perpetual foundations that they get focussed on family legacy. We must tread carefully here.

I suspect that if Henry Ford resurfaced today, given some of his unusual world views, he possibly would not be thrilled with the progressive nature of the Ford Foundation!

A growing number of foundations in the USA are shifting to limited life. The best-known example is The Atlantic Philanthropies (AP), which has a booklet on its learnings: *Operating for Limited Life.*[3]

Another example is the Bill and Melinda Gates Foundation. The Gates Foundation's constituent documents state that the foundation will close within 20 years of the death of the survivor of Bill and Melinda, however, Bill Gates stated in an interview in 2022 at the *Forbes 400 Philanthropy Summit* that the foundation will likely close in 25 years.[4]

There are few examples of limited life foundations in Australia. The Stegley Foundation was founded in 1973 by Brian and Shelagh Stegley, the founders of Stegbar Windows. It disbursed its assets and closed its doors in 2001. It was a terrific role model for others in Australia, but few have followed in its footsteps.

One client of mine with a sizeable foundation opted for limited life, primarily for two reasons:

1. they wanted to significantly address the issues that they were tackling within a 20 year period, whilst their cognitive faculties were in good shape

2. due to their humility they took the view that their name did not need to live on via the family foundation for 200+ years.

One of the more interesting quotes I know is related to limited life foundations. It came from former AP Chair, Frank Rhodes, paraphrasing Samuel Johnson, "There's nothing like an imminent hanging to

---

3. https://www.atlanticphilanthropies.org/insights/insights-books/operating-for-limited-life

4. https://www.forbes.com/sites/giacomotognini/2022/09/23/exclusive-bill-gates-reveals-the-bill--melinda-gates-foundation-aims-to-run-for-just-25-more-years/?sh=3cc734ac452f

concentrate the mind."[5]

Limited life brought a whole new mindset to the afore-mentioned client's team. It was both an exciting yet daunting task. Capital had to be spent wisely to maximise outcomes, otherwise it was lost. The team loved the challenge, but were also sitting on the edge of their seats!

One of the highlights of this approach was that there was no budget for each focus area. The money was spent on the best ideas. If there were few good ideas, then little was spent. If there were a stream of strong measurable ideas, we could pin the ears back and go for it!

I have seen evidence of a lower sense of urgency at perpetual foundations. Program managers know that they have a certain annual budget for their focus area. They work hard to make good grants, but the desperation is not always there, as they know there will be another similar budget allocation in the following year.

I would suggest to clients that they consider the life span of the family foundation to be a maximum of 30-40 years. This provides plenty of time to engage the second and third generations, but also provides the benefits of limited life.

Philanthropy is not for everybody. Of course, if the second and third generations aren't interested in becoming engaged with the foundation, then the foundation should spend down at a faster pace.

Assessing potential funding partners

- when talking to a potential funding partner (grantee), if the initial indications are that you are mission-aligned, first seek a summary of what they are trying to achieve, to minimise their time. This might be 2-4 pages and would include: their vision, mission, governance (including board and executive team bench strength – at the end of the day, you are backing people), what success looks like, any strategic partners, how they will measure impact and the milestones along the way

---

5. https://news.cornell.edu/stories/2016/06/olin-lecture-reflects-philanthropy-chuck-feeney-56

- if the above looks promising, don't ask the potential partner for a grant application on your pro forma, as this results in grant applicants filling out endless different types of forms, taking a considerable amount of time. Simply ask for their business plan, including forecast cashflow, goals, how they will measure impact, the milestones along the way and the quarterly KPI reporting that they provide to their board. Review the plan for reasonableness and discuss it with them

- ensure you both understand what the measurables will be, how it will be shown that the change is due to the partner's behaviour/activity (cause/effect), the partner's role in the system, and whether it is cost effective and if possible sustainable[6]

- should the issue be funded by government? If yes, then consider what philanthropy's role is. If it needs to be funded by philanthropy, determine the right tool e.g. grant, debt instrument, equity instrument

- be clear the partner is measuring outcomes and not outputs.

Reporting/evaluation

- don't ask partners (grantees) to provide a special acquittal report for you: such a report for a donor is a poor use of resources for the grant recipient. Ask partners to forward the quarterly impact reports that they provide to their board

---

6. A market based solution is not always possible but it does provide in-built systems to assist longevity

- for material sized grants be prepared to not only fund some form of evaluation of the work performed, whatever is appropriate for the situation (academic evaluation/return on investment/systems thinking[7]), but also ensure that evaluation is used as a strategic tool by partners to monitor progress

- agree the reporting process pre grant approval

- encourage partners to share problems that arise, and be open to mid-course corrections

- disseminate learnings to relevant parties to scale successes and minimise risk of failures being repeated.

Site visits

- get out of the office and into the dirt regularly to see what is really happening on the ground and further build the relationship with your partner (grantee)

- stop and chat, unscheduled, to junior staff and the partner's clientele on location, to learn more

- a few years ago I had a fascinating client site visit with m2m (Mothers to Mothers) in Nampula (Mozambique). We were able to see first-hand some of the issues young mums with HIV (which they had passed to their infants) were facing on a daily basis, and how the local 'mentor mothers' with lived experience were assisting. From the ivory tower in Melbourne that would not have been possible

- a visit to a First Nations Australians ranger program in Arnhem Land taught me about the local conditions and the flexibility that the rangers required in order to develop various seasonal business models to make the program sustainable

---

7. Rockefeller Philanthropy Advisors, *Assessing Impact*, p. 8

- a visit with an environmental group (EG) to a ranger program in Cape York showed me that the EG had not spent enough time developing trust with the ranger group, which was likely to result in flawed outcomes

- an externally curated education tour of USA foundations led to the Sidney Myer Fund CEO, Leonard Vary, introducing the unique Kenneth Myer Innovation Fellowships (see chapter 22 for more detail).

Operations

- for efficiency, seek relevant grant management software that caters to your needs, but time needs to be spent determining exactly what your needs are. If you are not going to seek online grant applications, then you don't need the software that focusses on that feature

- in the early days we had a number of clients that developed an online portal in order to maintain the key records of the foundation (constituent documents, strategy, minutes), and to provide easy access. In later days Google Drive served this purpose

- run a biennial anonymous survey of your partners (grantees) to receive frank feedback and learn how you can become more efficient and effective.

Warren Buffett

It is difficult to leave a 'best practice' chapter without touching on Warren Buffett. Buffett is always concerned with the 'ABC' of large organisations, including foundations: 'Arrogance, Bureaucracy, Complacency'. All large foundations in Australia should take note.[8]

As his wealth escalated, Buffett watched the early successes at the Bill and Melinda Gates Foundation. He appreciated the importance of the focus areas, could see the foundation infrastructure in place and he trusted his friends Bill and Melinda to execute. So he decided to gift the majority of his wealth to his friends' foundation. Since 2006 Buffett has gifted USD36 billion to the Gates Foundation, a foundation which doesn't have his name in it. There is humility right there.[9]

This is an interesting model for others to consider.

And finally

A lot of this chapter has been common sense. However, in my experience the behaviour is not common in the Australian philanthropic sector. Some final comments:

- I challenge sector leaders, foundation CEOs, PAF founders and others to insist on discipline, focus, rigour, evidence, impact measurement and taking risks

- buy a Philanthropy Australia ('PA') membership, assuming it can articulate how its strategic plan will lead to more and better philanthropy. You will be supporting the peak body, which is important for sector growth, and you will meet like-minded donors which may fast-track project collaboration.

Getting the basics right is fundamental to maximising outcomes, but the greatest attention must be given to getting strategy right.

---

8. https://www.gatesfoundation.org/ideas/articles/warren-buffett-philanthropy

9. https://www.gatesnotes.com/Commitment-to-the-Gates-Foundation

Chapter 20

Best practice giving—strategy

"The essence of strategy is choosing what not to do." – **Michael E. Porter**

A foundation's strategy is its detailed plan for achieving success. Social change is hard work. Without a strategy outcomes most likely won't be maximised.

Logic model

Peter Frumkin best summarises how a foundation should approach its task to seek effectiveness. A logic model articulates how a foundation will achieve its mission. A logic model comprises:

1. Theory of change
The heart of the logic model – the activities, outputs and outcomes that will lead to change

2. Theory of leverage
The mechanics of the process e.g. grantmaking and program tactics

3. Theory of scale
The philanthropic leverage – amplification of impact.

Of course logic models can be flawed if you get the assumptions in the causal change wrong.

Frumkin's 'philanthropic prism' stipulated that there were five elements to strategic giving which donors need to think through:

1. the donor's personal style: level of engagement and visibility

2. public benefit to be created: your areas of focus

3. type of activity: grantmaking and program tactics

4. the type of giving vehicle: this will depend on personal circumstances

5. timeframe: perpetuity or limited life.[1]

There is little point developing theories of change in isolation. Former Rockefeller Foundation President, Peter Goldmark cautions us: "My feeling is that a theory of change is not much good unless a grantee owns it."[2]

The Philanthropy Framework

In 2019 Rockefeller Philanthropy Advisors (RPA) developed *The Philanthropy Framework.*[3] With the growth of the philanthropic sector in the USA and boards seeking more focus on outcomes, the framework was developed to provide a structure to maximise impact. The framework comprises three core elements:

1. charter: the foundation's form of governance and decision-making protocol

2. social compact: the agreement with society about the value it

---

1. Peter Frumkin, *Strategic Giving,* The University of Chicago Press, 2006, p. 174-216

2. Rockefeller Philanthropy Advisors and Stanford Social Innovation Review, *Powerful & Innovative Ideas for Grantmakers, Investors, and Nonprofits*, 2006, p. 17

3. Melissa Berman, Renee Karibi-Whyte & Olga Tarasov, *The Philanthropy Framework*, Rockefeller Philanthropy Advisors, March 2019

will create

3. operating model: the approach to resources and systems needed to implement strategy.

Elements of Frumkin's work were used in RPA's thinking. With knowledge and resources fragmented, consideration of these elements will assist boards to know who they are, navigate a complex world and contribute to the public good, as well as assist with the evolution of the philanthropic sector.[4]

RPA went further in 2022 with the release of a new tool to assist foundation boards with strategic clarity by developing 'operating archetypes'. The stated archetype helps funders maximise impact as it articulates how a foundation might deploy resources to implement its vision and strategy. RPA determined eight operating foundation archetypes:

1. talent agency: build promising people and entities closest to the issue

2. think tank: provide research/papers to policy makers and implementers

3. campaign manager: bring together actors/stakeholders to develop solutions

4. field builder: fill gaps and drive advancement

5. venture catalyst: risk capital to give voice to those unheard or unsupported

6. designer: craft/find partners to test scalable models

7. underwriter: support causes that are personally important

4. Melissa Berman, Renee Karibi-Whyte & Olga Tarasov, op. cit., p. 46

8. sower: desire to have a broad-ranging impact across many areas in a broad field or specific geography.[5]

RPA's, *Operating Archetypes* report provides very useful case studies on each archetype. Boards can use this approach to help determine their funding style, given their resources, skills and networks.

Effectiveness

The success of a foundation will depend on its effectiveness. Phil Buchanan is the President of the Centre for Effective Philanthropy in the USA. I like Buchanan's simple view that foundation effectiveness comes in many forms, but it does require four elements:

1. clear goals

2. coherent strategies

3. disciplined implementation

4. relevant performance indicators.[6]

Innovation is important. Effectiveness is more important. I suggest scaling effective strategies, as opposed to constantly looking for innovation.

The right strategies will vary depending upon the larger context in which a foundation operates. Good strategy will constantly evolve, based upon learnings. Buchanan suggests we should remember Warren Buffett's words: "Beware geeks bearing formulas."

5. Olga Tarasov, Melissa Berman and Renee Karibi-Whyte, *Operating Archetypes*, Rockefeller Philanthropy Advisors, 2022

6. Phil Buchanan, *Giving Done Right*, PublicAffairs, 2019

Creativity

Anheier and Leat argue that 'creative foundations' increase the problem-solving capacity of society. They mount the case that often the triggers for creativity—such as structural instability, diversity and spontaneous communication—do not apply to endowed, resource independent foundations. I see this at some of the older foundations in Australia. Anheier and Leat argue the critical factors required for a creative approach are:

- a commitment to mission—this is often driven by a personal connection

- a culture of self-criticism—'doing good is not good enough'

- regular radical review—a thorough radical review at least biennially, looking outward as well as inward

- awareness of a changing environment—and how this might affect a foundation's beneficiaries and mission

- permission to change—having the ability to change tack, hopefully enabled by broad remits via a foundation's constituent documents.[7]

Systems change

We often work in isolation, making bets on which for-purpose entities can make an impact to solve an issue, independent of others. When setting strategy you need to be mindful of the system that you are working within. This is known as taking a systems change approach.

- identify the issue—what is the problem (and associated

---

7. Helmet K. Anheier & Diana Leat, *Creative Philanthropy*, Routledge, 2006, p. 202

problems)?

- develop the key actor map—who is working on the solutions?

- convene with allies—what can we learn from others?

- define the objective—what constitutes success?

- develop feedback loops—systems will only change if entrenched patterns that drive the system are changed

- determine your unique point of leverage, where you can maximise impact given your skills, resources and networks.

The Omidyar Group's, *Systems Practice* is an excellent introductory guide to systems change.[8]

To be successful you will need to find systems entrepreneurs and intermediaries, who play an important role in the ecosystem, coordinating the efforts of multiple organisations towards a common goal. Such entrepreneurs in Australia often struggle to receive the long-term unrestricted funding they require, as the results from their work are not always immediately apparent and donors often seek immediate impact.[9]

Ford Foundation President, Darren Walker, says it is not always the size of the investment that matters: "I've learned that getting the right ecosystem in place enables grantmaking to sustain its impact—and helping build that ecosystem doesn't always involve a big bet."[10]

I think the President of the Rockefeller Brothers Fund, Stephen Heintz, has a particularly interesting analogy for philanthropic strategy:

---

8. The Omidyar Group, *Systems Practice*

9. SVA Consulting, *Insights on Australian field-building intermediaries and their funding journeys towards sustainable impact*, September 2022

10. Alison Powell, Willa Seldon & Nidhi Sahni, *Reimagining Institutional Philanthropy*, Stanford Social Innovation Review, Spring 2019

*"We can think of philanthropy like acupuncture. We have
tiny needles available – where do we insert them in order to
trigger a systemic change? The focus of our work has to be
around triggering change in the public and private sectors."*
[11]

If grants are made in the context of a broader strategy, the results can
be far-reaching.

Being catalytic

In 2009 American Mark Kramer, from FSG Advisors, wrote a well-known
piece for the Stanford Social Innovation Review titled, *Catalytic
Philanthropy*. Essentially 'being catalytic' means making change.[12]

Kramer argued that 'catalytic philanthropists' had the ambition to
change the world and were effective, in contrast to most donors, due to
four distinct practices:

1. take responsibility for achieving results i.e. get involved. The
   urgency of the issue, particularly where there was personal
   significance, energised donors and they actively recruited
   collaborators. The donors took responsibility for finding
   solutions. Kramer stated that donors have the connections and
   capacity to make things happen in a way that most for-purpose
   entities don't

2. mobilise a campaign for change i.e. get others involved.
   Catalytic philanthropy cuts through divisions by stimulating
   cross-sector collaborations and mobilising stakeholders to
   create shared solutions. Systemic reform requires a relentless

---

11. Stephen Heintz, *Achieving social change: what role for grantmaking?*, Alliance Magazine,
    March 2014, p. 48

12. Mark Kramer, *Catalytic Philanthropy*, Stanford Social Innovation Review, Fall 2009

and unending campaign that galvanizes the attention of the many stakeholders involved and unifies their efforts around the pursuit of a common goal

3. use all available resources i.e. don't just make grants. Catalytic donors use a variety of unconventional tools for social change, including corporate resources, investment capital (such as impact investing), advocacy, litigation and lobbying

4. create actionable knowledge i.e. gather and package knowledge effectively. Catalytic donors don't just rely on grant applications to provide them with information. They gather knowledge about the problem they are tackling and use this to inform actions.

Some years ago Peter Goldmark stated that, "In philanthropy I would argue our product is change."[13]

I do agree with Kramer that many donors need to be more strategic to create change. However, care needs to be taken that it is not just the donor driving the approach. Most donors do not have the time or resources to undertake what Kramer calls, 'catalytic philanthropy'. In addition, responsibility for a strategic approach to a community issue needs to be with the many community stakeholders, including the donor. The inspiration doesn't have to come from a donor. Many resources have been wasted by donors whose business success has led them to believe they have all the answers in the community sector. Take a catalytic approach, but work to seek solutions with those with lived experience and subject matter experts.

---

13. Rockefeller Philanthropy Advisors and Stanford Social Innovation Review, *Powerful & Innovative Ideas for Grantmakers, Investors, and Nonprofits*, 2006, p. 5

Ceding control

We discussed the power imbalance earlier. Powell, Seldon and Sahni suggest simple methods to ensure power is shared:

- list grantees whose work is crucial to the impact sought and determine whether more can be done for them to ensure success, including a big bet

- ensure appropriate deference to these core grantees on matters of strategy

- determine who else is active in the space (funders, intermediaries, for-purpose leaders), who could complement your work, and partnerships that could accelerate impact.[14]

One client I worked with had a very simple philosophy, focussed on 'People, Model, Momentum'. The client was seeking to back ideas that ticked three boxes:

- people—back bold, ambitious people

- model—support scalable models

- momentum—support where there were observable measures of success i.e. the plan is working but needs capital to scale up the outcomes.

The strategy included a portfolio approach of some safe bets, but also bigger, riskier bets.

---

14. Alison Powell, Willa Seldon & Nidhi Sahni, *Reimagining Institutional Philanthropy*, Stanford Social Innovation Review, Spring 2019

Common failings

The most common failings of foundations that I see are:

- lack of discipline, resulting in lack of strategy and focus, and trying to be all things to all people

- lack of understanding of the issues being targeted

- looking for a short-term solution

- lack of collaboration with others, including sharing learnings

- refusing to pay for overheads (this includes appropriate overheads for foundations)

- inadequate theories of change

- not measuring impact.

Don't be satisfied with doing good

I like Doug Balfour's giving philosophy as detailed in his highly recommended book, *Doing Good Great.* Doug doesn't want people to be satisfied with just doing good, as the needs are too great to create just moderate impact. He argues that one should have an investment mindset, with rigorous due diligence and making decisions with the head and not the heart.[15]

Most families that I have worked with over the last 20 years have been intelligent, self-made people. I have learnt a lot from many of them. I have found it extraordinary the number of times they have made giving decisions with their heart and not their head. The discipline and rigour, which they used to create wealth, is sometimes left at the foundation boardroom door.

---

15. Doug Balfour, op. cit.

Greater focus on strategy

Liz Gillies, CEO of the Menzies Foundation, has been championing the sector to have more focus on strategy for many years. At the Philanthropy Australia conference in 2022 Liz stated, "We need more focus on strategy and less on process."[16] A challenging report for the Australian philanthropic sector issued by the Melbourne Business School in 2017 (co-authored by Liz) saw the enormous opportunity for change, but that it would rely on philanthropic boards having, "… a greater focus on the strategic impact of philanthropic initiatives and a higher priority … to clarify their strategic intent and measure their performance against this strategy."[17]

Develop a clear strategy and test it with others. Know who you are and what you do. Be clear on what success looks like and how to measure progress. Collaborate with like-minded donors, seek leverage and be clear how you operate so you don't waste grantseekers' time.

Social change is hard work and can be demoralising. We must remember that we are dealing with some of the most difficult issues that our community faces. If there were simple solutions, they would have been solved by governments or markets long ago. It will need commitment, determination and a sense of humour! It can also provide some of the most satisfying moments of your life.

---

16. Philanthropy Australia conference, *Masterclass 5: Evaluating for Impact*, 6 September 2022

17. Liz Gillies, Dr Jodi York & Dr Joanna Mink, *Philanthropy: Towards a Better Practice Model*, Asia Pacific Social Impact Centre, 2017, p. iii

Chapter 21

Best practice giving—the board

"If not now, when? If not you, then who?" – **Hillel the Elder**

I have learnt a lot from sitting around many board tables over the years, often as a director, and sometimes as secretary or adviser. I have worked with some of the smartest, most respected people in the country, primarily self-made people.

The boards I have been privileged to be involved with include The Myer Foundation, Sidney Myer Fund, Philanthropy Australia, Catherine Freeman Foundation, Reichstein Foundation and many private family foundations. Some of the directors I worked with had decades of corporate and for-purpose board experience, were ASX CEOs, Chairs and Directors, university Chancellors and were some of the leading governance experts in the country.

From this experience I have formed views on best practice for foundation boards. Getting it right will maximise community outcomes.

Board structure

The foundation board structure should ideally include:

- diversity that reflects the community in which you operate
- subject matter experts on the issues that the foundation is focussing on, or at least there should be an advisory board with such skills, and preferably those with lived experience

- at least two independent directors and preferably more, to ensure there is rigorous discussion on strategy and implementation.

I am aware of several cases where the foundation's responsible person (RP—independent director) was beholden to the founders as they were the family lawyer or accountant. As the founders were clients of the RP, the RP was unlikely to stand up to decisions made by the founders, if need be. In one case the RP was a friend of the founders' child, so the founders knew they would be able to 'control' the RP if necessary.

With one client, the appointment of two independent directors to the foundation board led to a lot less irrelevant family discussion in board meetings, and a lot more focus on the foundation's strategy and impact.

In my experience there are many foundation boards that don't have the necessary expertise and/or energy to tackle the foundation's mission. With one CEO I joked that perhaps at the next board meeting the CEO should walk in and hang a defibrillator on the boardroom wall at the start of the meeting, as it might reinforce the message that it was time for a number of retirements.

Induction pack

Upon joining, a board member should receive an induction pack including at a minimum: constitution/trust deed, board charter including conflicts of interest policy, the rules and guidelines relating to the foundation structure (e.g. PAF, private charitable trust), a document detailing the minimum expectations of board members, overarching foundation strategy, investment strategy, any policy documents, and bios of directors and executives.

A useful reference for directors and trustees is David Ward's, *Trustee Handbook*.[1] It is a 'plain English' introductory guide for trustees. David has also written handbooks specifically for Private Ancillary Fund and Public Ancillary Fund trustees. Directors and trustees must also

---

1. David Ward, *Trustee Handbook: Roles and Duties of Trustees of Charitable Trusts in Australia*, Philanthropy Australia, Third Edition, 2017

be mindful of the Australian Tax Office's ancillary fund guidelines, if relevant, and the ACNC governance standards for registered charities, and relevant trust and common law.

Board focus

Many books have been written on board governance. The basics are primarily common sense, but I have seen many cases where foundation governance is poor. The focus of the board must be to:

- ensure strong governance is in place in order to exercise their fiduciary duties with integrity and good faith

- ensure the right skills and experience required to target the mission are seated around the table

- ensure the entity has the right constituent documents. Ideally this would ensure the right structure is in place to fit the foundation goals, with broad constituent documents, but a tight strategy. The Collier Charitable Fund Trustees inherited neither (see below)

- develop an appropriate strong board charter

- agree and document the minimum expectations of all board members

- appoint the right CEO for the role and provide an environment for that person to thrive (where the foundation has a CEO)

- with the CEO, develop the vision, mission and strategy for the foundation

- determine what success looks like

- with the CEO, develop short-, medium- and long-term goals, for the foundation, with relevant milestones, in order that progress can be measured

- ensure the CEO has a mechanism to measure impact

- ensure appropriate time is spent in meetings on strategy. One meeting a year should be set aside for a strategy review. At least once every two years this should be facilitated by an external person who has the ability and authority to challenge the board's approach. If the strategy is flawed all else is in vain

- bring candid and constructive advice to the table

- bring new ideas aligned to the mission to the table for the CEO to consider

- ensure that meeting agendas, papers and minutes are distributed on a timely basis

- ensure board meetings are primarily focussed on achieving the mission, removing roadblocks, and consideration of risk mitigation, with operational matters covered via dashboard reporting

- ensure an appropriate succession plan is in place for the Chair and CEO. This is particularly important for foundations where the family is no longer engaged. Appropriate periods of service longevity should be stipulated and adhered to. There are examples of foundations where Chairs and/or board members have held their position for well over a decade, which is often inappropriate

- annually evaluate the performance of the CEO

- biennially self-evaluate board performance.

Remuneration

For larger foundations, consideration should be given to remunerating directors in an appropriate way. I have never understood why directors dealing with some of the most pressing issues in the country should be expected to do so pro bono. I think payment also provides a stronger sense of contract; an obligation to prepare. I have seen foundation board members turn up to meetings with little preparation and little to say, but taking more than their share of the chicken sandwiches.

Where directors decline a fee, with a number of clients I suggested that in lieu of receiving a payment, directors have the ability to approve a grant to the eligible charity of their choice amounting to an annual fixed sum.

Poor governance impacting outcomes

Here are two examples of poor governance resulting in outcomes not being maximised.

1. Paul Ramsay Foundation

I never met Paul Ramsay AO, and he will likely leave an extraordinary legacy to the country via the Paul Ramsay Foundation. At the time of writing it was the largest foundation in the country (by corpus size). However, if he had the right advisers around him prior to his death he would have:

- documented broadly what he sought to achieve with the foundation. I understand that the lack of clarity considerably slowed down the foundation's strategy development and implementation over a number of years

- established the right foundation structure to achieve the outcomes sought—he didn't, resulting in significant time and effort to change the structure, slowing down the foundation's progress

- established a foundation board with the appropriate skills and experience to develop a vision, mission and strategy in the for-purpose sector—I gather he didn't, as there was a significant board restructure, again slowing down the foundation's strategy development and implementation.

2. Collier Charitable Fund

The Collier Charitable Fund is an example of a complicated constituent document. The Collier sisters, Alice, Annette and Edith, established the Collier Charitable Fund in 1954 in order to continue, in perpetuity, the sisters' giving. This is a very noble ambition that we would like to see more of. Unfortunately, the Wills of the Collier sisters have made the process complicated. The Wills are quite specific and clarify the seven designated funds across a range of focus areas to be supported, and the proportion of funds to be distributed for each purpose.

This has resulted in the inefficient process of the Fund receiving hundreds of grant applications each year across a range of focus areas, with only a modest percentage being funded, primarily with small grants despite the Fund's sizeable corpus.[2]

Over 100 years ago in England, Joseph Rowntree established the Joseph Rowntree Foundation. He was quite visionary for the time and took the view that he didn't want to 'rule from the grave' and restrict the scope of the trust he established to the mindset of his era. "I hope that … these trusts may be living bodies, free to adapt themselves to the ever-changing necessities of the nation …"[3].

Regular questions to consider

Boards must be regularly asking the important questions:

- are we clear about our strategic priorities and how to measure progress?

---

2. https://www.colliercharitable.org/

3. Professor Dorothy Scott, op. cit.

- are we providing strong leadership?

- do we have the right mix of skills on the board?

- are we happy to ask ourselves, including executives, the hard questions?

If we get the board governance right, we are well on the way to maximising outcomes for the foundation. Let's now look at great philanthropy case studies.

Chapter 22

Best practice giving—case studies

"I am no longer accepting the things I cannot change. I am changing the things I cannot accept." – **Angela Davis**

I find case studies are a useful way of seeing how theory can be put into practice. This chapter includes vignettes of best practice philanthropy that I have seen from around the world over the last two decades. Where possible I have included links to the subject. This will allow the reader to consider and explore the examples at their own pace and at their own level of detail.

Australian philanthropy sector doyen, Dorothy Scott, described the abolition of slavery as the example, *par excellence*, of visionary philanthropy for three reasons:

1. people committed themselves to the cause knowing that they were unlikely to see slavery abolished in their lifetime

2. initially, only a minority saw slavery as morally wrong, and generally suffered as a result

3. the abolition of slavery marked a very significant milestone in human history i.e. the dignity of a human being not to be the property of another.[1]

Within the case studies that I discuss, not everything these families, foundations and for-purpose entities are doing is perfect, and not all have succeeded, but they have vision, boldness, passion and a plan. There are some terrific models here for others to consider, follow and improve on.

Australia

DAK Foundation

https://dak.org.au

When self-confessed old hippies, Dave and Kerry Rickards, sold their business they wanted to use the capital constructively for the community. After testing a number of ideas they established a foundation. They realised they would get better 'bang for buck' by focussing where there was greater need: overseas. DAK has a small team focussing on eyesight restoration, women's health and essential medical equipment. DAK funds over 40 projects worldwide.

What I like: the passion of the founders, and their focus on what they considered to be the greatest need – the health needs of those in low-middle income countries.

Anonymous foundation

Arthur and Maureen had built a business and were soon to have a liquidity event. Prior to the cash hitting their account, with the assistance of an Excel spreadsheet, they determined 'how much was enough', their needs to maintain their simple lifestyle and their surplus wealth. Once

---

1. Professor Dorothy Scott, op. cit.

the cash was received, they transferred the significant surplus to their limited life foundation and developed a strategy for their giving for the next 20 years, focussing on important issues that they were passionate about, seeking measurable results.

What I like: they determined their surplus, narrowed their focus and sought to create significant change in a short amount of time via a limited life foundation, whilst they still had the energy and the mental capacity to act.

Colonial Foundation

https://colonialfoundation.org.au

Colonial is a rare example in Australia of a foundation with real focus, making fewer but larger unrestricted grants and working with partners for the long term. A great example is Orygen Youth Health Research Centre (mental health). Colonial provided significant funding to Orygen over 20 years which transformed the organisation. This led, in part, to CEO, Patrick McGorry AO, becoming the Australian of the Year in 2010, resulting in a greater national focus on youth mental health, with extra funding for the issue from Federal budgets ensuring the emergence of headspace.org.au.

What I like: the discipline, focus and fewer but larger unrestricted multi-year grants using advocacy to create change.

Kenneth Myer Innovation Fellowships

https://www.myerfoundation.org.au/grant-opportunities-list/myer-innovation-fellowships

Funded by the Sidney Myer Fund and The Myer Foundation, these Fellowships seek to bring new talent to the social sector to target social and environmental challenges. Fellows are provided $120,000 for their 12 month commitment which gives them the luxury to develop a sustainable action plan for their big idea.

What I like: the entrepreneurial approach and the acceptance of risk. If one in ten Fellows succeeds, it is a success.

GenV

https://www.genv.org.au

GenV is a partnership between the Paul Ramsay Foundation, the Murdoch Children's Research Institute and the Victorian Government seeking to understand pathways linking disadvantage to pregnancy and childhood outcomes. In the largest childhood research project ever in Australia, GenV follows babies and their parents across Victoria that could help treat, predict and prevent health problems in an entire generation, thereby reducing the number of children experiencing disadvantage across Australia. The research will more readily inform practice, policies and resourcing.

What I like: this is a unique, bold, state-wide collaborative approach to using data sets targeting better health and wellbeing outcomes across an entire generation. It has huge scale potential.

Cumming Global Centre for Pandemic Therapeutics

https://www.doherty.edu.au/cumming-global-centre-for-pandemic-therapeutics

In late 2022 Canadian Geoff Cumming announced a $250 million pledge to establish the Cumming Global Centre for Pandemic Therapeutics within the Doherty Institute, in a joint venture with The University of Melbourne and The Royal Melbourne Hospital. The Centre will seek to develop treatments for pathogens of pandemic potential and advance the science behind antiviral therapeutics, to transform the management of future pandemics.

What I like: big picture, global approach with the right partners, with significant leverage to bring in other donors. The public nature of the launch will inspire other high-net-worth individuals in Australia to act.

Watertrust Australia

https://watertrustaustralia.org.au

Water management is a major issue in Australia, and likely to become more important over time. Launched in 2021, Watertrust Australia seeks to provide an independent source of water and catchment policy advice, leading to improved management of Australia's land and water management. It has been funded by a coalition of long term philanthropic funders.

What I like: it's early days but I like the focus on one major issue and the long term collaboration of several key players, including the independence that philanthropy brings.

ClimateWorks Centre

https://www.climateworkscentre.org

ClimateWorks Centre (CWC, originally ClimateWorks Australia) was established in 2009 via a partnership between philanthropy (The Myer Foundation) and Monash University. At the time there was a lack of independent, quality research on climate change and net zero roadmaps in Australia that business and government could trust. CWC bridges research and climate action to assist the system-level transitions required for net zero emissions across Australia, SE Asia and the Pacific.

What I like: that this idea morphed from a conversation around the Shelmerdine family kitchen table into a game-changer for independent advocacy for climate policy in Australia.

Tuckwell Scholarship Program

https://tuckwell.anu.edu.au

The Tuckwell Scholarship program was founded in 2012 by Graham Tuckwell AO and Louise Tuckwell AO, who launched the program with an initial gift of $50 million. The program aims to transform undergraduate scholarships in Australia. Scholars are selected on the basis of intellect, character, leadership and their commitment to Australia. The Tuckwells expanded their program in 2016 when they committed to building two new halls of residence which will deliver an estimated $200 million to the program over the next 30 years.

What I like: the size and public nature of the gift were transformational in the Australian philanthropic sector, inspiring others into action.

Private client

One client I worked with was keen to develop their First Nations Australians strategy. We brought in an adviser who had experience working with First Nations People. The adviser reviewed the work the client had done previously and then commenced a strategy overhaul. We assembled a group of 'Critical Friends', six Indigenous Australians, who guided our work. When the new strategy was completed, we appointed a First Nations Person to be the First Nations Lead and implement the strategy. We continued to have biannual check-ins with Critical Friends so they could monitor our progress.

What I like: collaborating with First Nations Australians, those with lived experience, to guide the work and then appointing a First Nations person as First Nations Lead to implement the strategy.

The Alfred Felton Bequest

https://www.eqt.com.au/philanthropy/the-felton-bequest

When he passed away in 1904, Alfred Felton bequeathed the bulk of his estate to charitable projects including acquisitions of artworks for the National Gallery of Victoria. It is estimated that these artworks are now valued at well in excess of $2 billion.

What I like: whilst the bequest is not solely arts related, the bulk of the funding has been used for one issue—to establish the NGV as an internationally significant institution.

Cochlear implant – Australia's Top 50 Philanthropic Grants, 2013

Professor Graeme Clark AC was pioneering the cochlear ear implant. However, he did not have the funding to retain his key engineer. In 1978 modest philanthropic funding from The Clive and Vera Ramaciotti Foundations ensured the work could continue. This enabled the development of the cochlear implant, which led to hearing impaired patients understanding speech.

What I like: the implants were a world-wide game changer for hearing impaired people. A high risk small grant enabled the research to continue at a critical stage.

Our Place

https://ourplace.org.au

Based upon evidence that education lifts aspirations, businessman Julius Colman AM was concerned with education within disadvantaged communities in Victoria. He sought out one of the most disadvantaged communities to develop a holistic place-based approach to supporting the education, health and development of all children and families by utilising the school platform. The pilot site was Doveton College which commenced operation in 2012. A key part of the plan was the holistic approach to a child, including early learning, health and development, high quality schooling, with wrap-around health and well-being services and engagement activities for kids. It also provides adult education, learning and employment opportunities.

What I like: it's still early days but I like Colman's entrepreneurial approach to seeking a solution to a major community issue: review the evidence, test via a pilot and use long term philanthropic funding to leverage government to scale to eight other sites.

Maranguka Justice Reinvestment

https://www.dusseldorp.org.au/partner/maranguka-justice-reinvestment-project

Maranguka and Just Reinvest NSW partnered in 2012 to develop a justice reinvestment 'proof of concept'. The aim was to reduce Aboriginal incarceration by implementing strategies that address the drivers into the criminal justice system, led by the community and informed by data. Maranguka is directed and guided by the wishes of the Bourke Tribal Council. The initiative has been backed by the Dusseldorp Forum and the Vincent Fairfax Family Foundation who have been funding core operating costs for many years.

What I like: listening to those with lived experience and taking a long term, place-based systems change approach to a critical issue, whilst widely sharing the learnings.

CAGES Foundation/Maari Ma Health Aboriginal Corporation

https://www.maarima.com.au/news/40/25/ENDURING-PARTNERSHIP-WINS-NATIONAL-PHILANTHROPY-AWARD

CAGES has funded Maari Ma for over a decade, getting to know the community and supporting a model of care that suits the needs of families in far west NSW.

What I like: with humility, CAGES decision making has been heavily influenced by those with lived experience, and they have provided long term funding.

Fay Fuller Foundation

https://www.fayfullerfoundation.com.au,
https://www.ourtownsa.com.au/file/rkos421mu/Health-report-Digital-FINAL-lowres%20(3).pdf

The Fay Fuller Foundation (FFF) focusses on supporting the health and wellbeing of the South Australian community. In 2018 FFF commissioned a comprehensive report on the Health Needs and Priorities in South Australia. The outcome was Our Town, an 11 year, $15 million initiative in partnership with The Australian Centre for Social Innovation and Clear Horizon. Our Town seeks to build the capabilities of regional towns to, "… develop community-based responses to mental health and wellbeing, with an eye to scaling what works, and influencing regional policy".

What I like: it is still early days, but putting the power in the hands of those with lived experience in the community, supported by long term multi-year funding, with an aspiration to scale successes.

ten20 Foundation

https://probonoaustralia.com.au/news/2019/08/collective-impact-and-empowering-communities-the-legacy-of-the-ten20-foundation/

GordonCare provided child protection services for 125 years for disadvantaged children and young people. Its board could see that existing responses to child vulnerability weren't addressing the root causes of the issue, so they made the bold decision to move from service provider to catalytic funder. They sold their assets and launched a 10 year investment initiative to spend down its $10 million corpus, focussed on developing community led solutions to help vulnerable children. The money was primarily provided to, "…backbone organisations and leaders so they could run their own projects and create change from inside their communities", as well as influence government policy to better support place-based approaches. A key part of the initiative was the launch by ten20 of a field-building intermediary, Opportunity Child (OC). OC was an intermediary providing a breadth of functions to an emerging field of place-based systems change, focussed on outcomes for children experiencing vulnerability.

What I like: a bold approach to an old issue, throwing out an old model of care and targeting a new bold preventative approach to entrenched social issues via place-based systems change. The 'end game', assisted by the spend down approach, was to empower local communities and shift government policy.

UKARIA

https://www.ukaria.com

Ulrike Klein AO had a vision to build, "… a place of inspiration, where artistry is nurtured and celebrated, and new work is born …" The result is the UKARIA Cultural Centre in the Adelaide Hills. UKARIA includes a concert hall purpose-built for chamber music, as well as a space for residencies, for artists to draw inspiration from nature to create.

What I like: the vision and passion to build something special.

Who Gives a Crap

https://au.whogivesacrap.org

When three mates discovered that over two billion people don't have access to a toilet, they decided to take action. In 2012 they started Who Gives a Crap, a certified B Corp, selling toilet paper, tissues and paper towels. They donate 50% of their profits to help build toilets and improve sanitation in low-middle income countries. As of mid 2023 they had donated over $11 million.

What I like: developing a sustainable model to target a major issue. The buying of an everyday product results in a positive impact on our community.

Bennelong Foundation

https://www.bennelongfoundation.com

Established in 2002 by Jeff Chapman AM and Carena Shankar, the Bennelong Foundation primarily supports community health, cultural inclusion and education and training that build pathways to employment. Jeff and Carena decided many years ago to use their business smarts to generate wealth to be used to support communities into the future. The idea is to create wealth over several decades through the family office, with the Foundation being the end beneficiary of all the assets i.e. the sole purpose of the family office is to generate wealth for the Foundation. Part of the magic is that this has also created an opportunity for all staff of the businesses to be part of this wealth-creating journey that will benefit many generations of the community to come.

What I like: Jeff and Carena's humility, but even more impressive is the building of significant businesses for the benefit of the community. Jeff and Carena's drive for wealth creation is not for themselves, but for the community. This unique model in Australia will inspire others to do similar, which will have a significant long term benefit for our country.

Global Ventures

https://scgv.org

In 2022 Save the Children established Global Ventures (GV). GV seeks to take innovative finance and new technologies to scale in Australia and around the world. Its impact investing funds are providing patient capital to social entrepreneurs to avoid the funding 'valley of death' and assist child wellbeing, leveraging Save the Children's global platform to accelerate portfolio impact and financial returns. One early investment example is THINKMD, a USA public benefit corporation, which has developed clinical intelligence and analytics which can provide, via digital technology, 'physician-based knowledge and skills' providing 'better health to anyone anywhere'.

What I like: bold, innovative approach to seeking patient capital to tackle child wellbeing.

Stella

https://stella.org.au

Founded in 2012, Stella provides a range of initiatives that actively champion Australian women writers, tackling gender bias in the literary sector. Its flagship program is the annual Stella Prize, a major literary award. Stella is a voice for gender equality and cultural change in Australian literature. In 2022 the Stella Prize was secured in perpetuity via a clever campaign to raise the final $2 million needed to endow the Prize. The campaign was time-bound and linked to the 10th anniversary of Stella. This included a $1 million match from Paula McLean (one of the largest donations to date to Australian literature) and a significant gift from the Helen Macpherson Smith Trust, a rare Australian philanthropic foundation named after a woman. Women donors of all levels around Australia were galvanised to give to the campaign.

What I like: the female-led philanthropy focus, and the clever funding campaign to galvanise both small and large donors, resulting in the initiative now being sustainable.

Overseas

Growald Climate Fund (USA)

https://www.growaldclimatefund.org

Founded by a fourth generation Rockefeller family member, the Growald venture philanthropy fund has a modest corpus but has played a leading convenor role for many larger foundations in the USA, UK, Europe and Australia. It initially had a small team, but the Executive Director successfully connected climate innovators with financial resources. Growald then encouraged foundations world-wide with greater resources to get on board, with Growald coordinating bi-annual meetings of funders to assess strategy, finesse plans and push for larger financial commitments.

What I like: the Fund's humility ('we strive for impact over recognition'), agility, advocacy and focus on one critical issue, with the use of leverage by a small team with modest financial resources, and the outsized impact it has been able to create.

European Climate Foundation (Europe)

https://europeanclimate.org

ECF plays a unique role in paving the way to a net zero emission world. It is a thought leader across the climate movement, developing the tools to reduce carbon emissions. It is a network enabler bringing people together to collaborate and advocate. It is also a strategic grantmaker providing significant funding to a broad range of actors within the system. All done with a sense of urgency.

What I like: big picture vision, systems thinker, and collaborative approach via pooled funding from foundations world-wide.

Children's Investment Fund Foundation (UK)

https://ciff.org

CIFF, established in 2002 by Chris Hohn & Jamie Cooper in the UK, takes a strategic approach in a transparent way, backed by rigorous due diligence and data, to improving the lives of children worldwide.

What I like: CIFF uses the smarts and financial resources of the founders, with a focus on impact measurement. In addition there is total transparency, with detail on all existing funding partners on their website, including grant size and nature of the work.

Bernard van Leer Foundation (The Netherlands)

https://bernardvanleer.org

Founded in 1949, from 1965 van Leer has focussed on early childhood development, particularly those growing up in circumstances of social, economic and environmental disadvantage around the world.

What I like: laser focus for decades on one issue, building significant internal expertise, disseminating the learnings, and seeking to scale successes.

KR Foundation (Denmark)

https://krfnd.org

KR seeks to address the root cause of climate change by focussing on what they consider to be four critical areas of work where they can have an impact. This fits within the Danish Government's ambitious commitment to reduce greenhouse gas emissions by 70% by 2030.

What I like: focus on one issue (a big one) and their rigorous due diligence to ensure they are maximising impact.

Blue Meridian Partners (USA)

https://www.bluemeridian.org

BMP was incubated at the Edna McConnell Clark Foundation (EMCF). EMCF for many years has taken an investment approach, often aggregating capital with multi-year relationships. BMP takes a long term approach and seeks to find successful strategies addressing social problems facing families in poverty and then targets significant external resources via pooled funds.

What I like: big picture, seeks scale, collaborative approach, and the shared learnings and costs via pooled funds.

Skoll Foundation (USA)

https://skoll.org

Founded by Jeff Skoll, Skoll seeks to catalyse transformational social change by investing in and championing social entrepreneurs targeting solutions to some of the world's most pressing problems.

What I like: they know who they are, and they use the Skoll World Forum to build a world-wide network to collaborate on big ideas and promote successful social entrepreneurs. And they have had the discipline to pursue this course for 20 years.

Jasmine Social Investments (New Zealand)

https://www.jasmine.org.nz, https://www.bigbangphilanthropy.org

JSI seeks to fund high-performing social ventures and social entrepreneurs who are solving a basic need of the very poor. Rigorous due diligence, through an investment lens, is performed on the ground and shared with other potential donors.

What I like: the discipline to stick with their plan, the focus on impact at scale and sharing of due diligence with Big Bang Philanthropy (and others) to leverage their work.

Segal Family Foundation (USA)

https://www.segalfamilyfoundation.org

Segal supports local grass roots organisations working across Sub-Saharan Africa. Most of their partners are in East Africa where they have built a team.

What I like: Segal organises an annual conference of its partners and other potential donors, to share ideas and leverage its impact. The conferences alternate between Africa and the USA. I attended one of these conferences in Nairobi and was impressed by the buzz in the room, and the hive of break-out activity between partners and donors.

MacKenzie Scott (USA)

https://yieldgiving.com

MacKenzie Scott's approach to giving is to get on with it! Since 2019 Scott has gifted USD14 billion to 1,600 charities (an average of USD8.75 million each). Initially her anonymous team took a pro-active approach and would prepare due diligence and make decisions. She has since commenced a process, via Yield Giving, calling for applications for specific types of organisations or certain locations. She calls her approach, 'yielding' control.

What I like: a humble, non-bureaucratic approach to wealth redistribution and trust in those on the ground—shifting the philanthropic power imbalance. The simple process and large unrestricted funding limits the burden on grant seekers so they can focus on their mission. She is also following Chuck Feeney's mantra of 'giving while living', seeking to give the lot away! Time will tell how strong the outcomes are from this approach.

Yvon Chouinard, Patagonia founder (USA)

https://www.patagonia.com.au/pages/ownership

Clothing company, Patagonia, has long cared for the planet, initially by using materials less harmful to the environment, then donating 1% of sales and then becoming a B Corp. Yvon Chouinard, the founder of Patagonia, took a giant step in 2022 and transferred the family shareholding in Patagonia to a for-purpose entity. He said: "Earth is now our shareholder".

What I like: instead of selling the business or taking the company public, Chouinard decided to donate ownership of the company to a charitable trust and a for-purpose entity to ensure profits are used to tackle climate change for the life of the business.

The Audacious Project (USA)

https://www.audaciousproject.org

Audacious seeks to catalyse social impact on a huge scale. It is housed at TED, supported by social impact adviser, The Bridgespan Group, and backed by some of the world's largest foundations. Audacious works with proven social entrepreneurs and asks them to think bigger. The Audacious team then assists these entrepreneurs to develop multi-year plans and present them to major donors.

What I like: bigger, bolder thinking rolled up with collaborative efforts to seek social change on a larger scale.

MacArthur Foundation – Lever for Change (USA)

https://www.leverforchange.org

In 2019 MacArthur established Lever for Change (LFC). It was the result of MacArthur's 2017 100&Change Challenge, which provided USD100 million to applicants for a bold solution to a significant social challenge anywhere in the world.

LFC customises philanthropic grant challenges that award a minimum of USD10 million and provides opportunities to help donors to find and fund bold solutions capable of accelerating social change.

What I like: big picture thinking, a small number of big bets supporting creative people and leveraging other donors whilst seeking to accelerate social change.

"Plan P" (Confidential at the time of writing)

Plan P is a bold new initiative that seeks to develop and fund USD1 billion ideas targeting major global issues. Collaborations would include initiatives like the Audacious Project (see above). Plan P will target massive capital sums, influencing thinking of major donors, showing how bold giving should be possible, including from those new to their giving.

What I like: bold thinking, billion dollar ideas, leveraging donors by simplification of big ideas, and collaborating with the right players. Raising the 'philanthropic bar' and seeking USD1 billion ideas to become the 'norm'.

PART IV: SECTOR TIPS

Chapter 23

Tips for families to get started

"Never confuse net worth with self-worth. There is no relationship between the two." – **Chuck Collins & Pam Rogers**

Pause before you run

A family that is seeking to create constructive change in the community needs to consider a number of issues. This is an exciting moment! You are about to embark on a wonderful journey with your family. The journey may have moments of frustration, but it will hopefully lead to some amazing new experiences and learnings for the family, possibly some life-changing moments for family members and most importantly some successful outcomes for the community.

You don't necessarily need to establish a family foundation to create constructive change in the community. You can simply work with appropriate community partners, review their goals and plans, volunteer with them and then write cheques. However, in my experience, if you are seeking to invest $1 million+ over time, having a family foundation structure:

- generally results in a more strategic approach being taken as there are foundation meetings organised at convenient times dedicated to focussing on community impact

- generally ensures that due diligence is performed, meeting papers are prepared and discussed, with actions agreed and documented via minutes

- makes it easier to engage and give a voice to other family members

- makes it easier to track your impact as most of the giving is done through one vehicle.

Structured giving does not have to be via a family foundation. It could be done via a sub fund, a giving circle or some other form of collective giving.

Consideration needs to be given to a range of issues prior to getting started:

- why you give

- the current giving style of the family

- the giving goals of the family, including your giving focus

- the type of structure, if any required, which will be driven by the family goals

- which family members will be engaged and how

- how decisions will be made

- the time commitment involved

- the financial capital to be initially committed

- the individual and collective skills the family has

- external expertise that will likely be required.

Seek advice

Seek advice from philanthropic advisers or those with experience in the sector. Such advisers need to understand your goals, the different types of foundation legal structures, and the advantages and disadvantages of each. If possible, speak to other families who are ahead of you on your journey, so you can learn from their successes and mistakes. The Philanthropy Australia website has detail on the different types of giving structures available to families, as well as other useful resources.

Getting the right advice upfront will save time and minimise poor decisions, allowing you to quickly maximise impact with your mission. For example, a structure such as a Private Ancillary Fund is inexpensive to establish, and depending on your exact needs should cost from $5,000 to $7,500. I have seen examples where ridiculous sums ($35,000 in one case) have been charged by opportunistic suppliers or those establishing such vehicles for the first time, and charging the client for the pleasure of learning how to do it.

In my experience some are reluctant to pay for philanthropic advice. However, when you amortise the cost over what you are seeking to distribute over the following ten years, the expense is usually immaterial. You seek tax advice from an expert; why wouldn't you do the same with something more important?

Leave funds aside for distribution from your personal account, to enable you to provide support to people and organisations that are not eligible charities, but are doing great work targeting issues in the community.

Minimise individual family member discretionary giving. In my experience, the families that work together on common goals will get more satisfaction from the family giving. A family foundation won't heal all family rifts, but it does provide a unique opportunity for outward-focussed conversations and for all family members to use their different skills to assist goal attainment.

Talk to families who are working in the area in which you are interested e.g. if you are interested in climate change, the Australian Environmental Grantmakers Network has developed a *Climate Change*

Funding Framework that will allow you to tap into work done by experts, thereby fast-tracking your impact. If you are seeking to give offshore, the Australian International Development Network can share its expertise. If you wish to give via a gender lens, Australians Investing in Women has significant experience.

Resources

There are numerous resources to help frame your early thinking and get started. These include:

- a number of chapters of this book, particularly:

    - 'How much is enough?'

    - 'How much to leave the kids?'

    - 'Engaging the next gen in the community'

    - 'Educational tool for the next gen'

    - 'Philanthropic vision'

    - Part III - 'Best practice giving'

- *Inspired Philanthropy,* Tracy Gary with Nancy Adess: a manual providing a step-by-step guide to assisting you to create a giving plan

- Philanthropy Australia: membership based, PA is the sector peak body
  https://www.philanthropy.org.au

- Alliance (UK magazine): "Provides a useful, independent and practical commentary on global philanthropy trends"
  https://www.alliancemagazine.org

- Stanford Social Innovation Review (USA magazine): written by and for social change leaders, SSIR, "covers cross-sector solutions to global problems"
  https://ssir.org

- The resources listed in the appendices to this book.

Have patience and aim high

Don't be afraid to start slowly, build relationships and test ideas. Your confidence will grow. It is a journey, with twists and turns. During this journey you will meet some incredibly impressive and uplifting people. Have patience, be bold, bring discipline and aim high. You will also have a lot of fun.

"Remember these words of advice from Anjali Sharma and Ashjayeen Sharif: don't be scared to reach for goals that might seem entirely absurd. You're far more powerful than you think you are".[1]

---

1. Claire O'Rourke, *Together We Can,* Allen & Unwin, 2022, p. 296

Chapter 24

Tips for foundation CEOs

"Culture eats strategy for breakfast." – **Peter Drucker**

Be self-aware

The role of the foundation CEO is critical. The role is primarily to confirm the mission and develop strategy (with board input), build the right team, build and maintain a strong culture and implement the strategy in order to maximise impact.

You must be self-aware and know your strengths and weaknesses. Play to your strengths and recruit to cover for your weaknesses. Everyone has a different leadership style. Mine was to provide guidance and then autonomy. Discuss the issue at hand, listen, guide, and then get out of the way so team members can develop and thrive. It is important to allow people the space to flourish. But always be available to chat if team members wish to check-in.

It is important to keep the ego in check. In an earlier chapter we talked about the power imbalance in the philanthropic sector and humility. The CEO is the face of the foundation, so it is important that the CEO shows the team what acceptable behaviour is. Many years ago I was meeting a foundation program manager at this person's office. As I stepped into reception, I saw seven very large framed photos on the walls. The foundation CEO was very prominent in six of the photos! Pointing at each photo, I counted out aloud at each 'CEO sighting' and then looked at the receptionist, who sheepishly grinned and looked away.

I have heard regular comments over many years from for-purpose team members, regaling stories of arrogance from foundation team members. The philanthropic sector needs to really understand that it can achieve nothing without its partners who are on the ground, implementing on a daily basis. Nothing! There is no room for arrogance. And this understanding needs to be driven by the CEO.

Drawn from my experience over 20 years in the philanthropic sector, the following tips will assist CEOs to maximise their impact.

Board

- hold regular meetings with the Chair to discuss strategy and execution to ensure you are on the same page. If I was starting over, this would be more of a focus for me second time around

- work with the Chair to ensure the board composition will maximise the chances of success

- check-in from time to time with individual board members for general advice, to build your relationship and to see whether they are holding back on particular issues

- encourage the Chair to biennially self-evaluate the board. This will assist having the right board in place, operating in a way that assists the CEO develop and implement strategy.

Strategy

- every year hold a strategy review meeting with the board to check that the mission, strategy and execution are on track and everyone is still on the same page. Every second year this session should be facilitated by an external person who can challenge your approach

- within the agreed strategy, have quarterly team action plans, with accountabilities, so the team is spending time on the right issues each quarter. This ensures day to day actions align with medium to long term goals of the foundation.

Staff

- recruit from outside the philanthropic sector. The sector has a history of 'chair-hopping', with staff moving between foundations. Everyone has a certain way of thinking, including ideas and people that they are biased towards. Fresh blood will bring new ideas into the sector

- recruit people with lived experience, strong values, passion and curiosity who are smarter than you. Ensure you test for this during the recruitment process. And then test this with your own referees, not just those offered up by the candidate

- encourage sensible risk-taking and embrace failure. As one client put it, "I have no issue with noble failure. I'm not so impressed with dumb failure"!

- don't let staff get too comfortable in their roles. I have noticed that once someone gets a job on the 'grantmaker side' they sometimes believe that it is easier on that side than the 'grantseeker side'. They stay in the role for many years and don't seek other roles. If there are limited opportunities for them to grow in the role and/or the organisation, perhaps you need an exit plan for them

- efficiency and effectiveness are critical to success. Cyril Peupion's, *Work Smarter: Live Better* provides practical tips on how to change teamwork habits. Peupion paraphrases Peter Drucker: "Efficiency can be defined as doing things right…Effectiveness can be defined by doing the right things."[1] Work out 'how' to work. And then determine 'what' to work on. This book is one of the simplest and most practical management

---

1. Cyril Peupion, *Work Smarter: Live Better*, Peupion Pty Ltd, 2010, p. 14

books that I have read

- implement a quarterly team culture check. There are various Apps that make this a quick and efficient process, allowing trends to be spotted. You can also develop your own through Google Forms or SurveyMonkey. This will provide a regular checking of the 'pulse of the room' on important culture issues agreed by the team

- have regular check-ins with team members. This might be a 5 minute chat at the water cooler every few days. Or it could be a fortnightly walk around the block. Determine what works best for each team member. I was having a walking check-in with a colleague one day when we strolled past a cemetery. I said, "Do you mind if we pop in, as I believe Sidney Myer is buried in here?" So there we were discussing Sidney's approach to giving over his grave! A great 'teachable moment' right there

- organise team off-sites to check in on strategy, progress and each other. If I was starting over, this would also be more of a focus for me

- develop a succession plan so that when you leave there are 1-2 internal candidates for your role

- you don't build strong team culture if you are at the home office five days per week.

Board papers

- share the draft agenda with the Chair well before papers are due to be finalised, so there are no surprises

- include a summary table up front with the key decisions for the meeting, including a 'grants for discussion' summary with dollar value

- papers need to be concise, preferably PowerPoint, Slides or similar for readability

- appendices should be accessed via links

- upon distribution of papers, encourage minor questions from board members to be circulated prior to the meeting so they can be dealt with pre meeting, so more time is spent in the board meeting on the big issues

- papers should only be soft copy. This is far more efficient and better environmentally.

Minutes

- should be drafted pre meeting, leaving gaps for decisions made. This ensures that they can be completed (in draft) and sent to the Chair within 24 hours of the meeting, and then circulated (in draft) to the board within two days of the meeting. I have seen many examples where minutes take weeks, and on some occasions, months to be circulated. This is totally inappropriate. Minutes are a critical record of decisions made so need to be drafted immediately.

Other

- the office should be paperless for efficiency, as well as the environment

- ensure the team has the right IT tools to maximise efficiency

- move on before 10 years in the role. Sorry, but your time is up and fresh ideas are needed! Craig Connelly has a similar view. He was the Ian Potter Foundation CEO for numerous years. He says, "We had implemented a number of positive changes at Potter and I felt after seven years it was time for me to move on, with a new CEO to come in with fresh ideas".[2]

- your team is likely to be working on difficult, wicked problems. Make sure you celebrate the successes along the way. A key internal slogan within the Andersen insolvency team in the 1980s was, "You are only as good as your last job." This resulted in me being slow to celebrate the successes as I was always looking ahead. Make sure the team has some fun!

Set the right strategy, hire the right team, build the right culture and monitor it, and the outcomes will flow.

---

2. Conversation with author, 30 March 2023

Chapter 25

Tips for philanthropy advisers

"The value of a man resides in what he gives and NOT in what he is capable of receiving." – **Albert Einstein**

The role of philanthropy adviser

With the immaturity of the philanthropic sector in Australia, philanthropic advisers are a newish profession in this country. The importance of the role is often misunderstood, with donors and family offices not always grasping the technical skill and emotional intelligence required to perform the role.[1] I recall situations where I was in meetings and tax advisers provided grantmaking advice to my clients. I would circle back later and say that I was happy for that to continue, as long as I could provide tax advice to their clients!

The imminent growth of the philanthropic sector in this country will require a strong, growing and well-trained philanthropy adviser cohort to ensure capital is effectively deployed and outcomes maximised.

Bill, a Sydney client, once said to me, "To succeed in life you need to be able to create relationships and influence people." This is good advice for philanthropy advisers. The role of philanthropy adviser is an unusual one. You are part family adviser, part psychologist, part convenor, part family mediator, and part connector of money to ideas.

UK Philanthropy adviser, Rebecca Eastmond, describes the role of the

---

1. Emma Beeston and Beth Breeze, op. cit., p. 214

adviser as one who assists clients to determine what makes them angry about the world and then helping them to do something positive about that issue.[2]

A self-aware adviser will recognise that: "It is an extraordinary privilege being part of the process of creating some positive change in the world."[3]

Every family has its quirks. The philanthropy adviser business can involve quirky families with wealth, so you may need patience and tolerance. (It is interesting to write this as Ange suggests that I could work on both these traits!)

Selling philanthropy

It is not easy to 'sell' philanthropy. The hard sell will not work. Most people don't like being told what to do. This is particularly the case with self-made high-net-worth individuals (HNWIs). What I found most effective was not altruism, and saying that giving was the right thing to do. I had some success by tapping into the selfish side of people. The carrot that I found to be most effective was discussing with mums and dads the extraordinary educational tool that a family foundation could be for the next generation (see chapter 14).

Seek speaking events, consider the audience, and make sure you have something interesting to share. Tell stories. There must be three great takeaways for the audience. Don't be bland, and use humour to lighten the mood. When talking to journalists, of course you must be factual, but use words and phrases that are unique and jump off the page. Make sure you are concise and ensure you get your three key points across. If you are 'good copy', it will get a run.

Find journalists who write on community issues, and feed them information in a user-friendly way. Journalists are time poor and will appreciate it. When they next need a comment on a community issue they will call you for comment. Provide constructive feedback on their articles and then feed in messages for future articles e.g. "I like the way

---

2. Emma Beeston and Beth Breeze, op. cit., p. 68

3. Ibid., p. 26

you highlighted … did you know that …"

In his first speech after being announced as 'Australian of the Year' in 2011, Simon McKeon AO said he would use his new platform to highlight the work of for-purpose organisations in Australia. He also said, "Australians were generous". I didn't know Simon at the time. However, I guessed his email address (got it on the third attempt), congratulated him on his appointment and speech, but then provided him the giving statistics which suggested Australians weren't so generous. Despite his inbox being full of congratulatory messages (I used a 'catchy' title in 'subject') he replied to my email overnight, wanting to know where my stats were from. Once I provided the reference, he was able to share those statistics in a number of wonderful speeches he made throughout his year in the spotlight.

Never stop networking. You can't meet enough clever and passionate people, you will learn from others, you will know who to collaborate with, you will meet your next 'new hire', and you will grow your client base. Seek connections with those who could be doing more for the community and provide them exciting opportunities to do so.

Be brutally disciplined with pursuing leads. Establish a system that works for you. With one prospect I checked in twice a year for seven years. He eventually agreed to establish a foundation.

Top tips

My top tips for being a philanthropy adviser are:

- be genuine, otherwise people will see through you. You only get one chance at a first impression

- be very clear on exactly the nature of your services i.e. what you do and what you don't do

- be aware of the adviser eco-system and who is good at what they do. This will lead to collaborative opportunities

- listening is critical, so you can guide families where they wish to go. Don't plan in your mind how to reply when someone is talking to you. Listen to what they are saying. Embrace silence. Many people don't like silence. It allows for reflection. I love silence. Use it as a tool. People often fill silence with what is really on their mind

- be acutely aware of what the family is trying to achieve, and then understand the relevant structures within your domain so the right structure (if needed) is established. I have outlined elsewhere the adverse ramifications of establishing the wrong structure

- help families discover what their passions are, and then guide them in that space

- over time try and steer families from personal whims to critical community needs

- you can't be an expert on all issues, but be curious, read widely on community issues and know who the relevant experts are

- strong written and verbal communication is important in order to share ideas. You need to condense large amounts of material on complex issues into a few pages. Most people won't read a 15 page summary

- provide an opinion; this is what you are a paid to do. Make sure you have the reasons to support your opinion. I have seen many 'advisers' sit on the fence

- encourage:

  - best practice giving (see chapter 19)

  - focus on just 1 or 2 areas

  - fewer but larger grants

  - multi-year unrestricted funding

- impact measurement

- consideration of spend down

- take the time to help others on their mission. The favours are sometimes returned. I assumed that everyone I met had an uncle or aunty worth $50 million. You just never know where the next lead will come from

- be tolerant, as you will likely have clients that:

  - don't put the same priority on giving as you do

  - could do so much more than they do but choose not to

  - ignore your advice and the family giving strategy and just give to the 'Save the Donkeys Society'

  - simply don't wish to be strategic and disciplined about their giving

  - don't wish to fund all the programs and organisations that you would

- most clients will tick one (or more) of the above boxes at some stage. That is okay, but if they are doing it with over 25% of their giving, it might be time to find some new clients

- keep clients up to date with the expertise that you are providing them e.g. the wins their partners are having, governance compliance, annual/since inception giving summaries

- get used to rejection. A high percentage of people will reject you

- be powerful advocates for more and better giving

- make it fun! This will keep families engaged.

I summarise the adviser role here: "Our goal (as an adviser) was not to tell families what to do, but to guide them through the process. I saw my role as a guide, a knowledge sharer and an inspirer."[4]

Determine the client's exact needs. Then provide amazing service at good value so they have an outstanding experience and tell others about it. This will grow your business and the size of the philanthropic sector, resulting in positive outcomes for the community.

Be self-aware

In 2023 Beth Breeze and Emma Beeston released in the UK, *Advising Philanthropists*, a very useful toolkit for the philanthropy adviser. In it they discuss the dangers of being an intermediary, occupying the space between the donor and the potential grant recipient. They quote Joel Orosz' seven temptations of philanthropy:

1. "Believing the flattery: being exposed to constant praise can make it hard to critically appraise your performance

2. Surrendering to the whims of arrogance: flattery can lead to an overblown sense of self-worth and stop you listening to and considering others

3. Surrendering to cynicism: you treat every compliment with suspicion

4. Regarding the foundation's money as your own: because your role in the process means you have forgotten this is money for the public good

5. Doubting the worthiness of all applicants: you are so analytical that you believe no applicant is worthy of funding

6. Finding value in all applicants: this can make it hard to say no and result in delay as you put off making decisions

---

4. Emma Beeston and Beth Breeze, op. cit., p. 30

7. Taking the easy way out: examples include cutting corners such as skim-reading proposals and not responding to enquiries because you are busy".[5]

Satisfying

Eight years of insolvency experience early in my career taught me not to believe anything at face value, but to think through it, and test it. Develop a healthy scepticism.

In the early years it was hard to make a living from providing philanthropic advice. This is changing as the sector grows.

Being a philanthropy adviser can be a frustrating role at times. However, the comments that I have had from many families on how they appreciate how I helped their family commence their structured giving journey are incredibly satisfying.

Be proud of what you do. You are helping build a stronger community. This is a critical role. There is a shortage of strong philanthropic advisers in Australia. Please add to the list.

---

5. Emma Beeston and Beth Breeze, op. cit., p. 45

Chapter 26

Tips for fundraisers

"Wealth creation comes partly from standing on the shoulders of the stable society around you." – **Daniel Petre**

Making miracles happen

Beth Breeze is a delightful English woman who is the Director of the Centre for Philanthropy at the University of Kent. Beth loves fundraisers! Whilst they can get short shrift from some, she strongly advocates for them. In her lecture, *The New Fundraisers: What kind of people raise money for good causes?,* she says, "Fundraising matters … fundraising is the activity that drives what charities can do."[1] In the UK alone, fundraisers (paid and volunteers) raise billions of pounds each year.

Beth has a great quote in the lecture from one of the individuals she interviewed for a previous book she has written, *The New Fundraisers.* "I love fundraising. The passion I feel about what I do is because I'm giving someone with money the opportunity to do the best thing they've done all year, or all decade – or ever!"[2]

And one more: "(Fundraisers) … make miracles happen – in the hospital, in the classroom, in the research laboratory, on the stage, and amid some of the most desperate conditions around the world."[3]

---

1. https://www.youtube.com/watch?v=Bs89hvK45HA

2. Ibid.

3. Ibid.

Fundraisers, or grantseekers, have a tough gig in Australia. With 60,000 charities in the country, including 32,000 deductible gift recipients (DGRs), they seek funding to drive the mission of their entities within a competitive field.[4] This is particularly so when Australian individual taxpayers on average give just 0.4% of their income to DGRs.[5] Something that has fascinated me with donors is that often their first question is, 'Are you a DGR?' (Which provides the donor a tax deduction.) So instead of first checking the mission of the entity, they check to see whether they will get a tax deduction! I know several people who have raised funding for non-DGRs. Now that is hard work!

In my experience sometimes Australians are good at finding reasons not to give. We need to find better ways to inspire people into action. A small sample of the reasons provided for not giving are included below, with my usual response:

- "It's not a DGR": no, but you can see the impact we are having

- "The admin costs are high": well, to achieve our mission perhaps administration costs should be higher. Investors don't look at the administration costs for a listed company. We are seeing a shift away from donors' emphasis on admin costs and towards impact

- "I think 10% of the funds going to that charity overseas are being misappropriated": well isn't that wonderful that 90% of your gift will help those children in need

- "I'm not convinced about the board and executive team": this looks like an opportunity for you to bring your extensive skills to the board and help them get back on track.

---

4. https://www.acnc.gov.au/for-public/understanding-charities/are-there-too-many-charities-australia

5. McGregor-Lowndes, Balczun & Williamson, op. cit., p. 99

Top tips

After many years working with donors and interacting with for-purpose entities I have some suggestions for fundraisers:

- In line with Beth Breeze's comments above, put your shoulders back and hold your head high. You are making miracles occur. So be proud of it

- Take your time to build trust and a relationship with donors. They usually do not like to be rushed. Get to know them, their decision drivers and seek to determine what their goals are. I know of stories where grantseekers have cultivated relationships over many years prior to the first gift arriving, and even longer prior to a large gift landing:

  - how do they operate and think?

  - what are their passions?

  - what type of giving do they prefer?

  - what size gifts have they given in the past?

  - why do they give? Personal experience, guilt, ego, status, business, spirituality, role modelling for peers/family, mental stimulation, to feel good about themselves or simply to create positive change?

  - who is the decision maker? It is dangerous to presume, and could ruin your relationship if you do, as you may be showing disrespect for all parties involved. I once saw a male for-purpose CEO pitch directly to the husband and ignore the wife. You can guess the outcome

  - how do they like to be communicated with? Calls, Zoom, email or meeting face-to-face? What level of frequency of communication do they like?

- do they like to be thanked, and if so how? Is a polite letter required or a marching band? I know one donor who loved having his photo in the monthly newsletter. I know another who so disliked photos that he was obsessed with always standing next to the photographer, so he would never be in photos! Either is fine, as long as you are aware of the preferred approach

- do they want to meet other like-minded donors to share ideas, or wish to operate from the shadows?

- do they like to hear new ideas from sector leaders at quarterly lunches?

- how much detail do they need within a pitch? Do they want the 20 page business plan or a 2 page summary?

When formulating your pitch, at a minimum I suggest you:

- articulate your vision

- state what success looks like

- explain your organisation's role in the system, as it is unlikely that you will be acting on your own

- share how will you measure impact. Not activity, but impact

- outline the milestones along the way, so that the donor can watch progress.

You need to articulate your vision and share brilliant stories. Go and make the miracles happen!

Chapter 27

Tips for wealth advisers

"All of us have an obligation to support the more needy people in our society. I think it adds to the glue that holds us together. I wouldn't want to be part of a society that was only interested in chasing dollars or shareholder value." – **Geoff Harris AM**

The state of play

Wealth advisers can play a unique role in significantly growing the philanthropic sector in Australia. Many of their clients have the capacity to give in some structured way, so advisers who have a knowledge of the sector are able to drive client satisfaction and assist sector growth. Wealth advisers, financial planners, lawyers and accountants can all influence their clients to think more about the use of their wealth, the impact it can have on families and the community, and the educational tool a family foundation can be for the next generation. And it is good for business too! Those not thinking through these issues, and how it impacts their business, are missing a major opportunity.

In my experience, generally wealth advisers have not shown strong interest in the philanthropic sector. A large percentage of wealth advisers are driven by financial incentive schemes to increase funds under management, with limited incentivisation to discuss giving with their clients.

Philanthropy teams within wealth advisory firms are common in the USA and the UK. Some wealth advisers in Australia are following suit, but many still don't provide such a service. As wealth continues to accumulate, I predict that by 2030 it will be unusual for a wealth adviser in Australia to not have at least one philanthropy team member. It will also be unusual for a wealth adviser to not have established their own corporate foundation. The next generation is looking for such actions.

A huge inter-generational wealth transfer has commenced in Australia. The Productivity Commission estimates that this wealth transfer over the next two decades could be as high as $3.5 trillion.[1] With this enormous inter-generational wealth transfer commencing, wealth advisers will need to manage the significant risk of losing clients due to their limited relationship with the next gen.

Reluctance to engage

From the advisers that I have spoken with over the years it appears that many are reluctant to raise giving with their clients primarily for two reasons:

1. They don't want to be seen to be 'preaching' to their clients, and possibly put their clients in an awkward position.

Sandy Clark, former director of The Myer Family Company, once said to me when I was a little reluctant to raise the issue of foundation establishment with a family friend, 'Peter, do you think the family would be interested in the information you have?' I thought that of course they would be. (And they were. A foundation was established, although I was hoping for a larger one!).

This is a similar situation with raising the possibility of establishing a structured giving program with a client. Once you are armed with information on the opportunities for the client and their family, it will likely open a very rich conversation. And that is the worst case scenario; a good conversation. The best case is the adviser assisting the client establish some form of structured giving strategy and working with the client's family, via managing the corpus, for many years.

---

1. Productivity Commission, *Wealth Transfers and their Economic Effects*, 7 December 2021, p. 62

2. They don't have a strong knowledge of giving and different giving structures, so they don't have the confidence to raise the issue.

Seek out experts on the sector to build your knowledge base. Philanthropy Australia has some guides that provide information on the sector and different types of giving structures.

Business opportunity

Wealth advisers should employ a philanthropic expert, part-time if need be, to assist develop conversations and strategies with clients. This is adding value to the client and enables the philanthropic expert to play a complimentary team role. It provides a point of difference, and shows that your business is not just focussed on making money, but is also concerned with the family's personal growth and community issues.

There are many benefits for wealth advisers to develop a philanthropic advisory business with their clients:

- philanthropy is a door-opener. With my 'philanthropic hat' on, I found I could get through most family office doors. In Australia, many people provide wealth management services, but few provide philanthropic services

- philanthropy provides a unique opportunity to open a different conversation and get to know your client better

- many philanthropic structures require an independent director. The family foundation will provide opportunities for you to become an independent director, attending board meetings and assisting with strategy implementation. This is a very satisfying way to build a long term relationship with clients

- if the wealth advisers are managing the capital in the family foundation, then they are meeting the next generation, the children, at each quarterly foundation board meeting. This provides an incredibly unique opportunity to build a strong relationship with the next generation of the family. You are sitting around a table with your client's children discussing some of the more important issues on the planet. It is a unique experience. Many advisers and commentators, including CNBC, are aware that a high percentage of heirs will remove the financial advisers for several reasons, including that the next gen has no relationship with the advisers[2]. Even if you have little interest in the pressing needs of our community, surely losing a big chunk of your business will get you interested!

- your business' foundation can collaborate with clients and co-fund projects and attend site visits together (you can also get staff and suppliers involved)

- your community engagement alongside your clients is great publicity for your business.

You will need to be genuine. It is obvious to clients when you are not, and it will reflect poorly on your reputation.

There are many in the wealth management sector who have created significant wealth in recent decades. There are some excellent examples of leaders in the sector playing a major role in giving, raising funds and providing pro bono services to for-purpose entities. However, there should be many more such role models. They are in a powerful position to influence their colleagues, their peers, their clients, their sector, their friends and the broader community.

Some advisers can only see the short term and won't see the long term business opportunity that philanthropy provides, let alone the community benefit. You may need to introduce staff incentive schemes with appropriate KPIs for advisers to encourage client giving.

In my experience the advisers who focus more on giving are those who volunteer in the community and sit on for-purpose boards. As I presented to wealth advisers, I could always pick those in the room who were interested in what I was saying. They were always engaged

---

2. CNBC, Financial Advisor 100, *What the coming $68 trillion Great Wealth Transfer means for financial advisors*, 21 October 2019

in the community in some way and were keen to learn how they could use philanthropy to get their clients to do the same, whilst building a closer relationship with them. They knew it was the right thing to do. They knew it was good for business. Through your business' foundation, opportunities can be provided to staff to get further engaged with their community via volunteer days. This might open their eyes to a new world.

Good for business. Good for the community.

Strong bonds with clients

I formed a strong bond with most of the families that I worked with. This bond continues years later. We shared some incredibly uplifting moments. I was invited into boardrooms, family dining tables and sometimes kitchen tables to discuss family values and giving strategies. Often these were intimate family conversations.

With one large family dad suggested that the only time everyone was home was at breakfast time. So some foundation meetings were held over breakfast. On one occasion I was trying to remember all the children's names as they sat at the very large kitchen table and reached for their favourite cereal. One of the sons entered the room with a girl following close behind. I was sure I had already said good morning to all the daughters. With a raised eyebrow I glanced at dad, whose sheepish smile confirmed that the eldest son had a new special friend. What to do with her name in the minutes?

Philanthropy provides a unique opportunity to open doors and build close client relationships. Get on the front foot. Hire the best available leader in the philanthropic landscape and build your expertise, before your competitors do. I see philanthropy as a major business opportunity for wealth advisers. Some will win, others will fall behind.

PART V: SECTOR REFORMS REQUIRED

Chapter 28

Constructive critique of the Australian philanthropic sector

"The highest use of capital is not to make more money, but to make money do more for the betterment of life." – **Henry Ford**

When I joined the Australian philanthropic sector in January 2003 it was very small. There were only a handful of foundations with a corpus in excess of $100 million and there were very few full-time staff. The sector has grown over the last two decades and is heading in the right direction, but unfortunately many philanthropic practices remain unchanged throughout the last 50 years. Nancy Roob, CEO of the Edna McConnell Clark Foundation in the USA, agrees:

> *"The fundamental structures and operating models of foundations haven't changed much over the last several decades. This is largely due to the combination of no outside force requiring them to change and few variations on the basic operating model to inspire innovation."*[1]

A project by the Melbourne Business School in 2017 seeking a better practice model for philanthropy found a major disconnect between

---

1. Alison Powell, Willa Seldon & Nidhi Sahni, *Reimagining Institutional Philanthropy*, Stanford Social Innovation Review, Spring 2019

perceptions of grantmakers and grantseekers around philanthropic practices in Australia, with donors having a far more favourable view of philanthropic practices than grantseekers.[2]

From my experience, greater focus on the following issues will create a stronger philanthropic sector, maximising the impact of capital allocations, resulting in materially better outcomes for the community.

Foundation Boards

- foundation board composition needs to change. They often only include one independent director who has little experience in dealing with issues the foundation is targeting. The sector has discussed board diversity, but there has been little action. Boards rarely include those with lived experience who are often better positioned to find solutions to issues

- I have seen many examples of ill-discipline by foundation boards. This includes very clever, self-made people who sometimes leave their smarts at the foundation board meeting door, and operate by 'gut feel and heart'

- discipline, strategy, implementation and impact measurement must be driven by committed boards if we wish to maximise community impact.

Strategy

- most foundations that I have seen have not had the discipline to minimise their focus areas, nor develop a measurable plan for change. Most large foundations in Australia are funding across numerous focus areas, with relatively fixed annual budgets across their program silos, sometimes trapped by history. With the focus spread too broadly, the impact is reduced. It would be preferable to focus on only one or two areas to maximise impact.

---

2. Liz Gillies, Dr Jodi York & Dr Joanna Mink, op. cit., p. iii

I applaud MacKenzie Scott's approach to giving, trusting those on the ground, but imagine the impact if she had tackled one focus area with her distribution of USD14 billion (to date)

- there are many reasons for the lack of focus and professionalism of the sector in Australia:

  - the sector remains fragmented and primarily voluntary in nature, which can result in it simply expressing the wishes of the founders

  - its independence: foundations have little accountability. There is no pressure to learn, collaborate and succeed

  - risk aversion: donors often want the instant satisfaction of knowing that they have made a difference. This can result in a short-term focus across multiple focus areas

  - ego: many in the sector wish to lead initiatives, yet few wish to follow, via collaborations with others

- in 2013 a report commissioned by Danish foundation, Realdania, drew on a 3-part philanthropy hierarchy devised by FSG (philanthropy advisers) and used the common metaphor of fishing with:

  - traditional philanthropy and grantmaking equivalent to giving a hungry man a fish

  - strategic philanthropy equivalent to teaching a man to fish

  - catalytic philanthropy equivalent to reforming the whole fishing industry and improving the lives of the poor as a result[3]

---

3. Monday Morning, *Catalytic Philanthropy, More Engagement – Greater Impact*, 2013, p. 6

- The conclusion was drawn that traditional philanthropy (i.e. grantmaking) won't achieve social change, that grantmaking is associated with scattergun giving, with small average grant sizes, with little interest in long term results. Such commentary oversimplifies the real world. However, in my experience we still see a lot of these practices in Australia. I know of one family foundation with a corpus of around $100 million. Each year they write around 100 cheques (yes, they write cheques!) of, on average, $40,000, across a huge range of focus areas. Some would say that is terrific. I call it the 'spray and pray', or scattergun, approach. I would argue a more strategic approach would create far greater impact.

- we need a radical change in how funders invest. The Edna McConnell Clark Foundation shifted to large multi-year funding, but realised they alone could not create change, so they became fundraisers too. They created Blue Meridian Partners to build USD1 billion from a group of donors. They make investments of up to USD200 million each in for-purpose entities. The idea is to think big and be a marketplace for such portfolios. Harlem Children's Ground supporter Stanley Druckenmiller said, "I like to put all my eggs in one basket, and watch that basket carefully!"[4] For-purpose CEOs usually can't dream big, as they expect the funding won't follow.

---

4. Nancy Roob, *A New Normal for Philanthropy*, TEDxPennsylvaniaAvenue, 9 February 2017

Risk

- many foundations are risk averse. Foundations are in a unique position to take risks that governments and institutions sometimes cannot due to their stakeholders. This is the 'superpower' of philanthropy!

- this superpower should be better used to target issues in our community. If you are not failing, you are not taking enough risks.

Measuring impact

- few foundations measure the impact of their partners well. Some don't bother to measure impact, comforted by working with 'good people' who are mission-aligned

- there is often a reluctance for foundations to pay for an appropriate form of partner evaluation. This needs to change. Evaluation should be used as a strategic tool to drive behaviour

- few foundations evaluate their own performance, so wouldn't know if they are maximising impact

- the sector needs Philanthropy Australia and the large foundations to lead the way here, provide examples of impact measurement best practice (for large and small foundations) and disseminate the learnings.

Staff

- the sector is too insular. People grab hold of a grantmaker role and don't let go. It is deemed easier to be a grantmaker than a grantseeker. You have control, you make the decisions, you are less accountable, and you have a strong balance sheet. Not long ago one of the better known foundations had three program managers, and they had each been in their role for nearly a decade. Fresh thinking and ideas are needed

- the Hewlett Foundation sets tenure limits for program staff: a maximum of eight years. This ensures new perspectives are brought into the foundation, helps staff contemplate their legacy and ensures former staff share their learnings at other organisations

- too many foundation CEOs, particularly large foundations, are in their role for too long and are too comfortable. The level of urgency can wane

- in recent years in the sector there has been a merry-go-round of foundation CEOs swapping jobs. At my last CEO role, we recruited from outside the philanthropic sector for all roles, to bring in smart curious young minds with an investment mindset and fresh ideas

- the philanthropic sector needs more staff with lived experience and those from the other side of the fence i.e. they have worked within for-purpose entities, and understand issues at the grass roots level, so are better positioned to think through solutions

- you don't have to build a huge team and create an institution. I had a client who copied the Sandler Foundation (USA) model: fewer but larger grants enabling a leaner, non-bureaucratic and more agile team. The Colonial Foundation is a rare similar example in Australia

- I am aware of examples of family members being remunerated for working for the family foundation. If the salary is no higher than the market rate this is usually technically acceptable. However, I believe family members should not be able to be remunerated by the family foundation, whether it be for work as a foundation executive or director. For governance purposes, foundation staff should not be associates of the founders, as they may feel beholden to them. I also believe family members should forge their own careers, whilst being on the foundation board and contributing in that way.

Power imbalance

- we know there is a power imbalance when one party has a pot of gold, and another party is trying to access it. However, we must manage it better. Examples of arrogance in the philanthropic sector are common e.g. telling partners how to run their business including how to spend their funding, seeking plaudits, slow to return phone calls, taking months to make decisions

- foundation Chairs and CEOs must lead by example in order to create change and lift humility levels in the sector and build true partnerships

- more frank feedback from funding partners needs to be sought, including biennial anonymous surveys of partners and their interactions with the foundation.

Type of funding

- most philanthropic grants in Australia are still to fund projects for 1-3 years. Many of the oldest and better known foundations, decades later, are still operating in this manner. This is basically telling your partners, the experts in their field, how to spend their money and that they need to solve problems in 1-3 years

- the Ian Potter Foundation (IPF) is a good example of a foundation moving away from short term project funding to a high percentage of unrestricted grants. IPF's average grant duration increased from 13 months in 2015 to more than 36 months in 2022. And in 2022 more than 50% of grants awarded (by value) were for core funding support. Still a long way to go, but a strong move in the right direction. [5]

- many funders will still only fund a partner for 1-3 years. The CEOs of most for-purpose entities are running grossly under-capitalised entities. As a result they spend a significant amount of their time fundraising, taking them away from what they should be doing, which is tackling the mission of the entity. Many of these entities only have working capital for the next 3-6 months. Imagine running a foundation in that predicament

- in his thesis on charity/funder relationships, Tom Keenan argues that this short term funding, "... is creating and perpetuating ineffectiveness and inefficiency across the Australian charity sector and is largely ineffective when looking to address chronic disadvantage"[6] Tom states that the benefit of many small grants is neutral given the cost of winning the grant, resulting in billions of dollars being squandered each year.[7] Tom is scathing about this funding approach, and is particularly concerned about the "... absence of leadership to restore balance and morality to the funder/fundee relationship."[8]

- if you are mission-aligned and like their measurable plan, back your partners with unrestricted multi-year funding. This will provide them some budget certainty and allow them to get on with the job. I rarely see this

- the Colonial Foundation's funding of Orygen Youth Health Research Centre is a terrific yet rare example in Australia of significant funding for over 20 years, allowing Patrick McGorry to build Orygen and amplify the parlous state of youth mental

5. Ian Potter Foundation, *The Seahorse*, Issue 45, December 2022

6. Thomas W Keenan, op. cit., 2021, p.161

7. Ibid., p. 210

8. Ibid., p. 161

health in Australia

- some funders will only fund pilot programs. That's terrific, but even if there is some success from the pilot, they cease funding, to move on to the next 'shiny' project. Often the pilot sits on a shelf. At the very least in such situations, funders need to find other funders to assist scale the project. Preferably they would continue funding given the momentum gained

- I see and hear of regular examples of inappropriate grant funding exits. If a funder is to exit a partnership it needs to be done with an appropriate exit strategy i.e. over an appropriate timeframe with stepped grant funding. This provides appropriate notice to the partner and enables them to adjust their budget and have the time to replace the donor

- I'm aware of a recent example where a leading foundation had been funding a partner for many years. The funding had crept up to nearly 40% of the partner's budget. Obviously, there was risk associated with that, but there was a long-standing relationship and there had been successes in the community from the relationship. The partner was suddenly advised, with no notice, that the funding would cease at the expiry of the latest grant agreement in a matter of months. This was quite extraordinary and incredibly disrespectful. The CEO of the partner, only due to the close relationship with a foundation board member, managed to buy some time to rectify the budget via some extra funding from the foundation.

Accolades

- we need to celebrate giving, but the focus can often be on the accolades made when the gift is made, as opposed to when the issue is assisted or solved. We need to flip this

- I have no issue if donors seek naming rights. I do find it odd when naming rights become a major discussion and are offered for quite modest gifts.

Lack of limited life foundations

- there is a surprising lack of limited life foundations in Australia. A dollar spent today is worth more than a dollar spent tomorrow. Let's solve today's problems and the next generation can create wealth to work on tomorrow's problems, some of which we don't yet know about

- I have seen evidence of program staff at some foundations in cruise mode as they distributed their budgeted allocation each year. They were funding some nice programs, but there was no sense of urgency that we 'must get this right', as they knew there would be another similar allocation the following year

- the 4th generation never knows the first generation (the wealth creator) and in my experience the passion for the foundation can diminish after the 3rd generation

- I think the lack of limited life foundations in Australia is primarily due to the lack of consideration given to them. Again, we don't have role models to show us the way. We need a debate to consider changing the Private Ancillary Fund rules so that their lifespan is limited to a maximum of, say, 50 years. This will allow the benefits of three generations working together, with partners, to tackle community issues, but not allowing foundations to become institutional and bureaucratic over 100+ years.

Growing spotlight on the sector

As the Australian philanthropic sector grows there will be an increasing spotlight on:

- the lack of transparency in the sector

- the effectiveness of the sector given the tax concessions offered

- whether it is undermining democratic values

- how the wealth was created

- who is making the decisions on significant capital distributions and on what basis

- do the decision makers have the lived experience to suggest solutions

- what percentage of the wealth is being given away

- are the investment practices ethical?

"Ultimately, it's still the case that our sector prizes donor freedom over social justice as the apotheosis of philanthropy."[9]

I recognise that these issues are not clear cut. Is Elon Musk's drive to get to Mars of tremendous benefit to humanity, or a self-indulgent waste of money given the pressing humanitarian needs on planet earth? Time will tell. As the sector in Australia grows, it needs to be ready for greater scrutiny. Indulgent behaviour will be called out.

There is much to improve on. In particular:

- when will foundations in Australia bring discipline to the table and focus on just 1-2 issues?

- to maximise impact is it possible to get donors to think a little less about their preferences and more about humanity's pressing needs?

- when will the vast majority of grants be multi-year unrestricted

---

9. Charles Keidan, Executive Editor, *Alliance Magazine*, March 2023, p.3

grants, so the experts (the grant recipients) can get on with the job?

- when will more donors be comfortable funding systems change work, where the impact is not immediate?

- where are *The Audacious Project* type opportunities in Australia, seeking social entrepreneurs to think bigger, with $200 million ideas for like-minded donors to collaborate?

- when will we establish a large fully funded venture capital type intermediary for the for-purpose sector, where social entrepreneurs can seek ready access to capital, skills and networks to develop their model?

- who will establish Australia and the South Pacific's 'Skoll World Forum' equivalent, for donors and social entrepreneurs to collaborate and work on issues in our region?

- when will more foundations move away from targeting issues by drip feeding funding, to a limited life model where capital is disbursed towards solutions in a more timely manner?

- how will we get more families to think about giving considerably more offshore, to low-middle income countries, where many issues such as poor health and education are more prevalent and dire than in Australia?[10]

- will we move more resources to smaller organisations close to the issues we are trying to address, and listen and act on their advice?

- when will a significant number of influential families in each State across Australia step up and talk publicly about their giving, to be role models for others?

---

10. https://aidnetwork.org.au/

- in a country with Australia's extraordinary wealth, when will you need to give over $25 million p.a. to make the *AFR The Philanthropy 50* list? (You can currently make the list by giving $5 million).

There are many exciting opportunities here. We will need role models to show us the way. The existing well known, large foundations have a great opportunity to lead the way.

A few times over the years I have been advised that to increase giving levels in Australia we need to solve the 'giving challenge'. If people can see that they are creating change, then it will be easier for them to give significantly more. A venture capital type intermediary in Australia could lead to the unlocking of mega-gifts.

The supply of capital is there; this is a demand issue. How many for-purpose organisations in Australia really have the ability to accept gifts of $50 million, and match it with a tight, measurable plan to create change? This is partly linked to what American entrepreneur Dan Pallotta talks about—the market doesn't allow for-purpose entities to pay attractive salaries to attract staff to tackle some of our biggest issues. (Refer to chapter 34.) This must change.

Imagine

Imagine if we could empower the right social entrepreneurs with the resources (capital, skills, expertise, networks) to develop plans to take a systems approach to tackling the biggest issues in Australia. There is no reason that we can't action this.

Philanthropic foundations are in a unique position to drive this change. If we don't, we will continue to fail to address in a meaningful way the major issues facing our community. If we, as the leading lights within the philanthropic sector, fail to address these issues, we will have failed on 'our watch', as the sector will continue to make the same mistakes repeatedly.

Chapter 29

Transparency in the Australian philanthropic sector

"A lack of transparency results in distrust and a deep sense of insecurity".
– **Dalai Lama**

Transparency is important

Transparency generally builds trust and an ability to solve problems quicker. Transparency is important in the philanthropic sector for a range of reasons:

- openness improves performance

- increased data will allow learnings to be shared, provide better collaborative opportunities and less duplication within the sector, thereby maximising community impact

- foundations receive tax concessions, resulting in losses to Treasury, so there should be greater accountability of their activities

- foundation assets are not 'family funds', they are held in trust for charitable purposes, so at the least the charitable sector should be able to review annual accounts

- transparency will result in greater trust in the sector, which will enhance the sector's social licence to operate and keep at bay those who argue that philanthropy is harmful to society.

Krystian Seibert, former Philanthropy Australia Policy and Practice Specialist, summarises as follows:

"If we can pinpoint the contribution of philanthropy within specific communities, that is a powerful way of demonstrating its impact. It's powerful not only in terms of highlighting the role of philanthropy to the broader public, but also a useful tool when talking to elected representatives about the importance of a supportive policy environment for philanthropy."[1]

Current transparency levels are poor

Transparency levels in the Australian philanthropic sector are currently poor. If a situation arose in Australia where significant philanthropic funding was applied to seek government influence with no transparency and for spurious reasons, similar to that uncovered in Jane Mayer's, *Dark Money* (refer to chapter 17), it would be very detrimental to the growth of and support for the sector.

There has been little recent debate on the sector's transparency levels. It's the elephant in the room. For-purpose entities are very keen for increased transparency levels, but are reluctant to bite the hand that feeds them. They seek grant funding from foundations so they don't wish to raise an issue that might annoy their potential funders.

The main reason that we need greater transparency in the sector is to improve performance. Social Ventures Australia's, *Key trends and best practice in philanthropy,* a 2015 initiative with the AMP Foundation, highlighted:

---

1. Krystian Seibert, *Foundation transparency – how far should we go?* Alliance Magazine, 20 November 2018

"The research undertaken for this report highlighted the lack of comprehensive and consistent information available about the structure, activities and impact of many philanthropic entities, particularly in Australia. Until greater transparency and openness is achieved among Australian philanthropic entities, we will not have a deep understanding of what works and how together, we can have the most impact."[2]

Little in the sector has changed since then. The sector can do so much better.

The American philanthropic sector is considerably older and more advanced than the Australian sector. However, in the USA they had this debate around transparency levels in their sector over five decades ago. In the 1960s in the USA it was determined that the philanthropic sector required full transparency, and family foundations must annually lodge detailed financial information on the foundation's activities on a public portal.

The introduction of the Australian Charities and Not-for-profits Commission (ACNC) in 2012 has assisted transparency levels as most charitable entities now need to lodge a set of audited annual accounts with the ACNC, which can be viewed via the public portal on the ACNC website.

Philanthropy Australia (PA) has been trying to address the lack of sector transparency with *Foundation Maps: Australia* (FMA)[3]. Launched in 2018, FMA is an interactive and searchable funding map to help visualise who is funding what and where across Australia. The theory is that this will assist find who funds in a particular focus area and target group, and which for-purpose entities operate in a particular interest area/target group.

---

2. Social Ventures Australia, *Key trends and best practice in philanthropy*, 2015

3. https://www.philanthropy.org.au/about-us/publications/foundation-maps-australia/

Of course the success of FMA is totally dependent upon PA members taking action and voluntarily participating and lodging their grantmaking data *each* year.

FMA is only accessible to PA members. So if you are not a member, you cannot access the database. In practice I don't hear FMA being referred to or discussed widely within the sector, nor being promoted regularly by PA.

At the time of writing FMA only included data from 58 funders Australia-wide. Given it's not accessible to the public and includes only a small percentage of grantmakers in the country, it has limited value.

Private Ancillary Funds

Private Ancillary Funds (PAFs) are the only form of charitable entity in Australia that can seek to have their details withheld from the ACNC's public register[4] i.e. no transparency at all. (Some for-purpose entities can have information such as addresses withheld for safety reasons.) In the 2000s I was a key advocate for PAFs to retain their privacy for pragmatic reasons. I was arguing that we had around 800 PAFs (at the time) but given the wealth in Australia we should have 8,000. Clients at the time were telling me that privacy was paramount to them if they were to set up a PAF. Whilst I understood at the time that transparency levels in the philanthropic sector in Australia were not strong enough, I took the pragmatic view that removing PAF privacy would be detrimental to the growth of the philanthropic sector in Australia.

My thinking was, let's build the philanthropic sector, let's create the 8,000 PAFs, and then get the smart heads around the table to determine the appropriate levels of transparency in the philanthropic sector. Well, years later, with substantial further wealth created, and over 20 years since the implementation of PAFs, we still only have around 2,060 PAFs in the country. So it's not lack of privacy holding families back from establishing a PAF![5]

---

4. https://www.acnc.gov.au/charity/charities

5. Philanthropy Australia, *Insights from Australian Philanthropy's Response to the Covid-19 Crisis*, 27/2/23, p. 15

Most financial advisers are aware of the ability for PAFs to withhold their information, so that when PAF annual accounts are lodged with the ACNC, advisers tick the 'withhold information' box, so that whilst the ACNC staff can review the accounts, the public have no access at all to that PAF file. In fact, when you type the foundation name in the 'search' box the result is, "No charities found matching your criteria"! Totally invisible. You can't confirm the foundation's name or structure, let alone its size and the nature of its activities.

I had a client who for various reasons (primarily greater giving flexibility) established a private charitable trust. With such a structure you cannot have the information withheld from the ACNC's public portal. Why can that family not retain privacy simply due to the type of charitable trust structure that was established? There is no logic or equity to this.

After several years of reflection, I have now changed my mind; PAFs should be transparent, and at a minimum the following should be accessible on the ACNC public portal for each PAF:

- the entity name and directors' names

- the mission and focus areas

- whether it accepts unsolicited grant applications

- the annual accounts and audit report

- a list of grant recipients and amount granted for the previous year

- a contact email address.

The reasons are:

- funds held within PAFs are for charitable purposes, so we need to shine a light on their work

- eligible charities should be able to access the $7.6 billion that has been accumulated within PAFs[6]

- openness will improve collaborative opportunities and performance

- it will encourage PAF founders to improve mission clarity

- some of the larger PAFs will inspire other families to increase the size of their PAF

- I suspect that, once the public views the corpus size of a number of small foundations held by wealthy high-profile families, the size of some of these small PAFs would grow due to community expectations.

One philanthropic practitioner commented to me, "You can't be what you can't see". Her view was that removing PAF privacy would inspire other families to establish a PAF.

Some will argue that some PAF founders will close their fund if there is no longer privacy for PAFs. I suspect that this would be a small number. Perhaps this would be a good result for the community, as significant sums of money would leave PAFs and flow into the community.

As discussed in chapter 31, there is very little transparency on the activities of the 2000+ charitable trusts managed by Licensed Trustee Companies (LTCs). This needs to be addressed. Once we have full transparency of PAFs and LTC managed charitable trusts we will have a much clearer view of structured giving in Australia. This will inform better decision-making and result in stronger community outcomes.

As discussed above, the transparency debate was held in the USA

---

6. McGregor-Lowndes, Balczun & Williamson, op. cit., p. 26

decades ago. It is time we had the discussion here. It is a very popular topic with for-purpose CEOs who have no access to billions of dollars set aside for the community!

As the size of the Australian philanthropic sector grows, and if the sector does not take steps to improve transparency levels, the community will demand it. This will result in government stepping in to address the issue, to ensure there is appropriate accountability for the growing tax concessions available. We have a choice: do we as a sector act or do we await government regulation? Let's act; transparency will be a positive for the sector and will bring better community outcomes.

Chapter 30

The peak body – Philanthropy Australia

"And when we make charitable gifts, we almost always feel richer, not poorer, for having been given the opportunity to help." – **Beth and Seth Klarman**

Philanthropy Australia must lead the way

It is very important that Philanthropy Australia (PA) remains strong, with a clear vision, strong governance and is well funded by its members. As the philanthropy sector peak body it has the ability to lead the sector and shape what 'more and better' giving looks like.

Over the last 20 years I have worked with and supported six PA CEOs (Liz Cham, Gina Anderson, Deborah Seifert AM, Louise Walsh, Sarah Davies AM, Jack Heath) by providing regular assistance and advice. I have seen first-hand their passion and work ethic.

I have further tried to assist PA as a board member for three years, as a member of the Finance Committee for three years, and as a member of the Policy and Research Committee for six years. At the time of writing I have no formal PA role. I remain a PA member.

I have suggested to every grantmaker I have met over the last two decades that they sign up as a member of PA to support the peak body, help strengthen the sector and learn from and share with like-minded donors. I continue to do this.

So to be clear, I am a supporter of PA.

It's tough being a membership body, being pulled in different directions by the different needs of hundreds of members. Each member is different in purpose, passion, size, structure, focus and needs from PA. Like all membership bodies, PA does some things well, and needs to improve in other areas.

What PA does well

PA does a number of things well:

- In recent years PA has improved its advocacy for the sector by representing the for-purpose sector and the philanthropic sectors, lodging multiple submissions to government on behalf of the sector and encouraging members to do likewise. This has resulted in a number of important wins for the sector including:

  - strengthening the ability of for-purpose entities to be able to advocate to achieve their charitable purpose

  - improving the ability of community foundations to give to and support local charitable activities

  - advocating for community foundations to receive funds from Private Ancillary Funds (PAFs) (likely to be approved soon)

  - more flexible distribution guidelines for ancillary funds

  - assisting with the retention of franking credit refunds for income tax exempt charities

  - strong PAF and Public Ancillary Fund guidelines

- organising events for grantmaking staff to meet and share ideas

- developing guides to giving

- commencing building on-line tools to assist newcomers determine the best approach for their engagement

- running Chapter Groups, such as Australian International Development Network and Mannifera. PA provides some infrastructure which allows an early iteration for the passionate leaders of these groups to rally their supporters, build their networks, flourish and achieve their mission

- commencing sharing inspirational stories of giving to encourage others to do more.

Where PA needs to improve

PA has many areas in which it needs to improve:

- PA's mission of seeking 'more and better philanthropy' is spot on. This is exactly what the country needs. However, from my experience PA doesn't spend enough time on these issues. If the staff monitored how much time they actually spent on advancing 'more and better philanthropy' each week, I suspect the percentage would not be high enough. PA's mission of 'more and better philanthropy' needs to be expressed in the daily, weekly and monthly tasks of all staff

- organising and curating events that entice more directors and trustees to attend. These are the decision makers who need to be encouraged to focus on best practice grantmaking

- best practice grantmaking education. Along with growing the size of the sector, this should be PA's number one priority. Although improving, there is not enough focus on this, evidenced by the regular poor practices in the sector

- PA needs to be careful not to spend too much time promoting its views on particular community issues. That is the role of its members, who will have different views on various contentious issues. PA's "important principles" within its giving blueprint states that it will be "cause-neutral", and that, "… preference should not be given to one area over another in terms of where funding flows ..."[1]. There are several recent cases where PA has not adhered to this principle. 'Stick to your knitting' of 'more and better' giving

- as a membership body, whose members and potential members hold a variety of political allegiances, it needs to remain apolitical. It needs to work with all sides of politics. Numerous members and former members have commented to me on indicators that suggests the body has shifted considerably to the left in recent years

- PA needs to ensure that it represents and delivers for its membership base across the breadth of Australia. Over the years, families in Western Australia, Queensland, South Australia and Tasmania have commented that a lot of the content and leadership is driven out of Victoria and NSW. In order to change the giving culture across the country PA needs to invest more in the capacity of every State office

- PA appears to be building a heavy reliance on government to grow our giving culture. (Confirmed via its 2023 submission to the Productivity Commission's inquiry on Philanthropy.)[2] Government can assist in a minor way, but it is the peak body's role to lead a change in our giving culture, with its members and the broader community (refer to chapter 32)

- it holds too many general events. Staff spend a large amount of time organising events, and not all target more and better giving

- staff retention is poor. Over the last five years there has been a large turnover of staff, senior and junior. I'm not privy to all the reasons, but I do know that this is partly due to the general 'busyness' of staff who sometimes aren't convinced that their

---

1. Philanthropy Australia, *A Blueprint to Grow Structured Giving*, April 2021, p.3

2. https://www.pc.gov.au/inquiries/current/philanthropy/submissions

daily tasks target the mission

- it doesn't seek the frank views (via anonymous survey) of its members regularly enough.

What PA should focus on

PA should focus more on its mission of 'more and better philanthropy'. It could do this by:

- dropping 'philanthropy' from its name. Many people, particularly the next gen, do not resonate with the word 'philanthropy', which for some conjures up an image of an old white man writing cheques. Drop the word. PA should call itself something like 'Giving Australia'

- changing the board composition. It needs to include self-made entrepreneurs, who will better understand members and potential members, have experience growing a business, will take more risks and be better placed to drive the mission. At the time of writing the board is stacked with foundation CEOs

- dropping grantseekers as members. PA membership currently includes grantmakers and grantseekers. PA was incorporated in 1987, "as a peak body for philanthropists".[3] It should go back to its roots. Membership should be restricted to grantmakers only. Having grantseekers as members is mission creep, is a distraction to staff, is confusing for grantmakers and keeps directors and trustees away from important PA meetings for fear of being targeted by grantseekers. Grantmakers collaborate with grantseekers regularly; that is their job

- to achieve its mission of more and better giving PA needs to better focus on the giving side. As a senior sector CEO recently

---

3. Philanthropy Australia, *Constitution*, p.3

said to me, "PA needs to be able to speak with one voice, and that is the voice of grantmakers." The PA executive may argue that this would significantly reduce revenue from member fees (the membership list suggests a high percentage of members are grantseekers). However, if 'more and better' giving is done in an outstanding way, grantmaker member numbers will grow significantly

- once PA's membership reverts to just grantmakers, it can still bring together grantmakers and grantseekers in a trusted space at appropriate times, but in a more targeted way to consider specific issues

- being bolder in its efforts to grow giving levels in Australia: PA's target of increasing structured giving from $2.5 billion p.a. to $5 billion p.a. over the 10 year period could be achieved with just 7% growth p.a.[4] This target will probably be achieved organically. This target is lacking in ambition given the staggering wealth created in this country in recent decades. This target should be achieved by just a handful of families! PA's targets include capturing, "… a minimum one per cent share of the intergenerational wealth transfer for philanthropic purposes".[5] I'm not sure why this target is so low? If we want significant change in our community, we need to be bold

- having a much greater focus on the low giving levels in Australia by high-net-worth individuals (HNWIs). The lack of giving by HNWIs is a cultural issue, not a structural issue. PA tends to focus on structural changes required to grow the sector

- introducing Australia's Giving Pledge (see chapter 33)

- revamping the Philanthropy Australia Giving Awards. Work is needed on the type of awards, the rules, the judging and the

---

4. Philanthropy Australia, *A Blueprint to Grow Structured Giving*, April 2021

5. Ibid., p. 20

publicity, in order that it becomes sought after to win such an award, to inspire others to do more e.g. the top award, 'Leading Philanthropist', was recently given to a high-profile individual who appears to only give a small percentage of their wealth. Many considered this to be inappropriate for such an important award

- seeking new ideas to grow giving. I could see no new ideas in PA's 2021, *Blueprint to Grow Structured Giving*. It primarily consists of tasks that have been tried in the past. With significant recent funding commitments received from a group of PA 'Philanthropy Champions', perhaps these old ideas can be better implemented. However, they had not been implemented two and a half years after the release of the Blueprint

- analysing all staff tasks. If a task doesn't result in 'more and better' giving, then it should be ceased

- greater focus on growing the membership base. PA's 2020 Annual report indicates that total member numbers have dropped from 795 in 2016 to 764 in 2020.[6] (Later figures do not appear to be publicly available.) These member numbers include grantseekers. From the members' list, a high percentage of PA members are grantseekers. Grantmaking members probably comprises only 350-400 members. Given the 58,000 HNWIs in Australia, this is a small membership base, with significant upside to grow.[7] Exit surveys need to be held with every member to determine why they leave. The membership offering, and value proposition, should be so exciting that new members are knocking the door down to join

- addressing the harmful poor transparency levels in the sector (see previous chapter). PAFs should lose their privacy status and

---

6. Philanthropy Australia, *Annual Report*, 2020, p. 18

7. Credit Suisse, *Global Wealth Databook*, 2022, p. 130

PA either needs to get *Foundation Maps: Australia* firing or stop pretending that it is addressing transparency, and drop it

- addressing the issue with the Licensed Trustee Companies (LTCs) in Australia. (See next chapter.) Given generous sponsorships of various PA events each year by LTCs, PA may be facing a conflict of interest. Addressing the issue will definitely result in 'more and better' giving

- continuing to seek from government changes to the PAF rules in order that PAFs can give to community foundations, so that community foundations can play a larger role in place-based giving in times of need

- preparing a more contemporary version of the 2013 publication, *Australia's Top 50 Philanthropic Gifts*. For example this could be, *Australia's Top 50 Gifts in the 10 Years to 2023*. Great stories will inspire others into action.

Philanthropy Centre of Excellence

As a priority PA needs to establish a *Philanthropy Centre of Excellence*. Such a Centre would address many of the issues that I raised in my critique of the sector in chapter 28. If the right plan is developed for such a Centre, funding for the Centre would not be difficult to find.

The Centre could take the lead in:

- teaching and sharing best practice philanthropy principles and ideas, how philanthropy can be harmful, emerging trends and an understanding of the dynamics involved in creating social change

- coordinating true collaboration (not just co-funding) between the community sector, philanthropy and government so that we are not simply targeting problems via a range of uncoordinated and fragmented grants

- disseminating learnings, including successes and failures

- ensuring leverage is used via advocacy and encouragement of other donors

- determining appropriate measurement tools and providing case studies for small and large foundations

- building philanthropic infrastructure, which will provide valuable sector knowledge retention. Currently when senior people leave the sector, most of their knowledge leaves with them

- researching best practice philanthropic initiatives world-wide

- showcasing best practice philanthropy models and stories, not just to be more effective, but to inspire others to act

- training the growing cohort of philanthropic advisers that will be needed as the sector grows.

The difference between poor grantmaking, good grantmaking and inspired grantmaking can be taught, but rarely is. The Centre can address this.

The above actions will mitigate somewhat the 'giving challenge' we discussed in chapter 28 in the community sector. Several times over the years I have had debates with HNWIs who have said they would like to contribute more to solving community issues, but struggle to see how they could 'turn the dial' on an issue. If we take action on the above, capital will flow towards problems. The trick will then be to use it effectively.

If we were building a new philanthropy peak body tomorrow, it would look different to the one that exists today. This provides an exciting opportunity for the sector as we move towards more and better giving.

Chapter 31

Licensed Trustee Companies

"There was a marked imbalance of power and knowledge between those providing the product or service and those acquiring it." – **Kenneth Hayne AC, Commissioner, Royal Commission into Misconduct in the Banking, Superannuation and Financial Services Industry**

(The above quote was not referring to Licensed Trustee Companies, and The Royal Commission's Terms of Reference did not include Licensed Trustee Companies, but it might well have been.)

Background to Licensed Trustee Companies

Charitable trusts play a very important role in tackling community issues across Australia. This role will grow as our inter-generational wealth transfer continues.

One of the 'worst kept secrets' in the philanthropic sector is the conflicts of interest, lack of portability, lack of transparency and high fees charged to some charitable trusts by some Australian Stock Exchange (ASX) listed Licensed Trustee Companies (LTCs) in Australia. Many are aware of the issues here but look the other way as the two major LTCs, Perpetual (PPT) and Equity Trustees (EQT) disperse significant funds each year to charities, so are in a powerful position. Better to not bite the hand that feeds.

LTCs have a long history in Australia. Trustees Executors and Agency Co Ltd was the first trustee company established in Australia. It commenced operations in 1879 in Melbourne. Its primary role was to act as "…

executor, administrator and trustee and assisting with wills and estate planning".[1]

This is 'blue-blood territory'. EQT's former directors include former Prime Ministers (Sir Robert Menzies, Stanley Bruce) and a Governor-General (Sir Ninian Stephen).

Trustee companies were once 'trusted guardians', with a community focus, whereas today they are another arm of ASX listed, profit driven financial services companies. This raises issues which need to be carefully reviewed. "Directors of LTCs have a direct conflict between their fiduciary duties to shareholders as a Director and to the community as 'trusted guardian' of Charitable Trusts."[2]

EQT CEO, Mick O'Brien, said in 2021, "We are doing what regulators want and it's important we are close to them and understand them."[3]

LTCs are very different beasts today. Until the mid 2010s there were still around 30 LTCs operating in Australia. After a series of mergers and acquisitions over recent years most of these are now owned by PPT and EQT.

This is big business. These are large ASX listed companies, providing several financial services in addition to charitable trustee services:[4]

	PPT	EQT
Market capitalisation	$2.3 billion*	$0.7 billion*
Revenue (FY22)	$750 million	$112 million
Net profit (FY22)	$150 million	$24 million
Charitable trusts managed	>1,000	>650

*October 2023

---

1. Trevor Sykes, *The Bold Riders*, Allen & Unwin, 1994, p. 33

2. Charitable Alliance, *Submission to CAMAC Review of Charitable Trusts and Foundations*, December 2012, p. 4

3. Tim Boreham, *One of Australia's oldest listed companies follows a super new path*, Livewire, 26 May 2021

4. PPT and EQT, *Annual Reports*, 2022

There is limited data available on charitable trusts managed by LTCs. However, it is estimated that the charitable trusts they manage have an aggregate corpus in excess of $6 billion. This includes some of Australia's most iconic charitable trusts:

- The Felton Bequest

- Miles Franklin Literary Award

- The William Buckland Foundation

- The Wicking Trust

- Viertel Foundation

- Percy Baxter Charitable Trust

- Dafydd Lewis Scholarship.

EQT lists the names of the charitable trusts that it manages but provides no information on them. We don't know their size, their mission, where they provide their grant funding or the annual grant amount. Its website states that funds under management of charitable trusts is $2.4 billion.[5]

In FY22, total giving from EQT charitable trusts amounted to over $92.2 million. Over the last five years EQT has overseen nearly half a billion dollars of giving to the charitable and for-purpose sector.[6] It's interesting to note that in 2022 only 1.9% of grants were to the environment/climate change. In addition, despite stating that, "… SDGs provide a framework for us to create a better society …", only 2% of grants were for international programs.[7]

PPT's website states that it manages over 1,000 charitable trusts, which hold $3.6 billion in funds (as at 30 June 2022), and which distribute

---

5. https://www.eqt.com.au/philanthropy

6. EQT, *Annual Giving Review 2022*

7. Ibid.

$120 million p.a. But it does not provide any more detail on them. Nothing! For some of these charitable trusts, for-purpose entities can apply for funding, but in January 2023 applications for 2023 were already closed![8]

There is no transparency here even though they are charitable trusts holding over $6 billion established for the benefit of the community.

Illustrative case study

The community is losing out on significant funding each year, lost to high LTC fees. I think a case study could assist here, so I will use a fictitious example.

Aunty Dot never married, invested well, received a small inheritance, lived frugally and had an estate worth $10 million. She planned to leave it all to the Lost Dogs Home via a charitable trust. A LTC got wind of this and convinced her that they had the skills to ensure her wishes would be fulfilled and to do this the LTC should be the sole trustee of the charitable trust. Dot passed away and the Dot Charitable Trust for Dogs (DCTFD) was established via her Will.

The LTC established the trust, invested the $10 million into one of its LTC pooled investment funds and, in accordance with Aunty Dot's wishes, organised for two distributions p.a. to the Lost Dogs Home. Let's assume there is an annual grossed-up yield of 5% from the pooled fund. The LTC charges an investment management fee of 1% p.a. for the funds in its pooled fund. The LTC also charges an administration fee of 1% p.a., for what they call the 'pain and suffering' of being a trustee.

This is actually a quote I have heard from LTCs a number of times! When I was assisting our clients at The Myer Family Office (MFO) with developing and implementing their philanthropic vision, I did not feel 'pain and suffering'. In fact our team felt uplifted on a daily basis by the privilege of working with these families as they sought to tackle major issues in our community.

---

8. https://www.perpetual.com.au/wealth-management/not-for-profits/impact-funding/

The economics of Dot's wishes would be as follows:

- DCTFD corpus of $10 million

- annual income yield of $500,000

- annual investment management fee to LTC of $100,000

- annual trustee administration fee to LTC of $100,000

- net income annual distribution to the Lost Dogs Home: $300,000.

So you can see that 40% ($200,000) of the income is going to the LTC and only 60% ($300,000) assists the dogs. No laws are being broken here. LTCs are allowed to invest funds in their pre-existing investment funds and charge investment management fees. Under the Trustee Companies Act they can also charge an annual management fee of up to 1.056% (which would be higher than the example above). Aunty Dot would be staggered by such high fees for such a simple transaction with only one (or a few) specific beneficiaries.

EQT CEO, Mick O'Brien, has a different understanding to me of the for-purpose sector and the extent of the needs in our community. In 2021 he said in reference to the charitable sector, "The sector will chew up every dollar you give them, whereas if you set up a properly structured vehicle it will keep giving forever".[9]

There is certainly a lot of 'chewing up of dollars', but I think it is possibly the LTC sector that is doing a lot of the chewing. It would be interesting to know whether any LTC staff are incentivised to encourage perpetual giving. Why have a limited life foundation to solve community problems today, when the LTC can grow its funds under management, drip feed funds to the community whilst drawing significant and growing fees in perpetuity?

EQT's O'Brien again: "The interesting thing about a trustee company is that almost all of your clients really need your services. It's not as if you

---

9. Tim Boreham, op. cit.

have to sell them".[10]

He's quite right. When you have convinced people to establish a perpetual trust and that the LTC should be the sole trustee and exclude family members as co-trustees, you don't need to 'sell' to your clients; most of them are dead! With no transparency, and no-one watching, you can keep charging them high fees forever!

Changes to fee structure - 2010

The LTCs are influential bodies. After significant lobbying (remember O'Brien's, "… we are close to them …") by the then Trustee Corporations Association of Australia (TCA), the Corporations Legislation Amendment (Financial Services Modernisation) Act (CAFSMA) changed the regulation of fees charged by LTCs to charitable trusts nationally, effective from May 2010. The government committed to reviewing the impact of CAFSMA within a two year period.

Prior to these fee changes, fees were charged pursuant to the Trustee Companies Act in each State and Territory. Fees charged by LTCs tended to be capped at a percentage of income. This then limited fees to be based on income, not on rising capital values.

With the CAFSMA changes rolled out nationally LTCs could charge charitable trusts up to 1.056% of capital for trustee administration fees, which tended to result in a significant increase in the fees LTCs could charge, substantially reducing the funds available to distribute to the community. A fee based on a percentage of capital has no connection to the cost of providing the services. It also creates an additional conflict as it incentivises LTCs to grow funds when it may be more appropriate to increase grant distributions, or seek a balance between both options.

The CAFSMA changes would have a different outcome for each charitable trust but in many cases could result in a fee increase of 400% p.a., resulting in the LTC fees being up to 25% of total income of a charitable trust.[11]

---

10. Tim Boreham, op. cit.

11. Charitable Alliance, *Submission to CAMAC Review of Charitable Trusts and Foundations*, December 2012, p. 7

This was an exciting revenue proposition for the LTCs, and they acted promptly.

> *"The Charitable Alliance's direct experience suggests LTCs are demanding their entitlement (CAFSMA fees) to trusts which have multiple trustees, and as a result it is highly likely they are being charged to all orphan trusts where there are no independent trustees to monitor the fees that LTCs are indeed charging."*[12]

There are some major differences between the behaviour of LTCs and how we managed charitable trusts when I was at MFO:

- fees: at MFO we charged on a fee-for-service basis, by the hour. We felt it was the only fair way to charge, as with some clients we were doing considerable work each month, and with others we were seeing them only twice a year. An LTC-type fee based on percentage of corpus would have been totally inappropriate in most cases, and would have resulted in clients walking out the door due to the excessive fees

- portability: at MFO we did not write our name into the Trust Deed of clients as trustee, unless the client specifically requested it, which was rare. We were happy to back our fees and service levels. If clients were not happy with our fees or services, they were free to leave, as they should be. At LTCs they were locked in with no portability. If an LTC-managed charitable trust had co-trustees (usually family members) and the co-trustees wanted to move to another service provider, all trustees had to agree. I was aware of many cases where the LTC rejected that option, which preserved their fees. Without the unanimous vote of all trustees, the only way the co-trustees could remove the LTC

---

12. Charitable Alliance, *Submission to CAMAC Review of Charitable Trusts and Foundations*, December 2012, p. 6

was via court action. If the co-trustees lost the action, they would be personally liable for the legal costs. However the LTC could recoup its legal costs from the trust. In most cases this results in co-trustees (often family members) not taking action due to the risks involved

- clients: I didn't see a lot of evidence of LTCs seeking to grow the sector via working with families to establish foundations. The growth in the philanthropic sector since the introduction of private ancillary funds (PAFs) in 2001 has primarily been via PAFs. LTCs did not appear to be active in establishing PAFs, which had families that were alive. Families that were alive could monitor and question fee and service levels.

This is one of the last bastions in the financial services sector with a lack of portability. Our superannuation, insurance and our mortgages all have portability. We laugh when we reflect on the lack of portability of mobile telephone numbers decades ago!

Formation of the Charitable Alliance

CAFSMA crystalised a rising level of frustration from many independent co-trustees of charitable trusts. These trusts were important as they provided a tiny window into the opaque world of charitable trusts managed by LTCs. In addition there was frustration from the beneficiaries of charitable trusts, for-purpose entities, who suspected the distributions to them should be higher, or had seen distributions to them drop significantly. This was particularly the case where the beneficiaries were the sole beneficiaries i.e. the charitable trust had been established solely to benefit a particular charity, but they weren't getting the maximum benefit due to high LTC fees.

In 2012 the Charitable Alliance (CA) was formed to take action. CA was an alliance of very concerned trustees, advisers to and stakeholders of charitable trusts and foundations that:

- had an aggregate corpus >$1 billion

- provided support to the community of >$1 billion p.a.

- engaged with, and were focussed on, the support of those in need in communities around Australia.

CA was seeking to create a fair legislative regime for charitable trusts and foundations administered by LTCs. Its members included:

- Tim Costello AO as Chair of the Community Council for Australia, a for-purpose membership body which at the time represented over 50 charities, including a number of the largest in the country

- Royal Children's Hospital Foundation, Melbourne

- The Myer Foundation and Sidney Myer Fund

- Willian Buckland Foundation

- Danks Trust

- Helen Macpherson Smith Trust

- RE Ross Trust

- Reichstein Foundation

- Percy Baxter Charitable Trust

- Victor Smorgon Charitable Fund

- Baker IDI Heart and Diabetes Institute

- Simon McKeon, former Australian of the Year

- Liz Cham, ex CEO of Philanthropy Australia

- The author.

In mid 2012 CA wrote to senior federal ministers outlining its concern that the *charitable purposes* of Trusts administered by LTCs were being materially compromised by:

- conflicts of 'purpose' of ASX listed LTCs

  - fiduciary duty as a listed financial services company v charitable purpose of trusts

- high and often multiple fees charged by ASX-listed LTCs

  - materially reducing funds available for beneficiaries

- conflicts of interest where LTCs serve the role of 'trustee' and 'service provider'

  - Often multiple or all services

The major premise was that trustee companies were once 'trusted guardians' in the community but had morphed into ASX listed, profit driven financial services companies.

The three governance issues which CA sought to be addressed were:

1.Lack of transparency

Comments: it is understood/appears that:
Fees charged by LTCs were usually not disclosed publicly, despite the public being the beneficiary of charitable trusts.

LTCs may only rarely report related party transactions and/or fees, which may be a breach of basic accounting standards.

2. Lack of portability

Comments: it is understood/appears that:

There is no formal independent process to review the performance of LTCs.

Trusts may be the only sector remaining without true 'portability'.

LTCs can only be removed from their role via a court determination. Should an individual co-trustee (usually honorary) seek a change of LTC and fail, they may be liable for costs (yet professional LTC's costs are covered by the trust).

3. Lack of independence

Comments: it is understood/appears that:

LTCs regularly invest the Trust's capital in the LTC's own/related entity's managed funds for additional (high) fees without an independent competitive process. If correct, is the LTC as trustee breaching its fiduciary duty to its beneficiaries?

Funds under management fees are in additional to various other fees charged, including a legislated fee of 1.056% fee as LTC.[13]

After prompting from CA and others, the Federal Government requested the Corporations and Markets Advisory Committee (CAMAC) to review the CAFSMA fee arrangements.

Charitable Alliance submission to CAMAC Review of Charitable Trusts and Foundations

CA lodged a submission to CAMAC in December 2012. CA had received numerous case studies of over-charging and/or under-servicing from co-trustees (independent trustees, often family members) of charitable trusts. In order to limit the length of the submission to CAMAC, CA included only eight case studies which typified the many case studies that had been received. It was clear from the case studies that LTCs were advising co-trustees that the LTCs, under the new CAFSMA fee regulations, were 'entitled' to charge significantly higher fees, whilst providing no additional value to the charitable trust, or the charitable

---

13. Charitable Alliance, letter to Andrew Leigh, Shadow Assistant Treasurer, 10 May 2019

beneficiaries within the community.

CA's major recommendations were:

Pricing reform

- calculation of a maximum fee not to be linked to a % of capital, but of 5.5% of annual income

- allow a one-off establishment fee of a % of income (recognising the additional work to be done in year one)

- ensure LTCs are obliged to set 'just and reasonable' fees that reflect time and effort involved

- set a transparent mechanism for setting and reviewing total fees

- reduce the cost of the fee review mechanism by removing the need to go to a Court at first instance to resolve a dispute about fees.

Governance reform

- improve competition between LTCs through transparent reporting obligations from which valid comparisons can be made on pricing in the market

- LTCs be required to seek independent advice before investing the funds of charitable trusts in the financial instruments of companies related to the LTC

- prevent orphan trusts (i.e. trusts where the sole trustee is a LTC, with no family members involved to defend the donor's intent) from being created by legislating that LTCs receiving fees from a charitable trust must constitute a minority of the trustees of that charitable trust

- protect existing orphan trusts by requiring the appointment of new trustees and independent 'responsible persons'

- promote portability by ensuring someone has the power to

decide which LTC should manage a charitable trust (this could be a peer review body modelled on the ASIC Takeovers Panel)

- remove barriers to entry into the market of managing charitable trusts by creating a new class of Australian Financial Services Licence dedicated to the management of charitable trusts (only)

- implement a cost effective dispute resolution system to manage disputes between LTCs and other co-trustees (i.e. the same peer review body modelled on the ASIC Takeovers Panel).[14]

Philanthropy Australia (PA) lodged a submission to CAMAC stating the relevant governance standards be changed to include that fees relating to charitable trusts must only be fair and reasonable, that a signed annual report include explanation to support the former, and that in setting fees regard should be given to work performed and market rates. PA went further to state that if fees were excessive, the Australian Charities and Not-for-profits Commission (ACNC) should have the ability to replace the trustee. [15]

CAMAC recommendations

In May 2013 CAMAC released its report, *Administration of Charitable Trusts.* It put forward recommendations "… that seek to ensure that the administrative arrangements for these charitable trusts continue to promote the benevolent and philanthropic objectives for which they were established."

CAMAC's,

> "… starting point in considering these competing perspectives has been to ask why donors set up charitable

---

14. Charitable Alliance, *Submission to CAMAC Review of Charitable Trusts and Foundations*, December 2012, p. 2

15. Philanthropy Australia, *Submission to CAMAC Inquiry into Charitable Trusts and Trustee Companies*, 15 March 2013

trusts in the first place. It considers that the primary intent of each donor is to achieve the philanthropic or benevolent purposes or objectives for which the donor established and funded the charitable trust, within the time frame of the trust, and in an effective and efficient manner. This primary intent should be the policy cornerstone which underpins the regulation of charitable trusts generally."[16]

CAMAC recommended a two-stage reform process:

"Stage 1 essentially comprises three measures:

• the conducting of Stewardship audits of a cross-section of charitable trusts administered by LTCs, to address the present deficit of relevant and indisputable information on the state of administration of charitable trusts

• the introduction of a 'fair and reasonable' requirement for all fees and costs charged against a charitable trust

• changes to the judicial dispute resolution procedures to enhance access to the court and to broaden its remedial powers, including in regard to whether fees and costs charged against a charitable trust are excessive or whether an LTC should be replaced as the trustee of a charitable trust.

As well as responding to perceived difficulties or shortcomings in the current legal regime, these proposals are designed to promote a more open market by providing opportunities, where appropriate, to alter administrative arrangements in order to achieve the primary intent of the donor.

---

16. CAMAC, *Administration of charitable trusts*, May 2013, p. 1

Stage 2 would build on the information gathered from the Stewardship audits and any preliminary indications from the enhanced judicial dispute resolution procedure. It would focus on what, if any, additional changes to the regulation of administrative arrangements for charitable trusts are required to promote the primary intent of the donor." [17]

CAMAC was so concerned with the case studies that it had received from CA that it recommended a stewardship audit be carried out of charitable trusts administered by LTCs, as well as a requirement that LTC fees be 'fair and reasonable'!

"At the end of the inquiry, though, the committee found real problems with the way these trustees operated: their lack of transparency, the level of their fees and charges, and their unaccountability, even to co-trustees who were family members of the deceased." [18]

CAMAC noted in their report that of the 1,000 private ancillary funds established (at that time), 80% were managed by parties other than LTCs i.e. the market could see where the value and service was and voted with their feet, and it wasn't at LTCs. Sadly, for orphan trusts, they had 'no feet'.

Unfortunately, the vast majority of charitable trusts managed by LTCs are orphan trusts. CAMAC asked the LTC peak body, the Financial Services Council (the successor to the TCA) to survey its LTC members. According to this survey, of the 1,120 LTC charitable trusts at the time:

- 90% were sole trustee trusts, with a total capitalisation of some $2 billion

---

17. CAMAC, *Administration of charitable trusts*, May 2013, p. 1

18. Mike Seccombe, *The Saturday Paper*, 29 March 2014

- 10% were co-trustee trusts, with a total capitalisation of some $1.2 billion.[19]

One would imagine that these 1,000 orphan trusts, where nobody is watching and where there is no transparency, would all have received significant ongoing fee increases since the CAFSMA regulations were introduced in 2010.

With the lack of transparency within LTCs it is difficult to determine what the aggregate fee increases were each year. In 2012 CA conservatively estimated they could be $30 million p.a. I suspect it is higher, particularly if LTCs now manage charitable trusts with an aggregate corpus of over $6 billion. To be clear, that is around $400 million (conservatively) in extra fees charged by LTCs to charitable trusts in the 13 years since CAFSMA was introduced, instead of being distributed to the community.

> "The major finding of the CAMAC Report is that charitable trusts should not be treated in the same manner as other trusts. They are established for the benefit of the community and it is this benefit to the community that must be held as the primary purpose, the reason for their existence and the measure of their performance. It is also this primary purpose that bestows special status upon charitable trusts. These charitable trusts are not just another financial instrument or the property of financial services companies to be exploited for income purposes."[20]

Given the purpose of charitable trusts is to benefit the community, they should be managed within a charitable structure, not a structure whose role is to maximise profits for shareholders. Options to achieve this include establishing a new charitable structure or using an

---

19. CAMAC, op. cit., p. 17

20. Charitable Alliance, letter to Treasurer Joe Hockey & Assistant Treasurer Mathias Cormann, 11 April 2014

existing charitable structure such as Australian Philanthropic Services or community foundations.

Is anybody interested?

A decade later the CAMAC report has sat on a shelf with no recommendations actioned. This is a very disappointing outcome for the community. We need to address these issues now, before the huge inter-generational wealth transfer really kicks in.

As a community are we happy that the senior executives of a company (EQT) where a material part of their business is to administer charitable trusts for the community, in aggregate have received bonuses of millions of dollars in recent years?[21]

The Charitable Alliance had briefed a number of relevant Coalition finance-related Ministers on this issue in the decade subsequent to the CAMAC review, including Joe Hockey, Mathias Cormann and Josh Frydenberg. No action was taken. I suspect it was not a vote winner. The Current Assistant Minister for Competition, Charities, Treasury and employment, Andrew Leigh, has been briefed on the issue.

As a community, and as a sector, are we happy for this behaviour to continue? Should we take action to address this issue, or continue to look the other way?

---

21. EQT, *Annual Reports*, 2018-2022

Chapter 32

How to grow the philanthropic sector

"Don't judge each day by the harvest you reap but by the seeds that you plant." – **Robert Louis Stevenson**

The philanthropic sector in Australia has grown in the last 20 years but nowhere near the level of wealth creation. There is a huge opportunity to grow the sector. Over the years a number of helpful structural changes have been introduced by government. The sector seems to keep pressing for structural changes, but if we are to see generosity levels grow significantly in Australia it is cultural change that we will require.

Structural changes in the last twenty years

There have been many structural changes to the philanthropic sector in Australia over the last two decades to encourage higher giving levels. These helpful changes include:

- the establishment of prescribed private funds, now known as Private Ancillary Funds (PAF)

- tax deductibility for property over $5,000

- deductions for workplace giving

- conservation covenants

- capital gains tax exemption under the Cultural Gifts Program

- deductions for gifts of listed shares valued at $5,000 or less

- deductions for fundraising dinners and similar events

- five year averaging of donations

- educational scholarships

- new deductible gift recipient categories.[1]

Progress in the ten years to 2023

We have made some progress in the sector over the last decade. In a speech I gave at Philanthropy Australia's (PA) 2012 conference I called for a 'National Giving Campaign' to address the following issues:

- setting a benchmark for giving for 'mums and dads' as many things don't get done unless they are measured. I suggested tripling average giving rates at the time, so increasing giving to 1% of income – *not done*

- encouraging more families to consider the adverse impact of leaving significant income streams to children – *not done in a systemic way*

- encouraging more existing high-net-worth donors to talk openly about their work to inspire others (I suggested 30 families in each State) – *not done in a systemic way*

- introducing national giving awards to celebrate our giving – *done. PA established The Australian Philanthropy Awards some years ago*

---

1. McGregor-Lowndes, Balczun & Williamson, op. cit., p.16

- introducing a giving pledge in Australia – *an attempt has been made (refer to next chapter)*

- publishing a list of the 'top 50' philanthropic grants in Australia's history – *done, by our team at the Myer Family Office in 2013*[2]

- introducing an education campaign for financial advisers on different giving options – ad hoc campaigns have occurred, but *not done in a systemic way*

- boosting the resources of PA to grow the profile of the philanthropic sector by providing PA with DGR status – *done.*

Cultural change is required – the need for role models

It is clear to me that the reasons for modest levels of giving by most high-net-worth individuals (HNWIs) in Australia are primarily cultural:

- we rarely openly talk about our giving

- the 'tall poppy' syndrome still exists in Australia, and we don't celebrate individual 'success' as naturally as some people from other countries

- we are still learning to celebrate giving

- many of our philanthropic role models have long passed away e.g. Sidney Myer, Sir Ian Potter, Sir Vincent Fairfax

- we have few living exemplar philanthropic role models for others to aspire to.

There is minimal peer pressure or community expectation on HNWIs in Australia to give away material sums of money. Whilst the USA has a different history and culture to Australia, generally in the USA if you are

---

2. The Myer Family Company Ltd, *Australia's Top 50 Philanthropic Gifts*, 2013

financially successful, it is almost a given that you share it, and in fact you may be deemed a social pariah if you do not. There is peer pressure to act.

Upon the passing away of a 'successful' businessperson in Australia, there is discussion about their achievements in business, but there is little discussion about their contribution to the community philanthropically, or lack of. In comparison, in 2011 when Apple founder, Steve Jobs, passed away in the USA there was much commentary about his business exploits, and in particular his vision and how Apple products changed the daily lives of many of us. However, there was also a discussion about his lack of generosity, and he was marked down for this. I have not seen such a discussion occur in Australia.

Neil Balnaves AO is an excellent example of giving away a material amount of the wealth he had created (via the Southern Star Group) and then talking about it. Neil was ahead of his time and talked publicly about his giving soon after establishing The Balnaves Foundation in 2006. He had said to me many years ago that he didn't particularly want to talk about his giving, but felt he needed to be a role model for others to step up and act in a similar way. Sadly, Neil is no longer with us, but his legacy lives on.

Mark Wootton AO and Eve Kantor AO showed great leadership and foresight with their $10 million gift in 2005 to establish The Climate Institute, a think-tank focussing on progressive policies to mitigate climate change. At the time of the gift, this was a rare large public gift in Australia. Despite being a private couple, the public nature of the gift was to shine a light on climate change and encourage others to do more.

There was a shift in the Australian philanthropic sector in late 2012 with a series of large publicly announced gifts, which the country had not seen before. Leaders were stepping up to role model behaviour. It started with a $20 million gift from John Grill AO to the University of Sydney. This was followed in 2013 with gifts of:

- $50 million to Australian National University (ANU) – Graham and Louise Tuckwell

- $50.1 million to Queensland Institute of Medical Research – Clive

Berghofer AM

- $65 million to various Western Australia universities – Andrew Forrest AO and Nicola Forrest AO

- $12.5 million to Victoria University – Harold Mitchell AC

- $10 million to the University of Melbourne – Allan Myers AC and Maria Myers AC

- $10 million to the University of Melbourne – Greg Poche AO and Kay Poche AO.

Graham and Louise Tuckwell have been great role models for talking about their significant giving for the Tuckwell Scholarship Program at ANU. As has Simon Mordant AO in Sydney and Malcolm McCusker AO and Tonya McCusker AM in Perth.

We should celebrate what Andrew and Nicola Forrest are trying to achieve with significant community issues such as early childhood development, modern slavery and the use of plastic. They have said publicly many times their kids are not inheriting their wealth. They could simply be sitting on a $300 million yacht in the Mediterranean (as some do) or buying a USD150 million house in Los Angeles (as some have. As an aside, I do find it interesting that one would think a USD150 million house would be a good place to raise grounded children. Perhaps my dad had different values to his dad.)

I think it is very helpful that the Forrest's talk about their giving. I'm proud to say that I influenced Graham Tuckwell to go public with his and Louise's extraordinary initial commitment of $50 million to ANU (since increased to around $200 million over 30 years). At a PA conference several years ago Andrew stated that it was this public Tuckwell announcement that convinced he and Nicola to be more public about their giving, in order to encourage others. The Forrests are one of only three Australian families to commit to the overseas Giving Pledge.[3] (The others are Len Ainsworth AM and Melanie Perkins/Cliff Obrecht.)

---

3. https://givingpledge.org/

Recent efforts to grow the sector

We have few institutions seeking to grow the size of the philanthropic pie in Australia. The Myer Family Office (pre its merger with Mutual Trust), Australian Philanthropic Services (APS), Australian Communities Foundation, StartGiving and PA are good examples of entities actively seeking to grow the sector.

APS is a great story. It was launched in 2012, after being spun out of Social Ventures Australia.

Chris Cuffe AO was instrumental in its development and funded it (with support from several others) until break-even. Industry doyen, David Ward, has provided the technical expertise to APS since inception. It administers over 300 PAFs with an aggregate corpus of $1.8 billion. It has also established a rapidly growing APS Foundation, a Public Ancillary Fund (PuAF) with over 400 client sub funds with an aggregate corpus of over $200 million at the time of writing (after only a decade in operation).[4]

Australian Daniel Petre worked with Bill Gates at Microsoft in the USA in Microsoft's early days. Living in the USA, Daniel saw the culture whereby if you were financially successful you would share it. It was just a given. When Daniel returned to Australia in the mid-1990s he couldn't understand why we didn't have a similar culture, and why financially successful Australians often didn't feel an obligation to share their success. Daniel has funded numerous reports over many years to shed a light on the lack of generosity of HNWIs in Australia. He has been a courageous leader in this area, approaching a number of HNWIs suggesting that they could do more.

I think it is fair to say that after many years Daniel has given up on 'the older money' and is targeting the next generation in the innovation community. In 2022 he established StartGiving, a for-purpose entity, "… on a mission to make giving by successful tech founders the norm,

---

4. Chris Cuffe and APS, *Australian Philanthropic Services – The First 12 Years*, The Book Advisor, 2022

and the expectation."[5] Tech founders will be encouraged at an early stage to gift equity to their foundation. If the business is successful, the foundation's balance sheet will grow. Given Daniel's strong connections and respect in the tech sector I suspect he will have success, which will hopefully then flow on to other sectors of the community.[6]

Philanthropy Australia's giving blueprint

In March 2021 PA released, *A Blueprint to Grow Structured Giving*.[7] I applaud PA for putting a greater priority on growing giving levels in Australia. I took issue with the first sentence of the Blueprint Executive Summary: "Australia is a generous nation". Given the overwhelming evidence that suggests the opposite, I think the peak body was being incredibly polite. To create change we will firstly need a frank national discussion about where we are at, determine where we would like to head and then develop a plan to inspire people into action.

What really troubled me with the *Blueprint* was PA's goal of doubling structured giving over the decade to 2030. This was similar to an annual growth rate of around 7%. This should be achieved simply via organic growth. I thought this goal to be terribly unambitious and disappointing. Given the wealth created in recent decades, we should have been able to get that growth from just a handful of families, not the entire country!

At the time I had been contemplating what I should be doing in my life which would maximise my impact. I was so alarmed with the *Blueprint* goals that I resigned from my major professional responsibilities at the time to develop and implement Australia's Giving Pledge.

There are some good ideas in the *Blueprint* but many of them have been tried before. Perhaps they will be better implemented this time given PA received significant funding commitments from several members in 2022. There are two good ideas in the Blueprint (neither are new):

---

5. https://startgiving.com

6. *The Australian Financial Review Magazine,* May 2022

7. Philanthropy Australia, *A Blueprint to Grow Structured Giving*, April 2021

- access to superannuation: seek the government to allow bequests made to charities to be made from superannuation when people pass away, without the current tax penalty (up to 17%). PA estimates that, "... superannuation balances at death set to reach at least $130 billion by 2059 ..."[8] Accordingly, access to superannuation could have a dramatic impact on the income of for-purpose entities. However, the experts tell me that, given the significant amount of fiddling with this sector in recent years, you would need to get the superannuation industry on-side to make this happen and that is likely to be very difficult

- Living Legacy Trust: is a new tax incentive where a donor places an asset (e.g. property or shares) in a trust for the benefit of a charity upon the donor's death. The donor receives an income stream from the asset whilst they are alive. In return for irrevocably committing the asset to the charity, the donor receives a tax deduction when they place the asset in the trust based upon the asset's value.[9] This will be useful for some families, but will be too complex for many and is really a 'nice to have' rather than a game-changer.

In addition, the deductible gift recipient framework is a mess and should be cleaned up. We should ensure community foundations can generally have access to DGR 1 status in order that they can more easily fund local grassroots organisations, and ancillary funds should be able to distribute to each other, for example, to enable a PAF to distribute to a community foundation that may better understand the issues in a particular region.

These are 'nice to haves', not game-changers to grow giving levels. Rather than focussing on structural changes to the sector, it would be far more effective to educate families and their advisers about the excellent

---

8. https://www.philanthropy.org.au/news-and-stories/philanthropy-australia-cites-huge-op portunity-for-wealthiest-australians-to-lift-their-giving/

9. Philanthropy Australia, *A Blueprint to Grow Structured Giving*, April 2021, p. 18

structures that are already in existence.

Major opportunities to grow the philanthropic sector

1. Community foundations

Community foundations are grantmaking public charities operating for the benefit of a specific community, usually defined by geographic location. They bring people together, raise money, pool resources and manage funds to build long term assets to support a particular community's needs. They have an extraordinary capacity to make a positive impact as they can be on the ground, at the grass roots, in communities around the country, building relationships with local leaders and seeing where the gaps and crucial needs are. For that reason, place-based giving has always been important, and has become even more so since the pandemic. Post Covid-19, with hybrid working arrangements, people are spending more time in their local communities and as a result tend to value the local community more.

In Australia there are 40 community foundations striving to make their local community a better place to live, serving 156 local government areas. In aggregate they have approximately $500 million in funds under management as at 30 June 2021.[10] Since 2010 the growth of community foundations has slowed dramatically, with 26 established in the decade to 2009 and only 13 in the decade to 2019. Canada, with a similar population and land mass to Australia, has five times the number of community foundations that we do![11]

Community Foundations Australia (CFA), the community foundations peak body, has recognised that there is a lack of awareness among community leaders about community foundations and their benefits.[12]

---

10. Community Foundations Australia: https://www.cfaustralia.org.au

11. Philanthropy Australia, *A Blueprint to Grow Structured Giving*, April 2021, p. 10

12. Australian Community Philanthropy, *Community Foundations in Australia: a Blueprint for Growth*, April 2020, p. 16

CFA needs to deliver a bold measurable plan to dramatically grow the community sector. Such a plan should then be funded by philanthropy sector leaders. If managed well, the return on investment over the medium to long term would be enormous.

Sector leaders such as the Australian Communities Foundation (ACF), Foundation for Rural and Regional Renewal (FRRR) and the Lord Mayor's Charitable Foundation (LMCF), with CFA and PA, need to drive this initiative.

The Charles Stewart Mott Foundation (USA) saw the benefit of community foundations many years ago. They could see the local leadership role that community foundations could take. Former Mott President, William White said, "We have long been impressed by the simplicity and power that underlies the community foundation concept, which empowers people to support causes close to their homes and their hearts."[13]

Building the capacity of community foundations across the USA became one of Mott's major focus areas. To date it has provided over USD170 million to help expand community foundations worldwide, from only 300 worldwide in 1979, to more than 1,800 today.[14]

Mott is now looking to strengthen the community foundation field in Africa, Europe and Latin America. Mott has an incredible legacy. Mott's work is inspiring, yet it is not known in Australia. Promoting Mott's work here could flush out a 'Mott equivalent' in Australia. This is an amazing opportunity and legacy for a family to grasp.

Canadian Miriam Bergen's extraordinary CAD500 million gift to The Winnipeg Foundation (TWF) in 2022 for the benefit of the Winnipeg community will transform TWF's ability to serve its local community for generations to come. Again, this gift is not known in Australia. Bergen should be held up here as a role model for others to replicate.[15]

---

13. https://www.mott.org/work/civil-society/enhancing-community-philanthropy/

14. https://philanthropy.iupui.edu/news-events/news-item/paarlberg-appointed-charles-ste wart-mott-foundation-chair-on-community-foundations

15. https://www.wpgfdn.org/the-winnipeg-foundation/gift_announcement_nov2022/

2. Public Ancillary Fund sub funds

Some philanthropic intermediaries manage a public foundation, usually a Public Ancillary Fund, with sub funds for donors. Examples include community foundations, wealth advisers and trustee companies. A sub fund is a bit like a giving account. It can make structured giving more accessible as you don't need a significant capital sum to get started. Usually the entry point is between $2,000 to $50,000 (tax deductible), the sub fund can be established, usually free of charge, in the name of your choice within a couple of days. There are minimal ongoing administrative or governance obligations for the donor. All funds are pooled and donors then make recommendations for grants to eligible charities.

Research into sub funds by CSI Swinburne in 2019 based on 2017/18 data indicated there were only 1,995 sub funds in Australia. These funds in aggregate held just over $1 billion (an average of $0.5 million) and distributed around $57 million in that year.[16]

There is enormous scope to grow the number of sub funds, particularly via 'mums and dads' given the low cost entry point and their simplicity. Sub funds have been poorly marketed in Australia. Many in the community are not aware of their existence and many financial advisers still aren't aware of their benefits, so they are not able to share this with their clients. PAFs are reasonably well known, sub funds are not.

In around 2010 I told a room of philanthropic sector leaders that we should have 20,000 sub funds in Australia. This was met by hearty laughter from most in the room. All these years later I still don't know why that was funny! Again, sector leaders such as PA, CFA, APS, ACF, FRRR and LMCF need to drive this campaign.

---

16. https://researchbank.swinburne.edu.au/file/68f5d8fa-1441-42b6-b73d-939e70a2e354/1/2
019-seibert-snapshot_of_sub-funds.pd

3. Payroll giving

Payroll giving is one of the easiest and most effective ways for Australians to give. There are technology platforms now in place that assist employers to simply and efficiently implement workplace giving programs that include payroll giving e.g. Good2Give. Payroll giving is very effective. Employers can commit modest sums on a fortnightly/monthly basis, receive the tax benefit immediately and the sum can be matched by the employer. It provides employers with low cost opportunities for greater staff engagement and retention and provides charities with regular income streams and strong partnerships.

QUT research indicates that:

- only 4.1 million Australians are employed by employers providing payroll giving

- only 1.4% of taxpayers are using payroll giving (211,541 employees)

- the total amount given using payroll giving was only $53 million (2019/20), with an average annual donation of $248 (median: $100).[17]

With the right campaign, driven by Workplace Giving Australia, there is a huge opportunity for payroll giving growth in Australia.

4. Behaviourial economics

Behavioural economics can be used with individual taxpayers. On the Australian Tax Office (ATO) income tax assessment for individuals the ATO could state something along the lines of, "Taxpayers in your income bracket on average donate x% of their income to charities." Behavioural economics would suggest that most people don't want to be seen to be doing less than their peers, so there is a chance their giving would

---

17. McGregor-Lowndes, Balczun & Williamson, op. cit., p. 44

increase in the following year to be above the average. And so the momentum grows each year.

In a similar vein, the annual *AFR Rich List* should include an extra column on its list for each entrant: '% of wealth given away'. Some in the list will ignore this. However, there will be others that will be keen not to be at the bottom of the table of '% of wealth given away'. *The Sunday Times* in the UK has been providing this information for several years.

5. Bequests

We have already discussed the huge inter-generational wealth transfer that has commenced in Australia. Research in 2016 indicates that under 10% of Wills include a bequest to a charity.[18] As the average estate grows, there is an enormous opportunity for a sector-led plan to significantly grow bequests to for-purpose entities.

6. Inheritance tax

If there is no joy growing the sector, governments may turn to the last resort and apply the 'stick' approach i.e. the introduction of an inheritance tax. This is not something that I advocate, unless all else fails. In its *High Net Wealth Giving in Australia* report, the Centre for Social Impact stated that whilst Australia had not had an inheritance tax since 1979, most OECD countries had such a tax in place.

> *"An inheritance tax also provides greater incentive to give to charity. OECD analysis suggests charitable bequests decline by 12-20% when there is no inheritance tax in place."*[19]

---

18. John McLeod, *The Support Report*, JBWere Philanthropic Services, April 2018, p. 14

19. P. Flatau, L. Lester, J. T. Brown, M. Kyron, Z. Callis, and K. Muir, op. cit., p. 15

Huge opportunity

The opportunity to transform the size of the philanthropic sector in Australia is huge:

- with the Productivity Commission's estimate of the inter-generational wealth transfer over the next two decades being as high as $3.5 trillion[20], if 10% was gifted to foundations this would amount to $350 billion

- the aggregate wealth of the *AFR Rich List 2023* is $563 billion. If 10% is gifted to foundations this would equate to $56 billion, which would distribute at least $2.8 billion p.a.

- with 58,000 Australians with wealth of $10 million+[21], create another 15,000 PAFs with an average corpus of $5 million, which equates to an aggregate corpus of $75 billion which would distribute at least $3.75 billion p.a.

- extending the 1% giving pledge to all households with net wealth greater than $50 million could increase the pool of donations by up to $8.5 billion[22]

- with 112,000 Australians with wealth of $5 million-$10 million[23] create another 25,000 public ancillary fund sub funds with an average corpus of $100,000, which equates to an aggregate corpus of $2.5 billion which would distribute $100 million p.a.

---

20. Productivity Commission, op. cit., p. 62

21. Credit Suisse, *Global Wealth Databook 2022*, p. 130

22. P. Flatau, L. Lester, J. T. Brown, M. Kyron, Z. Callis, and K. Muir, op. cit., p. 14

23. Credit Suisse, op. cit., p. 130

- payroll giving: if we increased taxpayer participation to 10% then individual donations would increase over $350 million p.a., and much higher if this was matched by employers[24]

- inheritance tax:

  "It is difficult to determine how much revenue such a (inheritance) tax would generate. But it is clear it would add considerable resources to the charitable sector. Our calculations indicate a 5% inheritance tax with a $10 million net wealth threshold (excluding owner occupied housing equity) would raise between $2.3 and $3 billion annually for a Charity fund. Raising the threshold to $20 million would raise between $1.7 billion and $2.3 billion a year, while a $50 million threshold would generate between $1.2 and $1.6 billion annually".[25]

As discussed above, there have been significant structural changes to the philanthropic sector over the last two decades. It is not structural changes that we require to significantly increase giving by HNWIs. We now need cultural change. We need to celebrate our giving. Philanthropy has transformed our cities, but we don't know the stories. One of the most impactful ways to change our giving culture would be to implement a giving pledge in Australia. A pledge that would normalise material giving in this country, tell great stories and inspire others into action.

---

24. David Mann, CEO, Workplace Giving Australia, conversation with the author, 26 April 2023

25. P. Flatau, L. Lester, J. T. Brown, M. Kyron, Z. Callis, and K. Muir, op. cit., p.15

Chapter 33

Australia's Giving Pledge

"Every right implies a responsibility; every opportunity an obligation; every possession a duty." – **John D. Rockefeller and carved in stone at Rockefeller Plaza**

Attempts to grow giving levels

Many people have tried to grow giving levels in Australia amongst high-net-worth individuals (HNWIs) over the last two decades. My major efforts involved establishing the Philanthropic Services team at The Myer Family Office (MFO), finding opportunities to promote the benefits of giving, publicising great philanthropy stories, discussing different giving structures with financial advisers and talking to hundreds of HNWIs about the benefits of structured giving to the community and their family.

Many have tried similar or other avenues to grow giving levels. I know fundraisers who have been raising money for decades, trying a range of ways trying to convince donors to increase their giving levels. All the above are included in Philanthropy Australia's (PA) plan to grow giving.[1]

There has been some modest success. The philanthropic sector has grown over the last ten years in Australia, but nowhere near the growth of wealth creation. We are yet to develop a strong giving culture amongst HNWIs in this country. This provides us with a great opportunity.

---

1. Philanthropy Australia, *A Blueprint to Grow Structured Giving*, April 2021

It's a cultural issue

We know we have significant wealth in the country. We know we have made significant structural changes in the sector to drive growth in giving. We know that many have tried a huge range of ways to encourage HNWIs to increase their generosity levels. So why is the philanthropic sector in Australia not growing rapidly? As concluded in the previous chapter, we need to change our giving culture.

We need to be inspired into action. We need to, "… tap into the deeply held values and identities of a community with the power to affect the beliefs and norms of others in their social group".[2]

We need more HNWIs to give and to talk about their giving. If we could get respected HNWI role models across the country to give material sums, and regularly discuss their giving, it would become the 'norm' in society. People usually want to do the right thing, and be seen to be doing the right thing. If it becomes the 'norm' to give material sums and talk about it, then a lot more people will follow.

People are usually influenced by their peers. Whether you call it peer influence or peer pressure, it will be HNWIs that drive the change to our giving culture.

So in 2021, underwhelmed by the ambition in PA's *Blueprint to Grow Structured Giving*, I resigned from various responsibilities to focus on implementing Australia's Giving Pledge.

Australia's Giving Pledge – the plan

We need to inspire and show people the way. "People fail to act not because they do not have enough information, but because they don't care or they don't know what to do."[3]

Australia's Giving Pledge could transform the size of the philanthropic sector in Australia. The Pledge would change the giving culture of HNWIs

---

2. Ann Christiano & Annie Neimand, *The Science of What Makes People Care*, Stanford Social Innovation Review, Fall 2018, p. 29

3. Ann Christiano & Annie Neimand, op. cit., p. 33

in Australia by getting influential families around the country to act as role models. They would do this by publicly committing to give away a material portion of their wealth. Inspiring giving stories and community outcomes would be highlighted. This would normalise material giving in Australia.

The plan was to seek:

1. 'More giving': implement the pledge to initially bring in $20 billion+ into the philanthropic sector i.e. increase the level of capital in order that for-purpose CEOs could work on bold plans with larger budgets

2. 'Better giving': seek to ensure better deployment of capital. There was no point significantly increasing the size of the philanthropic sector if the capital was to be used poorly. This could cause harm to the community. The small Pledge team would provide opportunities to share with Pledge signatories best practice philanthropy and ideas to better collaborate with like-minded donors. It would operate similar to The Audacious Project (see chapter 22): catalysing social capital on a huge scale by working with social entrepreneurs backed by large donors.

We could show families 'what to do'.

We certainly have plenty of potential role models in the country to target:

- you needed $690 million in 2023 to make the *AFR Rich List*, a list of the 200 wealthiest families in the country[4]

- there are 141 billionaires in Australia (66 with >$2 billion).[5] At the time of writing I am only aware of three foundations with assets >$1 billion. (I'm aware of several more being planned)

---

4. Australian Financial Review Magazine, *Rich List*, 2023

5. Ibid.

- around 14,800 individuals earn >$1 million p.a.[6]

- Credit Suisse's wealth report advised that over 58,000 Australian families had net wealth of >$10 million[7]

- Treasury tell us there are 20,000 individuals with >$5 million in their superannuation fund[8]

- the top 100 superannuation funds in 2021 had aggregate assets of $12 billion.[9]

I needed to develop a detailed plan for the Pledge. A lot of the ideas around the Pledge were in my head and in Notes on my Mac. I discussed the idea with an old sector colleague, Mark Cubit. He immediately saw the vision and need. He wisely said, "Pete, if you take this idea to the big foundations or the sector peak body, they will take months to make a decision. I will provide you funding to get on with it immediately." There is great giving practice right there: clear vision, strategic thinking, a bold approach, risk-taking willingness, nimble action, great communication and a commitment to make things happen.

I spent several weeks documenting the plan. I had been thinking about this issue for years, and had even tested a similar idea ten years earlier with six clients whilst at MFO. They and the philanthropic sector weren't ready at that time. The clients all promptly rejected the Pledge idea for varying reasons. A decade later, it was terrific to test the detail of the Pledge plan with a smart head (Mark), particularly one that moved in the world of HNWIs and had worked in the philanthropic and for-purpose sectors for many years.

---

6. McGregor-Lowndes, Balczun & Williamson, op. cit., p. 99

7. Credit Suisse, *Global Wealth Databook 2022*, p. 130

8. Michael Roddan, *SMSFs with more than $5m surge 30pc*, Australian Financial Review, 6 September 2021

9. Ben Butler, *ATO reveals Australia's top 100 self-managed super funds and what they are worth*, Herald Sun, 5 April 2023

Feasibility study

The next step was to test the idea; a feasibility study was required. This would involve meeting with around 50 influential families across most Australian States and Territories. I needed to test the idea with those who would be signing up to the Pledge. This study would glean significant intelligence that would further shape the plan.

I provided the Pledge plan to a new entrant to the philanthropic sector; a family with considerable wealth. (Let's call them Carpenter.) Carpenter liked the plan and agreed to fund the feasibility study.

During the feasibility study I tested the idea that the Pledge commitment would be based on a sliding scale of family wealth i.e. for families with wealth of $30 million+ they would publicly commit to giving away 20% of their wealth in their lifetime or upon death, $100 million+: 25%, $250 million+: 30%, increasing to 50% for those with wealth of $500 million+.

During the two months of the study (September and October 2021) I met with 68 families. I had not underestimated the difficulty of the task of getting HNWIs to publicly commit to giving away a material percentage of their wealth—very difficult given the pre-existing giving culture in Australia. However, the initial results were very encouraging. Thirteen families agreed to sign the Pledge, with another 35 families in the 'maybe' category. Many of this latter category loved the idea, were already giving away material sums but were concerned about their privacy. I needed to increase the number of commitments so that there would be safety in numbers.

I reported the results of the study to Carpenter and recommended that given the very encouraging signs, the Pledge be funded for the following 5 months in order that I could:

- pursue another 40+ families who I was yet to meet with

- continue to target the very influential families in each State, who would bring other families along with them

- draft a plan to launch the Pledge

- develop a plan for the Pledge Secretariat, a small team that would run the Pledge and 'direct traffic' to ensure the effective deployment of capital e.g. connect like-minded donors and subject matter experts, and meet with the Bill and Melinda Gates Foundation to get their learnings from the overseas billionaires' Giving Pledge (GP),[10] which was managed by the Gates Foundation. This also included determining the appropriate skills and team, drafting a communications plan and budget and seeking funding for the Secretariat.

Carpenter agreed with the recommendations, so we marched on.

Further testing of the idea with families

By Christmas 2021 I had met with over 100 families, with 20 families committed to the Pledge and 51 families giving it serious consideration. Leading up to the Christmas break I was mulling over comments from families that the giving guidelines scale was too complex and onerous, the use of a definition of ultra high-net-worth family seemed too exclusive, and several families said they would commit only if there were 80+ signatories i.e. safety in numbers.

Of course, the Pledge would not be for everybody. I knew several very wealthy families who gave material sums, and were operating within the Pledge's parameters, but as they were not known publicly, they did not want to sign up. They were excited by the idea and wanted the Pledge to launch, but without their involvement. That was unfortunate, as their involvement could influence many others, but I understood and respected their position.

Some suggested that the Pledge be the Australian arm of the overseas GP established by Bill Gates and Warren Buffett. My view was that this would unlikely be successful for a variety of reasons:

---

10. https://givingpledge.org

- whilst the GP was a world-wide pledge, many considered it to be American. In my experience with Australian HNWIs, they really don't like to be told how to behave by Americans

- the GP was for billionaires. The AFR Rich List suggests we have 141 billionaires[11]. With over 58,000 Australians each with wealth of $10m+, why would we not want to inspire them to do more?[12]

- the GP was seeking families to commit to give away 50% of their wealth. Australia is not ready for such a sizeable pledge percentage, as proven by my feasibility study.

I found it disappointing that in NSW four high-profile, influential figures in the philanthropic sector in that State, all declined to participate in the Pledge without providing a logical reason. If they had participated, I'm sure they could have each persuaded at least another five influential families to come on board.

I thought it disappointing that two former PA Chairs rejected the Pledge, again without providing a logical reason. I am sure that if surrounded by the right role models, families would step up.

A few families said that a giving pledge 'did not resonate with them', and that their focus was 100% impact investing. That is terrific, but it seemed to me that they were seeking to grow their pie in a way that was non-harmful and helped the community, but weren't willing to share much of their pie. You could write another book on all the issues in the world that can't solely rely on impact investing to be resolved.

A number of high-profile families in the philanthropic sector would not commit to the Pledge and did not give a reason. They were already well known families, so privacy wasn't the concern. Were they getting the public plaudits for their giving, whilst distributing a small percentage of their wealth? Was a commitment to share 20%+ of one's wealth too high? The challenge is to get such families moving from 'good' to 'great'. Again, if we show families the way I'm sure they too would step up.

---

11. Australian Financial Review Magazine, *Rich List*, 2023

12. Credit Suisse, op. cit., p. 130

One family who is very vocal about their giving was outraged by my approach, stating they could not possibly sign the Pledge (without giving a valid reason) and would be made to look silly when the list didn't include their name! Thankfully it was my only irate call.

Tweaking the Pledge commitment

After reflection on the beach over the Christmas break, in the New Year of 2022 I tweaked the Pledge commitment to be less complex and, frankly, easier to comply with:

> *Signatories with net investable wealth (NIW*) of >$20m will publicly pledge to donate at least 20% of their NIW to eligible charities, or to their foundation, in their lifetime or upon death.*
>
> **Net investable wealth: investable assets excluding primary residence.*

Initially I wondered whether the revised 20% Pledge commitment was too lenient. Several families told me strongly that it was! However, I had reflected that the Pledge was a new concept in Australia. A country where the bulk of the wealth had only been created in the last three to four decades and the philanthropic sector was still immature. Most families gave considerably less than 20% of their wealth. If we could get 300+ families over the following few years to publicly agree to 20%, then this would be a great success, and would provide excellent momentum in building a 'giving norm' in our community, inspiring others and significantly growing the philanthropic sector.

I also thought that if this occurred, over the following years leaders could inspire Pledge signatories to do even more. "From little things big things grow …"[13]

The simplification of the pledge, and the lower commitment bar, built

---

13. Song written by Paul Kelly and Kev Carmody, 1991

on the earlier momentum that had been achieved. By March 2022 there were 40 signatories. This was amazing. There were 40 families (primarily influential names) from across every State in Australia (except Tasmania) who were willing to publicly sign a pledge to say they would give 20% of their wealth to eligible charities or to their foundation in their lifetime or upon death. This was possibly a game-changer for our giving culture. I was convinced that once the Pledge launched with 50+ families, that the second 50 families would be easier to sign up; again, safety in numbers.

The Fox family pledge

It was interesting that during this time the Fox family made their wonderful $100 million pledge to the National Gallery of Victoria (NGV). This could be a significant turning point in terms of naming rights in Australia. The family deserves some applause, as hopefully this will inspire other families to make larger gifts. It is interesting to note that given their wealth (according to the *AFR Rich List* estimate[14]), this pledge is 2% of their wealth. Now, if I was worth $10 million (ah, sadly not) and made a gift to the NGV of 2% of my wealth (i.e. $200,000), I don't think I would be on the front page of the newspapers. Of course this would be a far greater sacrifice for me, as obviously I would have a much smaller surplus of assets after the gift payment than a family worth considerably more than I.

To meet Australia's Giving Pledge (gifting 20% of one's wealth) the Fox family would need to make another seven similar pledges of $100 million each. Perhaps there are more gift announcements to be made.

Shortly after the announcement of the Fox pledge I had a meeting with the CEO of a high profile family foundation where the family seems to enjoy naming rights. I told the CEO that the game had now changed; no more naming rights for $1 million! (Which in their case was less than 0.02% of the family wealth.)

I had already held several meetings with a communications agency to begin to map out the Pledge communications strategy. We now needed funding to develop the brand, website and detailed comms strategy.

---

14. Australian Financial Review Magazine, *Rich List*, 2023

Pledge funding

In mid 2022 Carpenter advised significant funding would be provided for Pledge operations for the first three years, subject to board approval.

After waiting weeks for formal Carpenter board approval, unfortunately I was advised (8 weeks later) that Carpenter was to cease funding on most of their projects. Apparently, they could only put their foundation infrastructure in place to achieve their future giving goals if they ceased work with most of their existing partners.

This news was very upsetting, primarily as Carpenter provided no notice. There is nothing wrong with walking away from partners, but best practice philanthropy was to provide a staged exit over a reasonable and appropriate period of time (12-24 months), and preferably bring in other funding partners, so that the recipient partner would not lose momentum. The Pledge was provided no notice, so there was significant risk that the project would stall. I advised Carpenter that ironically it was their behaviour that the Pledge was trying to change! The Pledge was aimed not only at dramatically growing the size of the philanthropic pie, but also more effective deployment of capital, which included a focus on best practice philanthropy.

The Pledge had a strong plan and loads of momentum, but no funding to implement! I prepared a report on the Pledge status and Plan, plus a budget for the first two years of operation and sought support from 12 families/foundations (primarily Pledge signatories) to fund the Pledge over 2 years. Most families, whilst signatories and supporters of the idea, did not wish to fund the Pledge as growing giving was not within their giving strategy.

In September 2022 it was verbally agreed that two large foundations, in collaboration with PA, would provide the majority of funding required for the Pledge for years 1 and 2, subject to the two foundations seeking simple commitments from each other and PA. Paul Wheelton AM very quickly agreed to provide the bulk of the balance of the funding required. Paul and I had shared ideas on growing giving for 15+ years. His very quick support was not a surprise, but was much appreciated. He saw the Pledge as a 'no-brainer' to change our giving culture. We were back on track. Or so I thought.

Sadly, four months later these three partners were no closer to closing the deal. Despite all parties agreeing that the Pledge was exactly what the country needed to change our giving culture, and warnings that action needed to be taken to ensure momentum was not lost, there was still no action, nor funding on the table. The deal had been contingent upon one partner fulfilling a reasonably simple obligation on behalf of the other two parties. This was not able to be met.

Pledge shelved

Despite discussions with over 200 families, over 40 committed signatories Australia-wide, another 15 families highly likely to sign up upon seeing the full list of signatories, the Pledge had not managed to launch. There was a lot of disbelief from signatories and potential signatories.

The outcome was incredibly disappointing, particularly given the significant progress that had been made. The issue that most troubled me was that months earlier three senior CEOs in the sector had agreed that the idea and plan was good and had verbally agreed to fund it. Yet somehow, they couldn't manage to collaborate. This was a simple and inexpensive idea. How was the sector going to manage to collaborate on complex $200 million ideas?

I did receive a lot of correspondence from families stating how sad they were to hear that the Pledge would not launch. However, it had sparked, or fast-tracked, a conversation within their family and they were giving a lot more consideration to 'how much is enough?' and what the family was going to do with their wealth. Hopefully that will result in increased allocations to their giving in time.

The Pledge did not succeed in 2023. I'm yet to hear of a better idea to significantly change Australia's giving culture. I suspect it shall arise another day.

Chapter 34

How the for-purpose sector can help itself

"Efficiency is doing things right; effectiveness is doing the right things." – **Peter Drucker**

How many charities do we need?

The *Australian Charities Report (2022)* indicates that the for-purpose sector employs 1.38 million people. This is more than 10% of Australia's workforce. There were 3.4 million volunteers. The report is based upon data from 49,000 charities.[1]

The Australian Charities and Not-for-profits Commission (ACNC) states that in total there are around 60,000 charities in Australia[2], of which 32,130 had deductible gift recipient status.[3] The number of charities includes multiple listings from some organisations e.g. The Salvation Army has around 30 separately registered charities and Surf Life Saving over 300.

I admire these people as many of them wake up every day with an ambition to make the world a better place. Many other people wake up

---

1. Australian Charities and Not-for-profits Commission, *Australian Charities Report*, 8th Edition, June 2022, p.3

2. https://www.acnc.gov.au/for-public/understanding-charities/are-there-too-many-charities-australia

3. McGregor-Lowndes, Balczun & Williamson, op. cit., p. 13

and simply think about how to build their personal balance sheet.

There has been a debate rolling for some years about the size and structure of the sector in Australia. Do we really need 60,000 charities in a country of 26 million people?

Some say it is fine to have many new charities set up every year as they are being established by passionate people who will create impact in the community.

I take a different view. If we were starting with a clean sheet of paper seeking to target issues in the community, we would not seek to build 60,000 charities. This is a silly number of entities given our population; a charity for every 433 people. This provides significant opportunities to improve efficiency and effectiveness in the for-purpose sector.

If you plug 'cancer' into the search page of the ACNC, over 350 entities come up! Many of these entities will be doing great work, and some of them will be supplying irreplaceable local grass roots support services, but I suspect we would maximise community outcomes if we had significantly less entities via mergers. Better outcomes could result from:

- less duplication of work performed and improving the existing programs

- providing a better combination of programs to recipients

- stronger advocacy possibilities

- increased policy influence with government

- leveraging stronger managers across a broader network

- better collaboration with a smaller number of key enterprises

- adopting stronger systems and processes across a broader network

- increased scale and less inefficiencies due to the significantly reduced number of entities resulting in less compliance work (financial accounts, audits, ACNC lodgements), less fundraising competition, lower fundraising costs, and less staff and administration costs due to synergies with other entities.[4]

The number of charities grows each year. Prior to establishing another new charity we must search harder to see if similar work is already being performed by an existing entity. It most likely will be. Explore how you could bring your unique skills, brand, network and passion to this entity to assist your aligned mission.

Some of the larger charities are playing an important service provision role across the country. Many charities are providing essential grass roots local support services. However, there are many others with good intentions who are uncertain where they fit within the eco-system, or are simply poorly governed and drift along. Ego and 'founder syndrome', where the founder doesn't want to let go, often get in the way of mergers. Which Chair and which CEO will step aside? Does a loved brand need to disappear? Where there is no push from shareholders to improve performance, the status quo might win out.

A lack of knowledge of mergers and a lack of funding to do due diligence are also barriers to action.

Intermediaries needed

We need the infrastructure to enable inefficient entities to merge with entities with a similar mission. In the for-profit world there are market incentives, including intermediaries, that tend to ensure that inefficient companies fail or are taken over. This does not occur in the for-purpose world. Large donors could provide funding for a small team for three to five years to seek out merger opportunities within the sector. This could be transformational. Alternatively, if more efficient, a fund could be established that for-purpose entities could apply to, to assist with the

---

4. Paul Ronalds, *Put Ego Aside in Favour of Mergers*, Save the Children, Pro Bono Australia, 11 November 2015

costs associated with merger due diligence.

Mergers in the corporate sector are difficult. This is amplified in the for-purpose space where passion and staff longevity is often higher. Emotions run high. Therefore bringing different cultures together can be even more difficult. But we must try. If the vision is strong, and articulated well, it can work.

Save the Children is an example of a for-purpose entity that has merged with or 'acquired' a number of other for-purpose entities which has enabled it to expand its program reach and create significant financial savings. Save the Children has also established a back-office support services hub for other for-purpose entities in order to generate new revenue streams, and has established a number of social enterprises to generate income.[5]

Save the Children's then CEO Paul Ronalds, says, "NGO (non-government organisation) mergers, acquisitions and collaboration can deliver more and better services at a lower cost, while also increasing the number of beneficiaries."[6]

Chairs and CEOs will need to consider Harry Truman's great line: "It's amazing what you can accomplish if you don't care who gets the credit".

What is your end game?

For-purpose entities need to be very clear about their mission. Mark Kramer, prolific writer at the Harvard Business School on strategies for social impact, states many for-purpose entities function alone and, "… lack:

- infrastructure to learn best practice

- clout to influence government

---

5. Simon Miller, Sophie Coleman & Grace Williamson, *Diversifying Charity Business Models*, International In-house Counsel Journal, Vol. 13, No. 53, Autumn 2020, 1

6. Paul Ronalds, *NFP Mergers – Survivors are the Most Adaptable to Change*, Save the Children, Pro Bono Australia, 27 February 2017

- scale to achieve national impact".[7]

Boards must be very clear with their mission, strategy and measurement. Scale is not necessarily the answer. Gugelev and Stern argue, "… it's time for nonprofit leaders to ask a more fundamental question than 'how do you scale up?' Instead, we urge them to consider a different question: What's your endgame?" An endgame is the specific role that a nonprofit intends to play in the overall solution to a social problem, once it has proven the effectiveness of its core model or intervention.[8]

Gugelev and Stern believed there were six endgames for nonprofits to consider and it was the role of leaders to reach one of them. They outlined the six endgames as:

1. open source: a breakthrough idea that is easy for other organisations to adopt and integrate. Their future role is to serve as a knowledge hub

2. replication: a breakthrough product/model that is easy for others to adopt/deliver. Their future role is to franchise the idea, train and serve as a centre of excellence

3. government adoption: a model with high coverage potential. Their future role is offering services to government agencies and maintaining research/advocacy efforts

4. commercial adoption: a product/service with profit potential that solves a market failure. Their future role is maintaining advocacy and targeting hard to reach markets

5. mission achievement: defined outcomes relating to solving a discrete problem. Their future role is (where relevant) applying capabilities to additional issue areas

---

7. Mark Kramer, *Catalytic Philanthropy*, Stanford Social Innovation Review, Fall 2009

8. Alice Gugelev & Andrew Stern, *What's Your Endgame?* Stanford Social Innovation Review, Winter 2015

6. sustained service: a strong entity with a proven ability to sustain funding that fills a public service gap. Their future role is continued provision of a core service at an ever-increasing level of efficiency.

Gugelev and Stern's view was that, "The purpose of a nonprofit, like the purpose of an individual life, should derive from its inevitable conclusion".

The aim of a for-purpose entity is not to increase its budget—it is to achieve social impact.

One ('mission achievement') example is the Summer Foundation (SF).[9] SF is passionate about stopping young people with a disability from being forced into residential aged care. Its endgame is to change the system via a number of market interventions so that young people with a disability can be in control of where, how and with whom they live. SF is working towards reaching that target within 10 years, then closing its doors.

Boards should be thoroughly reviewing their business plans, considering how they will maximise impact and determining whether more impact could be made by merging with another entity.

The board

The board's role in achieving the mission is critical. Leadership and governance must be strong. Jim Collins' view was that moving from a 'good to great' organisation required disciplined people, disciplined thought and disciplined action.[10] This starts with the board.

In some cases there will need to be a detailed review of the board skills required for the entity to achieve its mission. Many charity board members are amazing, bringing extraordinary skills, experience and passion to the table. But in my experience there are also board members who are contributing the bare minimum.

Similar to foundation boards, the minimum requirements of a charity

---

9. https://www.summerfoundation.org.au

10. Jim Collins, *Good to Great and the Social Sectors*, Random House, 2005

board member need to be documented and provided to board members before joining the board. If the requirements are not met, they need to be warned by the Chair to lift their performance or exit. Boards need to biennially self-evaluate their performance.

Board members must take an interest in the organisation. They need to take the time to listen and learn from team members as well as customers/clients. Ask yourself: are you committed or just filling a seat?

In my experience from talking with for-purpose CEOs, often board members are not providing enough assistance to the CEO with fundraising. Many board members are not wealthy, and not all are well connected, but we must not forget the well-known saying from the USA: "Give, get, or get off." We all have connections, no matter how well (or poorly) we are connected with high-net-worth individuals ('HNWIs'). Board members must reach out to their networks (family, friends, school, university, sport, music, professional) that they have built over their life. Board members need to be spreading the word on the mission of the entity and its needs. If you don't ask, you don't get.

Many for-purpose entities cannot afford to pay directors, but it is interesting that for those entities working on the biggest and most difficult issues in the country, there is a community expectation that board members must volunteer! But if you join the board of a vacuum manufacturer you get paid! If the charity board can pay for board members, then I believe they should, as discussed in chapter 21.

Be prepared for the philanthropic wave

With nudging, the philanthropic sector in Australia will eventually explode in size. We will have over twenty $1 billion foundations, each distributing $50 million+ p.a. (hopefully more if they are limited life foundations) and 200+ large foundations ($100m+), each distributing $5 million+ p.a. As the philanthropic sector eventually professionalises, has bigger vision, seeks to better collaborate with government, and implements best practice philanthropy, it will have greater impact within the community.

The philanthropic sector has a growing understanding that it needs to provide the resources to for-purpose entities, if they require it, in order that they can develop strong, measurable plans, determine their impact and then scale.

As Dan Pallotta has discussed for many years, we need to recruit the best and brightest into the for-purpose world. This will mean that we will need to pay them appropriately. Salaries in the for-purpose world are often well below market rates. Why should one have to take a pay cut to work on the community's most pressing issues? They should get a pay rise!

> *"We have a visceral reaction to the idea that anyone would make very much money helping other people. Interesting that we don't have a visceral reaction to the notion that people would make a lot of money not helping other people. You want to make $50 million selling violent video games to kids, go for it, we'll put you on the front cover of Wired magazine. But if you want to make half a million dollars trying to cure kids of malaria you are considered a parasite yourself!"[11]*

Pallotta's brilliant 2023 documentary, *Uncharitable*, reinforces these themes and starts a bigger conversation around how we need to change our thinking about funding for-purpose entities if we really are seeking change in our community.[12] We have to move away from this double standard we have with for-profit and for-purpose entities. We need to move away from the constraints we put on for-purpose entities, and the focus on overheads needing to be low. Leaders in the philanthropic and for-purpose sectors need to push back on such misconceptions.

Having under-staffed, under-resourced and under-capitalised entities trying to solve the community's biggest issues is just bonkers! If we continue down this path little will change. We must recognise the opportunity to tap into for-purpose leaders' on-the-ground knowledge

---

11. Dan Pallotta, *The way we think about charity is dead wrong*, TEDx, Long Beach, California, March 2013

12. https://uncharitablemovie.com

when developing public policy to address issues in our community.

If we take the prudent approach, we will set for-purpose entities up for success. This will provide donors with great opportunities to invest in to help solve pressing social and environmental issues at a faster rate than currently.

As the philanthropic sector grows, we will need considerably more for-purpose entities in Australia that are in a position to create detailed measurable plans in order to receive gifts of $50 million+ and scale their organisations to achieve their goals.

Donors need to be guided by those with lived experience, those close to the community and for-purpose entities. The trick will be to ensure we have charities well placed to accept the challenge.

Chapter 35

Hope

"We have the wealth and intelligence to solve every issue on the planet, if we can be inspired to do so …" – **Peter Winneke**

My Dad often said one must have hope; if one does not have hope, you have little future. My optimism has been tested in recent years, particularly in relation to various world issues and poor local policies on climate change, First Nations Australians and our democracy. However, I am optimistic about the future. I see the next generation learning from the successes and mistakes of the previous generations, generally taking a more thoughtful approach to their life, and having less focus on wealth creation being *the* success indicator.

I believe we are on the verge of a new dawn in the philanthropic sector in this country. The sector has enormous capacity to grow so that it can eventually operate on a meaningful scale, with the capital being more effectively deployed to support governments, and for-purpose entities to address major issues in our community. I am optimistic that we will get there, but we need to nudge and cajole to get there quicker. We *can*:

- get families to give more consideration to how much is enough, a more meaningful use of their 'surplus' and the risks of leaving significant income streams to children

- highlight to families the enormous benefit to the community that a family foundation can be, and the incredible satisfaction that will be gained from it, as well as the extraordinary educational tool it can be for the kids

- better tell successful giving stories, which will lead to more role models, greater interest in giving, more families wishing to get involved, with material giving becoming the 'norm'

- learn from the mistakes and successes from offshore, particularly the USA, the United Kingdom and Europe where the philanthropic sectors are more mature

- maximise the opportunities in the philanthropic sector from increased transparency, collaboration and leverage with other stakeholders, including government.

Philanthropy can be a powerful change agent in society, targeting social ills. Foundations can and should support and lead social progress. As Franklin Thomas, ex-President of the Ford Foundation, said, "Philanthropy can be the research and development arm of society."[1]

We must get smarter with our use of capital to tackle issues in our community. We shall need courageous leaders to change behaviour. If we significantly grow the size of the philanthropic sector and can implement just a fraction of the smart strategies available to donors, the impact on our community, and that of our neighbours, could be considerable.

And it can be fun! Working with two or three generations of your family, working with smart and passionate for-purpose leaders having a crack at major issues in our community can be immensely satisfying.

Some questions to leave you with

- how is your legacy looking?

- how much purpose do you really have in your life?

- what upsets you? What are you passionate about? How could

---

1. Christine W. Letts, William Ryan and Allen Grossman, *Virtuous Capital: What Foundations Can Learn from Venture Capitalists*, Harvard Business Review, March-April 1997

you have an impact in that space? Who could you discuss this with to get the ball rolling? Who else could you inspire to get involved?

- how much really is enough? How much wealth does your family really need to live a comfortable and meaningful life?

- what would be a sensible amount to gift to your children, in order that they can 'learn to work' and build a productive life?

- what skills could you bring to a for-purpose entity? Don't underestimate your skills and networks. Determine the best fit for you

- if you clearly have surplus wealth, do the numbers, determine what it is. You will likely be surprised how high it is. Then determine a creative use for it in the community.

Gareth Andrews, former footballer and founder of Life Again, asks middle-aged people: "Have you done your best work yet?" I love it! "Have you done your best work yet?" Well, have *you*? Perhaps that is worth reflecting on.

Given your skills, connections, networks and passions, what could you get involved with that will result in your 'best work'? Once you get involved, I'm very confident that you will have a bit of extra spring in your step. That's what extra purpose in life does! And you will likely meet a terrific bunch of smart and passionate people that you didn't know existed. There is another world out there! I know; I found it. It will be challenging, but fun too.

John Kennedy, legendary Hawthorn Football Club coach, had a well-known saying. In his booming voice he would say to his players, "Do something. Don't just stand there; do something." (A saying he borrowed from my grandfather, Henry Winneke.)[2]

We have the wealth and intelligence to solve every issue on the planet. We just need to be inspired to do so. We can all, "Do something."

---

2. https://speakola.com/sports/john-kennedy-dont-think-do-1975

Bill Perkins, energy trader and author says that "... the business of life is the acquisition of memories."[3] Get the family together and start planning your philanthropic adventure. This will create amazing memories. Give while you live.

Let's pay attention. Let's not look the other way. Take action and inspire others to walk with you on your journey. Never lose your sense of outrage at the injustice in the world.

Imagine the impact we could have on so many aspects of our community if we could inspire thousands of families in Australia to strategically share part of their wealth.

Hopefully this book will stimulate thinking and provoke debate, which will assist in some small way to achieving stronger community outcomes. The opportunity for families to create positive change in the community is enormous and incredibly exciting.

---

3. Bill Perkins, op. cit., p. 192

Abbreviations/glossary

ACF: Australian Communities Foundation
ACNC: Australian Charities and Not-for-profits Commission, the sector regulator
AP: The Atlantic Philanthropies, Chuck Feeney's foundation
APS: Australian Philanthropic Services
ATO: Australian Taxation Office
B Corp: a for-profit company certified by the B Lab to meet rigorous standards of social and environmental performance, accountability and transparency
CA: Charitable Alliance
CAFSMA: Corporations Legislation Amendment (Financial Services Modernisation) Act
CAMAC: Corporations and Markets Advisory Committee
CFA: Community Foundations Australia, the peak body for community foundations
Community foundation: an independent philanthropic foundation usually working in a particular geographic area, providing services to its community and donors
Corpus: the net assets of a foundation
CSI: Centre for Social Impact
DGR: Deductible gift recipient, a fund or entity which can receive tax deductible gifts
Effective altruism: using evidence to determine how to maximise the outcomes from your giving
Family foundation: a charitable entity established by a family for the purposes of grantmaking
Family office: a provider of services to one or more families that

could include: estate and succession planning, wealth management, tax, accounting and philanthropy services

Focus area: an area of community need that a foundation is targeting

For-purpose entity: an entity with charitable purposes

FRRR: Foundation for Rural and Regional Renewal

FSC: Financial Services Council

GP: Giving Pledge, the worldwide billionaires' giving pledge established by Bill Gates, Melinda French Gates and Warren Buffett

HNWI: High-net-worth Individual. Defined here as having net wealth of $10 million+

KPI: Key performance indicator

Limited life foundation (spend down): a foundation that instead of operating in perpetuity chooses to distribute all its assets by a specified date

LMCF: Lord Mayor's Charitable Foundation

LTC: Licensed Trustee Company. Provides wealth management services such as administering deceased estates and administering charitable trusts. They are authorised under individual State/Territory legislation to carry out those duties and must comply with the relevant Trustee Act. e.g. Perpetual, Equity Trustees

MFO: The Myer Family Office

MFPS: MF Philanthropic Services, a division of The Myer Family Office

Orphan trust: a trust where the sole trustee is a LTC

PA: Philanthropy Australia, the sector peak body

PAF: Private Ancillary Fund, a form of family grantmaking philanthropic foundation with DGR status introduced in Australia in 2001. It cannot run charitable programs, nor solicit funds from the public

Private Charitable Trust: a privately controlled charitable trust operating solely for charitable purposes. It must fund charitable purposes, but grant recipients do not require DGR status. It does not have DGR status

PuAF: Public Ancillary Fund, a public fund with DGR status which must publicly fundraise and the majority of trustees must be representatives of the public

Responsible Person: defined by the ATO as an individual with a degree of responsibility to the general community

SDGs: Sustainable Development Goals. Adopted by United Nations Member States in 2015, they provide a shared blueprint for peace and prosperity for people and the planet

SVA: Social Ventures Australia

TCA: Trustee Corporations Association of Australia (precursor to the FSC)

The Audacious Project: seeks to catalyse social capital on a huge scale by working with social entrepreneurs and large donors

Unrestricted funding: funding that can be used at the discretion of the grant recipient

Will or testamentary trust: a trust set up in a person's Will which commences upon their death

Useful resources

Philanthropy Australia
Philanthropy Australia is the sector peak body which seeks 'more and better philanthropy'. https://www.philanthropy.org.au

StartGiving
StartGiving seeks to inspire a culture of giving from the innovation community to the charitable sector. https://www.startgiving.com

The Giving Pledge
This worldwide pledge is an open invitation to billionaires worldwide to publicly commit to give the majority of their wealth to philanthropy during their lifetime or in their Will. The website includes individual letters from most of the 200+ signatories stating the reasons for their giving. https://givingpledge.org

Australia's Top 50 Philanthropic Gifts
Compiled in 2013, this is a summary of some of the most effective gifts in Australia's history.
https://probonoaustralia.com.au/news/2013/10/australias-top-50-philanthropic-gifts-of-all-time

Pro Bono Australia
Provides a careers and jobs board, sector salary survey and a for-purpose news archive going back to 2001. https://probonoaustralia.com.au

The Life You Can Save
Based on the book of the same name by Australian philosopher, Peter Singer, this resource includes materials on deciding how much and where to give. https://www.thelifeyoucansave.org.au

More on effective altruism https://www.effectivealtruism.org

Bridgespan
A consulting for-purpose entity that seeks to make the world more equitable and just. https://www.bridgespan.org

Uncharitable
Dan Pallotta is well known for his 2013 TED talk: 'The way we think about charity is dead wrong' (see below). In the documentary, *Uncharitable*, Pallotta questions our fundamental beliefs about charities, and the multiple constraints we put on them, double standards in fact, which disadvantages them against for-profit entities. As a result, scale is difficult to achieve. Accordingly there is little chance of us solving the major issues in our community and around the world today. Pallotta advocates throwing out these unjust and flawed ways of thinking, and then dream about the world we want. Properly funded for-purpose entities have a big role to play in achieving this vision. https://uncharitablemovie.com

Dan Pallotta TED talk: https://www.ted.com/speakers/dan_pallotta

Career decisions
Your choice of career is the most important ethical decision of your life, and this website provides a career guide. https://80000hours.org

Useful articles and reports

Jeffrey C. Walker, *Solving the World's Biggest Problems: Better Philanthropy Through Systems Change*, Stanford Social Innovation Review, 5 April 2017

Alice Gugelev and Andrew Stern, *What's Your Endgame?,* Stanford Social Innovation Review, Winter 2015

Susan Wolf Ditkoff & Abe Grindle, *Audacious Philanthropy*, Harvard Business Review, Sept-Oct 2017

Nick Tedesco & Michael Moody, *The Future of Family Philanthropy*, Stanford Social Innovation Review, 12 September 2022

Rockefeller Philanthropy Advisors, *Scaling Solutions Toward Shifting Systems*, September 2017

Katie Smith Milway, Amy Markham, Chris Cardona & Kathy Reich, *Five Accelerators of Equitable Grantmaking and How to Harness Them*, Stanford Social Innovation Review, 27 April 2022

John Kania & Mark Kramer, *Collective Impact*, Stanford Social Innovation Review, Winter 2011

William Foster, Gail Perreault & Elise Tosun, *Ten Ways to make a Big Bet on Social Change*, Stanford Social Innovation Review, 10 May 2017

The Omidyar Group, *Systems Practice*

Joanna Levitt Cea & Jess Rimington, *Creating Breakout Innovation*, Stanford Social Innovation Review, Summer 2017

Nidhi Sahni, Laura Lanzerotti, Amira Bliss & Daniel Pike, *Is Your Nonprofit Built for Sustained Innovation?*, Stanford Social Innovation Review, 1 August 2017

Kevin Starr, *The Lazy Funder's Guide to High-Yield Philanthropy*, Stanford Social Innovation Review, 5 April 2016

Fay Twersky, *The Artful Juggler*, Stanford Social Innovation Review, Summer 2014

Social Impact Hub, *Field Guide to Impact Investing, For Australian Charitable Trusts & Foundations,* 2nd Edition, 2018

Julia Balandina Jaquier, *Catalyzing Wealth for Change, Guide to Impact Investing*, 2016

Mark Kramer, *Catalytic Philanthropy*, Stanford Social Innovation Review, Fall 2009

Alison Powell, Willa Seldon & Nidhi Sahni, *Reimagining Institutional Philanthropy*, Stanford Social Innovation Review, Spring 2019

Liz Gillies, Dr Jodi York & Dr Joanna Mink, *Philanthropy: Towards a Better Practice Model,* Asia Pacific Social Impact Centre, 2017

Ann Christiano & Annie Neimand, *The Science of What Makes People Care*, Stanford Social Innovation Review, Fall 2018

Useful books

Doing Good Great, Doug Balfour, Geneva Global, 2015
Balfour shares eight pillars of how to maximise outcomes from giving and implores us not to be satisfied with just 'good' outcomes.

Money Well Spent, Paul Brest & Hal Harvey, Bloomberg Press, 2008
The authors provide valuable insight into crafting and implementing an approach to achieve measurable results.

Strategic Giving; The Art and Science of Philanthropy, Peter Frumkin, University of Chicago Press, 2006
Frumkin explores how donors can think strategically about their giving to maximise the public and private benefits of philanthropy.

Give Smart, Thomas J. Tierney & Joel L. Fleishman, PublicAffairs, 2011
This book focuses on moving philanthropy from its 'natural state of under-performance' to rigor and better outcomes.

Generations of Giving, Kelin E. Gersick, Lexington Books, 2004
This book looks at 30 multigenerational family foundations in the USA and how these families think about and structure their giving.

Good to Great and the Social Sectors, Jim Collins, Harper Collins, 2005
Collins argues that discipline is the answer in the social sector, not business thinking.

The Life You Can Save, Peter Singer, The Life You Can Save, Tenth Anniversary Edition, 2019
Internationally renowned philosopher, Peter Singer, argues that affluent countries are acting immorally if they do not act to end poverty in low-middle income countries, which they know exists.

The Most Good You Can Do, Peter Singer, The Text Publishing Company, 2015
Singer again on how effective altruism is impacting ideas about living ethically.

Splendid Legacy – The Guide to Creating your Family Foundation, National Center for Family Philanthropy, 2002
Uses real (USA) case studies to assist families commence their philanthropic journey.

Robin Hood Was Right, Chuck Collins & Pam Rogers with Joan P. Garner, Norton, 2001
A practical guide, filled with brief case studies, to giving for social change.

Wealth in Families, Charles W. Collier, Harvard University, 2003
Collier discusses the role philanthropy can play in helping families convey both assets and values from generation to generation.

The Billionaire Who Wasn't, Conor O'Clery, PublicAffairs, 2013
The inspiring story of Irish American Chuck Feeney, who created significant wealth via duty free shopping and then gave it all away in his lifetime via his foundation, The Atlantic Philanthropies.
https://www.atlanticphilanthropies.org

Forces for Good, Leslie R. Crutchfield & Heather McLeod Grant, Jossey-Bass, 2008
The authors detail the six practices of high-impact charities.

The World We Want, Peter Karoff with Jane Maddox, AltaMira Press, 2007
A collection of stories from engaged citizens on building a better world.

Philanthrocapitalism, Matthew Bishop & Michael Green, A & C Black Publishers, 2008
In a thought-provoking, controversial piece, the authors examine the billionaires and business-style strategies that are attempting to change the world.

Creative Philanthropy, Helmet K. Anheier & Diana Leat, Routledge, 2006
Through case studies of selected foundations, the authors show theories in practice and argue how impact could be maximised.

Just Giving: Why Philanthropy is Failing Democracy and How it Can Do Better, Rob Reich, Princeton University Press, 2019
Reich mounts the case that whilst we laud wealthy donors, philanthropy may not provide the benefits we think it does and it may in fact be undermining democratic values.

Winners Take All, Anand Giridharadas, Allen Lane, 2019
Giridharadas argues that members of the global elite use their wealth and influence to preserve systems that concentrate wealth at the top, at the expense of societal progress.

Dark Moncy, Jane Mayer, Anchor Books, 2017
Mayer reveals the dark side of philanthropy, whereby significant sums were spent over many years by the Koch brothers, and other billionaires in the USA, to secretly fund right wing think tanks, academic institutions and media groups in order to pursue government influence.

A Tradition of Giving: Seventy-Five Years of Myer Family Philanthropy, Michael Liffman, Melbourne University Press, 2004
Liffman, a former CEO of The Myer Foundation, explores Myer family philanthropy through three generations and its impact on many Australians.

Enough, John C. Bogle, John Wiley & Sons, 2009
Bogle, the founder of Vanguard, shows that character, integrity and common sense are critical to running a business. He considers 'how much is enough' and believes that a life well lived is in service to others.

Advising Philanthropists, Emma Beeston and Beth Breeze, Directory of Social Change, 2023
Philanthropy advising is an emerging field and this book is an excellent addition to the knowledge and skills required to do the role successfully. It includes interviews with 40 philanthropy advisers from around the world.

Inspired Philanthropy, Tracy Gary with Nancy Adess, Jossey-Bass, 2007
This manual provides a useful step-by-step guide to align values and passions to create a giving plan.

Work Smarter: Live Better, Cyril Peupion, Peupion Pty Ltd, 2010
A great practical summary of how to work more efficiently and effectively in order to achieve more.

Acknowledgements

I am very aware that I have led a very privileged life. "Acknowledgements" really doesn't convey my gratitude, but it is a start. I have so many people to be grateful for.

Mum and Dad as I certainly won the parents' lottery, Jeffrey Sachs for opening my eyes, Chuck Feeney for being such an inspiration, a number of philanthropic and for-purpose colleagues who provided wonderful and useful comments for this book, some of whom are mentioned in the book and others who were happy to stay out of the spotlight, many for-purpose leaders whose passion and drive to make the world a better place continue to inspire me on a daily basis, a very tall man and his wife from whom I learnt a lot particularly around humility and maximising impact, the Myer family for giving me the autonomy to establish MF Philanthropic Services and pursue my dream, Graham Reeve for backing me, Rupert and his dad, the late Bails Myer for becoming the first clients, Roger Massy-Greene AM for taking a punt on me and for your wisdom, all my clients over the years as I have learnt something from all of you, Charles Lane and Andy Myer for giving me my first gig in the philanthropic sector, Mary Wooldridge for caring, John Emerson AM for your sound advice over many years, Rob McLean AM for your wise counsel, John Spierings for your passion and wisdom, Tim Costello and Peter Singer for inspiring me to never give up, Chris Thorn AM for your foresight and integrity, David Ward for always being happy to share ideas, John McLeod for your stats and graphs, Mark Cubit for your backing and encouragement of Australia's Giving Pledge, Dave Kennedy for introducing me to Chuck and for your regular encouragement, Pete Danks and the late and great Graeme Danks for your passion and courage to call out poor behaviour, Richard Leder OAM for your pro bono advice,

Mark Mentha and Mark Korda for teaching me during my insolvency days not to automatically believe everything one hears but to think through it (great training for philanthropy!), Simon Jones for taking a chance on me at Arthur Andersen, Paul O'Bryan and Anthony Garnham for your incredible friendship and many great conversations over the journey on 'how to fix the world', Christine Edwards and Kate Shea for challenging me with your editing skills resulting in a much better product, Bruce Springsteen for your beautiful songs, my young men Mike and Ed for being you and giving 100% most of the time, and Ange for your unconditional love and putting up with my constant gripes on the apathy in the western world, people lacking self-awareness, self-absorbed people, the lack of generosity, people not speaking their mind, inefficiency everywhere, and well, many other things...